Chicanx Utopias

Historia USA
A series edited by Luis Alvarez, Carlos Blanton, and Lorrin Thomas

BOOKS IN THE SERIES:

Felipe Hinojosa, *Apostles of Change: Latino Radical Politics, Church Occupations, and the Fight to Save the Barrio*
Patricia Silver, *Sunbelt Diaspora: Race, Class, and Latino Politics in Puerto Rican Orlando*
Cristina Salinas, *Managed Migrations: Growers, Farmworkers, and Border Enforcement in the Twentieth Century*
Perla Guerrero, *Nuevo South: Latinas/os, Asians, and the Remaking of Place*

« LUIS ALVAREZ »

Chicanx Utopias

POP CULTURE AND
THE POLITICS OF THE POSSIBLE

University of Texas Press AUSTIN

Copyright © 2022 by the University of Texas Press
All rights reserved
Printed in the United States of America
First edition, 2022
First paperback reprint, 2024

Portions of chapter 2 appeared, in a different form, as Luis Alvarez and Daniel Widener, "Brown-Eyed Soul: Popular Music and Cultural Politics in Los Angeles," in *The Struggle in Black and Brown: African American and Mexican American Relations during the Civil Rights Era*, edited by Brian D. Behnken; reproduced by permission of the University of Nebraska Press. Copyright 2011 by the Board of Regents of the University of Nebraska.

Portions of chapter 5 appeared, in a different form, as Luis Alvarez, "Border Reggae: The Possibilities of a Frontera Soundscape," in *Transnational Encounters: Music and Performance at the U.S.-Mexico Border*, ed. Alejandro L. Madrid (New York: Oxford University Press, 2011), 19–40.

Requests for permission to reproduce material from this work should be sent to:
Permissions
University of Texas Press
P.O. Box 7819
Austin, TX 78713-7819
utpress.utexas.edu

♾ The paper used in this book meets the minimum requirements of ANSI/NISO Z39.48-1992 (R1997) (Permanence of Paper).

LIBRARY OF CONGRESS CATALOGING-IN-PUBLICATION DATA

Names: Alvarez, Luis, 1972– author.
Title: Chicanx utopias : pop culture and the politics of the possible / Luis Alvarez. Other titles: Historia USA.
Description: First edition. | Austin : University of Texas Press, 2022. | Series: Historia USA | Includes bibliographical references and index.
Identifiers:
    LCCN 2021029658
    ISBN 978-1-4773-2447-9 (cloth)
    ISBN 978-1-4773-2448-6 (paperback)
    ISBN 978-1-4773-2449-3 (PDF)
    ISBN 978-1-4773-2450-9 (ePub)
Subjects: LCSH: Mexican Americans in popular culture—Political aspects—United States—History—20th century. | Mexican Americans in popular culture—Political aspects—United States—History—21st century. | Mexican Americans and mass media—Political aspects—United States—History—20th century. | Mexican Americans and mass media—Political aspects—United States—History—21st century. | Mexican Americans—Social life and customs—Political aspects—United States—History—20th century. | Mexican Americans—Political activity—United States. | Chicano movement—United States. | Utopias—United States. | Utopias in mass media.
Classification: LCC E184.M5 A663 2022 | DDC 973/.046872—dc23
LC record available at https://lccn.loc.gov/2021029658

doi:10.7560/324479

For Hesley and Indira,
for always reminding me of what is possible

Contents

INTRODUCTION *1*

CHAPTER 1. *Salt of the Earth* *17*

CHAPTER 2. Brown-Eyed Soul *42*

CHAPTER 3. *Chico* and *Kotter* *68*

CHAPTER 4. *No Human Being Is Illegal* *96*

CHAPTER 5. Border Reggae *126*

CODA. *Ngātahi* *152*

Acknowledgments *164*
Notes *167*
Bibliography *191*
Index *208*

Chicanx Utopias

Introduction

Chicanx popular culture has long been home to utopian visions and impulses.[1] Film, music, television, and art indexed the worlds inhabited by Chicanx folk and the ways they sought to make them anew. Chicanx dreams of the future linked seemingly disparate people and places, showed how pop culture and social movements shaped one another, and revealed that utopia sprang from everyday experiences. In the chapters that follow, I untangle race, culture, politics, and utopia from the often-hostile conditions of the nation-state and culture industry to illustrate that they were deeply intertwined.

Herein lie stories of people who weaponized pop culture's far-reaching medley of experiences, desires, and practices to combat economic and political conditions that were often stacked against them.[2] Inspired by Walter Benjamin's grounding of the utopian ideal in material culture, I examine how Chicanx pop culture forged a "politics of the possible"[3] and could not be separated from the social, economic, and political struggles that gave shape to everyday life. If "Revolution" was more plausible with a small "r" and an "s" at the end, the "small" politics of pop culture may not have been so small after all. From this vantage point, the signs and sounds of Chicanx popular culture recalled C. L. R. James's assertion that "a revolution is first and foremost a movement from the old to the new and needs above all new words, new verse, new passwords—all the symbols in which ideas and feelings are made tangible."[4] Utopia's fleeting presence was evident in the everyday practice of Chicanx pop culture as much as any endgame of political struggle or more expansive and organized movements. Such moments were not simply fantasy or always subordinate to capitalist markets, but were integral to social transformation that depended on utopian visions, even when those visions were never fully realized.[5]

Pop culture also silenced or obscured Chicanx voices and revealed instances when utopian visions clashed with one another or with the capitalist networks that presumed to, but could not, totally control cultural consumption. If pop culture was one avenue for Chicanx communities to contest capital and politics, its malleability and profitability made it tricky terrain from which to do so. It was easy to be seduced by capital or to fall prey to those with competing economic or political motives. With the saturation of postwar economic markets came increasing commercialization and the risk of Chicanx culture losing its meaning; excluding voices; and concealing patterns of violence, sexism, or structural inequity. In the spirit of Stuart Hall's seminal analysis of popular culture as contested and pliable in its political orientation, the history of utopia in Chicanx pop culture is not simply a case of resistance to or seduction by market forces or the status quo.[6] Rather, the story is a complex and, at times, contradictory mix of the two.

Postwar Chicanx popular culture was created and circulated in a world shaped by the rise of neoliberalism, globalization, and movements for civil rights and global justice. If, as some theorists have suggested, the postwar period fomented ethnocide and exploitation in lieu of democracy and freedom, Chicanx pop culture gave rise to utopia born from crisis.[7] David Harvey described neoliberalism as the belief that "human well-being can best be advanced by liberating individual entrepreneurial freedoms and skills within an institutional framework characterized by strong property rights, free markets, and free trade."[8] Such practices depended on privatization and deregulation fueled by a marked decrease in state involvement, as Arlene Dávila pointed out, "all in the guise of fostering more efficient technologies of government."[9] Dávila further explained how neoliberalism wrought new forms of "social control through legal/juridical implements and ideological control through cultural and informational institutions and representations."[10] The pop cultural expressions in this book dwelled among these macroeconomic and political shifts, which both veiled and exposed the dynamics of their production, circulation, and consumption. Sometimes Chicanx pop culture aligned with neoliberalism, and at others it chafed against it.

Amid such conditions, the increasing commercial reach of Chicanx pop culture fostered novel connections between Chicanxs and people, places, and movements across the United States and the world. Utopias emerged from such contact and exchange, including the selling, buying, and pervasive commodification of Chicanx culture. The postwar United

States was home to new mechanisms of surveillance, subjugation, and control at the same time as artists and musicians found room to maneuver in the interstices of culture and capital.[11] Depending on form and context, popular culture was widely accessible and contained both radical or more moderate messages. At times, Chicanx pop culture boldly challenged exclusion or alienation. At others, it distorted or suppressed ideas of liberation and was ruthlessly exploited for profit. In these moments, the arc of Chicanx utopias in pop culture echoed what Lauren Berlant labeled "cruel optimism," when that which "ignites a sense of possibility actually makes it impossible to attain the expansive transformation for which a person or a people risk striving."[12] Regardless of their trajectory, however, Chicanx utopias revealed the "conditions of possibility" and "imaginability" that sprouted amid postwar economic and political conditions. These Chicanx utopias may appear to be mere fragments of a much larger picture, but, when taken together, they reveal a longer and protracted struggle by ordinary folk to engage forces that were seemingly much bigger and more powerful than they were.

The following chapters contain three interconnected story lines. The first examines the racial and transnational crossings of Chicanx pop culture. This Chicanx cultural history was determined less by racial or territorial logic than by interracial, multiethnic, and hemispheric—even global—social and political currents.[13] Chicanx pop culture often centered the experiences of African Americans, Latinxs, whites, or Indigenous communities in its production or consumption. It was not uncommon for Chicanxs to draw their identity from their politics instead of their politics from their Chicanx identity. This means prioritizing the racial and spatial transgressions of Chicanxs and non-Chicanxs alike. It requires highlighting Black, Jewish, or Japanese engagement with pop cultural forms considered to be Chicanx and exploring Chicanx experiences with forms not normally viewed as their own. What might we learn from thinking about Chicanx pop culture from the outside in and the inside out? By viewing it as part of a relational and expansive cartography, we see how the outer edges of Chicanx pop culture engaged its inner workings and vice versa. Those presumed to be both inside and outside of the ethnic, racial, or national margins of Chicanx culture helped fuel its production and circulation to render a reordering of Chicanx identity and politics. From these disorienting angles, there are few assumptions about who is or isn't considered Chicanx, where Chicanx history happens, and what constitutes Chicanx politics. While claims to cultural authenticity were paramount for some, others disavowed any racial, ethnic, or national litmus test for a Chicanx identity that transcended such boundaries. These different sight lines help us see that Chicanx cultural history must account for how the Chicanx experience was imagined to be part of a larger matrix of struggle over race, civil rights, global justice, and everyday life.[14]

The second story line centers on how Chicanx pop culture engaged social movements. Chicanx film, music, television, and art were not simply reflective of politics but often, although not always, constitutive of politics. Akin to Daniel Fischlin, Ajay Heble, and George Lipsitz, I "see politics as cultural and culture as political." They reminded us that "when we learn to think about culture and politics as discrete and mutually exclusive spheres of existence, we neglect the political work performed by culture and ignore the inescapably cultural dimensions of political mobilizations and identities."[15] Chicanx pop culture was a crucial venue for Chicanxs and others to engage in and give shape to the Chicano and global justice movements or, as T. V. Reed pointed out, "the unauthorized, unofficial, anti-institutional, collective action of ordinary citizens trying to change their world."[16] It was home to ideas, relationships, and social experiments that didn't happen or weren't possible in other arenas of life. As Lipsitz argued, pop culture sometimes functioned as a dress rehearsal for political organizing and struggle beyond the dance hall, big screen, or exhibition space.[17] This had myriad results. On the one hand, Chicanx pop culture could serve as a venue for ordinary people to express and share their views of the present and desires for the future. On the other, its flow and messaging was conditioned by the drive for profit and conflicting politics that saturated its production. In both instances, Chicanx pop culture filtered the politics of the moment in which it was created, marketed, circulated, and consumed. In the pages to follow, I highlight the interface between pop culture and politics; show how cultural politics were part of civil rights; and chart "globalization from below" in the cultural expression of ordinary people. Ultimately, the stories in this book show why pop culture mattered to social movements and vice versa.

The third story line is how Chicanx pop culture was home to utopian visions and impulses. I elaborate below on meanings of "utopia," but I say "visions" and "impulses" here quite purposefully. The utopias embedded in Chicanx popular culture were not the kind of intentional planned communities or societies often conjured by the term. Instead, they echoed Ruth Levitas's claim that "utopia is the expression of the desire for a better way of being or of living, and as such is braided through human culture."[18] Chicanx utopias could be clearly articulated visions of the future but were also often impulsive or, to cite *Merriam-Webster*, "spontaneous inclination[s] or incitement[s] to some usually unpremeditated action."[19] They made up a kind of microcultural politics that Robin D. G. Kelley has described as "daily confrontations, evasive actions, and stifled thoughts that often inform political movements."[20] From this point of view, utopia takes an untold number of forms and requires close inspection to be deciphered. While people's hopes for a better life were reflected in the films, music, television, and art that were bought and sold as finished products, their visions of utopia were always part of a job unfinished. Chicanx pop culture echoed what Jill Dolan called "utopia in performance." Dolan argued that utopia is made of those "small, but profound moments" with which we have "fleeting contact"; that it is "always in process, always only partially grasped," and that its importance is "as an index to the possible, to the 'what if,' rather than a more restrictive, finite image of the 'what should be.'"[21] Many of the figures in this book did not reach any world-changing moment of transcendence in their experiences with popular culture, but they were a part of and helped create many small moments when a better world momentarily came into view. Utopia functioned as a continuum through which film, music, television, and art bore witness to how the "politics of small things" can challenge the power of big things.[22] Ernst Bloch's advice rings true: "One should observe precisely the little things, go after them. What is slight and odd often leads the furthest."[23] People often expressed utopia for as long as they could and, in the best of moments, made unequal relations of capital, race, or gender inoperable on the ground in creative, often temporary ways. Such utopian impulses were sometimes stifled or extinguished, but not always. They were sometimes co-opted or distorted, but not always. Chicanx pop culture encompassed a "politics of the possible" that did not simply reflect failed efforts toward an unattainable utopia or "real" politics, but consisted of the experiences that animated everyday life and things people did to make it better.

The everyday creation, circulation, or consumption of pop culture in daily life revealed utopia as much as any finished cultural product that was bought or sold. Lawrence Grossberg explained the everyday as "the uncatalogued, habitual, and often routinized nature of day-to-day living, what we don't think about while we're living it; it encompasses all those activities whose temporality goes unnoticed."[24] Lauren Berlant distinguished the "ordinary" as "an impasse shaped by crisis in which people find themselves developing skills for adjusting to newly proliferating pressures to scramble for modes of living on."²⁵ Over the course of this book, utopia reveals itself in everyday life and ordinary practices as much as the success, failure, or meaning of any film, song, or television show. In this way, Chicanx popular culture provides clues to a kind of utopian tool kit that included the labor, place, collaboration, and aesthetics required to build or, in some cases, simply make a gesture toward a better world. These elements were fodder for crafting new identities and politics that were rife with limitations and had no guarantee of producing positive results or even lasting very long but nonetheless animated Chicanx cultural history. Just as Stuart Hall remarked that hegemonizing is hard work, Chicanx utopias remind us that counterhegemonizing may have been even harder.²⁶

Imagination and ingenuity were crucial elements in Chicanx pop cultural utopias. The different people, places, and times in this book were linked in what Alicia Schmidt Camacho called a Chicanx cultural imaginary. The concept of "imaginaries" helps unravel the many strands of Chicanx pop culture because it illuminates the possibilities and limits of people's world-making aspirations.²⁷ Chicanx cultural imaginaries took different shapes, including film, music, television, and visual art. Depending on their form, some imaginaries made stronger links between communities than others, some were more readily translatable into political collaboration, some were easily hijacked for competing objectives, and still others revealed gender or racial tensions.²⁸ Chicanx cultural imaginaries were never guaranteed to be radical, and many rested on commercialized, for-profit cultural practices. Yet they showed how people engaged the world around them and often tried to change it for the better, recalling that social change must be imagined before it can be practiced.

My focus on Chicanx pop culture renders a particular engagement with utopian studies. At the risk of oversimplifying a more complex debate, I consider Chicanx utopias to be less "blueprint" utopias than "everyday" utopias. The utopian studies scholar Davina Cooper is instructive here. She described blueprint utopias as "utopian objects—including novels, buildings, and planned communities."²⁹ Conversely, she highlighted everyday utopias as "networks and spaces that perform daily life . . . in a radically different fashion." Everyday utopias are a "way of engaging with spaces, objects, and practices that is oriented to the hope, desire, and belief in the possibility of other, better worlds."³⁰ The utopias in this book were everyday utopias, springing from the popular culture that Chicanxs produced or consumed, and striking a chord with Kathleen Stewart's sense of the ordinary and its affects as

> a shifting assemblage of practices and practical knowledges, a scene of both liveness and exhaustion, a dream of escape or of the simple life. Ordinary affects are the varied, surging capacities to affect and to be affected that give everyday life the quality of a continual motion of relations, scenes, contingencies, and emergences. They're things that happen. They happen in impulses, sensations, expectations, daydreams, encounters, and habits of relating, in strategies and their failures, in forms of persuasion, contagion, and compulsion, in modes of attention, attachment, and agency, and in public and social worlds of all kinds that catch people up in something that feels like *some*thing.[31]

Chicanx utopias were visions or impulses that revealed as much about the moment in which they existed and the people that experienced them as any imagined future. They affirmed Bloch's observation that "the essential function of utopia is a critique of what is present . . . utopian consciousness wants to look far into the distance, but ultimately only in order to penetrate the darkness so near it."[32]

Encompassing people's joy, sorrow, frustration, and hope, Chicanx utopias were part of, and in turn shaped, daily life. To be certain, they were not blueprints for any intentional or planned Chicanx community. This distinction between "blueprint" and "everyday" utopias has been articulated by many other scholars in slightly varied fashion. In his extensive writing on utopia, Bloch differentiated between more wishful "abstract" utopias and more deliberate "concrete" utopias.[33] Russell Jacoby distinguished between "iconoclastic" utopias, which "resist precise definition" in their articulation of "a longing that cannot be offered," and "blueprint" utopias, which "map out the future in inches and minutes."[34] Miguel Abensour similarly noted the difference between "heuristic" and "systematic" utopias as exploratory hypotheses compared to literal plans.[35] John Storey characterized "blueprint" utopias as models of the future in contradistinction to "radical" utopias, which consist of "a restless desire continually on the move in search of somewhere better. It is a continuous human journey, not a fixed destination." For Storey, "something is not utopian because it depicts a better world that it seeks to convince us to construct from a blueprint; rather, its utopianism derives from how it defamiliarizes the here and now."[36] As Rachel Bowditch and Pegge Vissicaro reasoned, "everyday performative gestures" and "performances in public life embody utopian possibilities."[37] Ruth Levitas keenly observed that there is a growing literature on "mundane or everyday utopianism, where alternative or oppositional social practices create new, or at least slightly different, social institutions."[38] Chicanx utopias were embedded in the everyday, organic to daily life, ever shifting, and always incomplete.

Pop cultural utopias likewise amplify relational approaches to the study of race and ethnicity in Chicanx history. Chicanx utopias fostered community and identities that were interracial or transnational as much as they were singularly ethnic or nationalist, reverberating with Natalia Molina's explanation of the relational turn in Chicanx history. She noted that "a relational treatment of race recognizes that the construction of race is a mutually constitutive process and demonstrates how race is socially constructed, hence fighting against essentialist notions. Furthermore, it attends to how, when, where, and to what extent groups intersect. It recognizes that there are limits to examining racialized groups in isolation."[39]

My account here thus dovetails with historical studies that unearth conflict, cooperation, and shared living conditions between Chicanxs and other racialized groups.[40] Pop cultural utopias gave meaning to race, Chicanidad, and Latinidad by challenging—and sometimes reinforcing—popular conceptions of ethnic Mexicans as racially inferior or outside the bounds of the national polity. Frequently based on interracial exchange, they also highlighted how differential racialization and racial scripts, described by Molina as instances when racial thinking about one group impacted another, informed daily life for many Chicanxs.[41]

The relational aspects of my narrative highlight what Grace Hong and Roderick Ferguson have referred to as "strange affinities" and "coalitional possibilities" among Chicanx and non-Chicanx populations.[42] Black-brown connections, in particular, were central to Chicanx utopias because, to borrow from Daniel Widener, the political and cultural struggles of Chicanxs have sometimes unfolded in the context of larger movements for social change in which African Americans played a decisive role and vice versa.[43] This book thus owes a debt to historians who have shown how African American and Chicanx experiences have often intersected. Pop culture surfaced as a site where, as Gaye Johnson pointed out, Chicanxs and African Americans "used the physical places they inhabited and the discursive spaces they imagined to assert their common humanity and forge shared struggles grounded in mutuality and solidarity."[44] John Márquez reminded us that while such pop cultural bonds reflected shared experiences and desires, they were also informed by "the influence of black history and culture on the subjectivities of nonblack yet also nonwhite peoples."[45] These degrees of relationality, if we can call them that, never guaranteed oppositional politics or identities but did harbor their possibility.

Chicanxs have long engaged places and politics beyond their immediate surroundings and throughout the Americas.[46] Rather than do a deep dive into a specific site, I survey Chicanx pop culture in several places, some predictable and others less so. Los Angeles, New Mexico, and the US-Mexico border region figure prominently in chapters to follow, for example, but even if to a lesser degree, so, too, do places like Aotearoa (New Zealand), New York, and Tokyo. Analyzing how Chicanx utopias extended across racial and geographic boundaries reveals their variant registers of interracial politics, degrees of connectivity between groups, and political impacts of pop culture.[47] At the same time, pop culture's mixing of race, utopia, and social movements was dependent on place, often flourishing when it was rooted in local neighborhoods and institutions while more open to appropriation or manipulation when it was not. To be sure, Chicanx utopias were grounded in real places, in real time, and, as Michael Gordin, Hellen Tilley, and Gyan Prakash observed about utopias, they were "never arbitrary" and always drew on the resources present around them.[48] At the same time, trafficking in imagination and linkages beyond the constraints of one's most immediate environment made Chicanx utopias unconfined by the boundaries of a single community, shackles of the past, or even some unrealized future.

The history of Chicanx popular culture accounts for those whom Chicanxs jammed with, graced a screen with, or made art with.[49] It sheds light on cultural connections that inspired or were inspired by political organizing that crossed racial and ethnic lines. It shows us that life sometimes unfolded differently in the realm of pop culture than in other social or political arenas. Perhaps above all, it recognizes the utopias in Chicanx pop culture as one way "to reimagine the world and to reclaim the ways in which meanings in the world are produced, conveyed, and shared."[50] In the remainder of this book, I chart the utopian across forms of pop culture, including film, music, television, and art, focusing attention on how such expressions were differentially created, commercialized, circulated, and consumed. To put it another way, variant pop cultural forms produced different utopian visions with divergent possibilities and limits, intersections with social movements, and racial compositions. Some aligned with one another, and others collided. Chicanx utopias were not a monolith, but, to paraphrase the Zapatistas, part of a pop cultural world where many worlds fit.

More than just a political referent, the Zapatistas reverberate with many of the Chicanx utopias in this book. The dramatic emergence of the Zapatista Army of National Liberation (Ejército Zapatista de Liberación Nacional; EZLN) on January 1, 1994, alerted the international community to the Indigenous peoples of Chiapas and their extraordinary movement for autonomy and dignity in Mexico's southernmost state. Against the seemingly overwhelming power of state and capitalist forces, the Zapatistas shared their vision for a better world and inspired others across the globe to do the same. Part of their appeal was—and continues to be—compelling political and cultural practices that resonated far beyond the jungles and mountains of Chiapas. These included principles of "preguntando caminamos" (asking we walk), "mandar obedeciendo" (to command obeying), and a healthy recognition of how song, dance, and art generated politics. Such ideas fueled the Zapatistas' call for an "international of hope" and, more to my point here, echo in many of the Chicanx utopias I explore in the chapters that follow. Reading the Zapatistas as theorists and practitioners of utopia helps us see utopia as a process embedded in everyday life rather than any sort of political or social end game. Zapatismo reminds us that struggle and utopia are intertwined, that utopia is imagined and practiced by racialized groups, and that under the right circumstances, it can be mobilized as an anti-racist project.[51]

Blending Chicanx history with utopian, critical race, and pop cultural studies enhances our understanding of each. For those who study or aspire to utopia, this book points to a longer history of brown utopias. Utopia has received scant attention in Chicanx history, although a few scholars have recently considered Aztlán—the Chicano movement's reclaiming of the US Southwest as its political, geographical, and spiritual homeland—as a utopian project. Their studies interrogated how Chicanx religion, literature, and art generated visions of Aztlán as a world better than the one activists critiqued for its racism; inequality; and dearth of economic, educational, and political opportunities.[52] Chicanx pop culture charts utopian impulses that crossed racial boundaries, encouraging a more robust engagement with utopia in other fields, including African American studies. From escaped slave and maroon communities to intentional communities in Africa or Latin America, to Afrofuturism, to the success of the Oscar-nominated 2018 film *Black Panther*, there is bountiful literature in Black studies on utopia.[53] These include examinations of African American utopian experiments in early twentieth-century California and Baja California that often relied on collaboration with Mexicans and Mexican Americans.[54] This vibrant tradition demands we interrogate how Chicanx utopias have been imagined and practiced in concert with African Americans and others. The postwar utopian visions of some Chicanxs weren't only centered on Aztlán but were also aligned with the internationalist and multiracial organizing of civil rights and global justice movements. If, as Edward Chan and Patricia Ventura argued, "insufficient attention has been given to race in relation to utopia," one of my aims is to find moments when race and utopia came together in Chicanx pop culture to propel belief in a world with less segregation and white supremacy.[55] Part of what distinguished Chicanx utopias was their desire to stamp out racism or at least make its deleterious effects less palpable in daily life.[56] At the heart of this book, I mix subfields to show how pop culture gave rise to racial crossings, political exchange, and utopian dreams that might not otherwise be viewed in the same way, or even at all.

Lessons for Chicanx history are to be had as well. Throughout the book, I reject vertical, "silo" archetypes that isolate Chicanxs and embrace horizontal approaches that emphasize their many encounters with non-Chicanxs. From this perspective, Chicanx history moves in at least three directions: the "cross," as in cross-ethnically and cross-racially; the "intra," as in intra-ethnic relations of citizenship, gender, class, and sexuality; and the "trans," as in the transnational reach of the Chicanx experience.[57] There have long been circuits of Chicanx cultural politics that were not overdetermined by relationships with Mexicans or Mexico, for example, suggesting that paradigms of *"mestizaje"* and "borderlands" do not fully encompass the relational and transnational dimensions in Chicanx cultural history.[58] The ensuing chapters also make clear that postwar Chicanx cultural history is as much about continuity as it is about discontinuity. The conventional periodization of Chicanx history that emphasized rupture between the Mexican American, Chicano, and post–Movimiento Chicanx generations does not adequately explain Chicanx pop cultural utopias. Much of the literature underscored the discontinuity between World War II and later decades, especially the 1960s and 1970s, emphasizing the generational and political breach between efforts for accommodation and assimilation in the earlier period and the militancy and radicalism of the later period. Chicanx pop culture shines a light on the continuity of interracial living, social movements, and utopian dreams.

The people who appear in these pages creatively used available resources, and I try to do the same via wide-ranging archives and methods. I make use of labor and activist records, corporate and entertainment archives, government documents, print media, museum exhibitions, oral histories, and a rich public archive of music, lyrics, and film. Combining more "conventional" sources with examination of an extensive audio and visual catalogue locates Chicanx utopias at the crossroads of pop culture, social movements, and the economic conditions that shaped the lives of ordinary folk. These materials reveal narratives of triumph and retrenchment, resistance and accommodation, limits and possibility embedded in everyday utopias and pop culture. My focus on pop culture requires that utopia sometimes be analyzed in textual form as a vision embedded in commodities bought and sold, but, more often, I am concerned with how the production, consumption, and circulation of pop culture provides clues to everyday utopias. My aim is not to eschew more textual-based interpretations—methods I utilize in this book and have deployed elsewhere—but instead to interrogate the politics and experiences generated by and within pop cultural worlds. Like T. V. Reed, I am interested in "movements as sites for the production and reception of cultural texts" and, to borrow from Pierre Bourdieu, in how such texts relate to one another within an expansive pop cultural field.[59] While I tried to produce versions and interpretations of history that reverberate with people's own experiences, this is not a book about what utopia meant to participants in Chicanx pop cultural worlds. Most of them, in fact, did not claim to be utopian. And yet, their often brilliant cultural and political activity has much to say about utopian narratives in Chicanx history. This requires thinking about utopia as method in addition to analytical category or practical goal.[60] Michael Gordin, Helen Tilley, and Gyan Prakash reminded us that utopias are "not just ways of imagining the future (or the past) but can also be understood as concrete practices through which historically situated actors seek to reimagine their present and transform it into a plausible future." This, they observed, means thinking of "utopia as practice, as a technique used by historical actors for understanding their particular contemporary circumstances—and thus viable for the historian."[61] In this book, I scour pop culture and related archives for glimpses of when utopia was articulated by Chicanxs and others to make sense of, challenge, or make better the worlds they inhabited.

The chapters that follow offer a series of cinematic, musical, and artistic riffs on what seemingly disparate figures and moments might teach us about the Chicanx experience more than a comprehensive postwar history. They reveal how pop culture served as an incubator for utopian visions, underscoring how commercialized leisure exposed linkages and cleavages in Chicanx identities and politics. The first three chapters examine popular cultural moments during the Cold War, the Chicano movement, and the broader struggle for civil rights. They expose racial and gender fault lines of Chicanx utopias to highlight the successes and failures of coalition. These chapters include discussions of those who were not Mexican American but were involved in the production of Chicanx pop culture as means to question who and what was considered Chicanx and how Chicanx utopian visions in the 1950s, '60s, and '70s came to be. The final two chapters and coda investigate pop culture related to a broadly construed global justice movement. They show how Chicanx utopias developed in concert with African diasporic, migrant, and Indigenous communities around the world to underscore how globalization existed at the grassroots as much as among corporations or nation-states. Each chapter presents a unique story of Chicanx utopia that, when paired with the others, illustrates how race, utopia, and social movements blended together with shifting tenor and to varying degrees. They illustrate that civil rights had its global currents, race was long central to global justice, and the belief that "another world is possible" infused Chicanx popular culture from the 1950s to the 2000s.

Chapter 1 considers the pro-labor, communist-inspired 1954 film *Salt of the Earth*. Based on the true story of a largely Mexican American miners' strike in New Mexico in 1950, *Salt* is often cited as part of the Chicanx canon of radical cultural politics. I examine how the filmmakers, labor organizers, and cast and crew involved in the film struggled to perform anti-racist and feminist utopias on- and off-screen. This chapter underscores the fact that utopia required hard work, in this case, the labor of filmmaking. *Salt* revealed how Cold War Red-baiting both spawned and stunted utopian possibilities, especially when we consider African American involvement in its production, its celebration of the hetero-normative nuclear family, and filmmakers' reluctance to engage US imperialism.

Chapter 2 probes brown-eyed soul music in Los Angeles during the 1960s and early '70s. Mexican American bands such as Cannibal and the Headhunters and Thee Midniters were part of a multiracial audio and political thicket that blended Black and brown with a mix of rock, soul, jazz, R&B, country western, Mexican, and Caribbean rhythms. Making music alongside the urgency of civil rights in Los Angeles, they provided a utopian soundtrack for the Chicano movement that flouted segregation and offered glimpses of a life in which race was lived differently. Tracking the longer history of brown-eyed soul from its seeds in the 1940s to its legacies in the '90s, in this chapter I assert that utopia was not simply a vision of the future. It was also rooted in histories of place, politics, and, at least in this case, popular music that informed people's aspirations for a better world.

In chapter 3, I tackle the racial and ethnic "revival" in 1970s network television. I ponder the on- and off-screen politics of *Chico and the Man* and *Welcome Back, Kotter*, prime-time sitcoms with Chicano or Latino characters. Shedding light on what race relations in America could be after the civil rights movement, both programs promoted racial utopia and the resolution of racial conflict as achievable goals. Each also had tens of millions of viewers each week, made big profits, and drew the ire of activists for their racial politics, including casting leads with actors who were not Chicano or Latino. This chapter illustrates that utopia was defined by its limits as much as by its possibilities, risked silencing marginalized voices, and was conditioned by whiteness and demands of the consumer market.

In chapter 4, I survey poster art in the immigrant rights movement since the 1980s. I tell the story of *No Human Being Is Illegal: Posters on the Myths and Realities of the Immigrant Experience* (*NHBI*), the traveling exhibition by the Center for the Study of Political Graphics (CSPG) in Los Angeles, from its initial installation after the 1986 Immigration Reform and Control Act (IRCA) to subsequent versions following California's Proposition 187 ballot initiative in 1994 and the May Day immigrant rights marches in 2006. In the face of ever-evolving immigration policy, anti-immigrant hysteria, and global economic restructuring, *NHBI* offered utopian visions of a world in which dignity triumphed over dehumanization. This chapter shows that the utopian imagination thrived on collaborative networks and produced its own unique aesthetics. *NHBI*'s utopian streak reflected the global dimensions of immigrant rights and the extensive grassroots connections of the CSPG and the artists and activists involved in the exhibition.

I explore reggae music in the US-Mexico borderlands in chapter 5. Since the early 1990s, a vibrant reggae scene flowered on both sides of the border from San Diego/Tijuana to El Paso/Juárez and beyond, revealing how Chicanx and Mexican youth found common social and political ground playing Afro-Caribbean-inspired music. Dozens of bands, frequent concerts and festivals, specialty shops, radio shows, and recording studios emerged amid the militarization of the border, anti-immigrant hysteria, and cultural tourism. Border reggae fueled a pop cultural diaspora not based solely on race or place-based identity but on shared struggles in the wake of global capital. This chapter illustrates that utopia in the neoliberal epoch emerged amid dystopian conditions and was rooted in local places while simultaneously being a cross-border phenomenon.

The "coda" analyzes *Ngātahi: Know the Links*, the six-part "rapumentary"/documentary series by the Maori hip-hop artist and videographer Dean Hapeta. Although Chicanxs were included in the films, they were neither their creators nor their central focus. Nonetheless, *Ngātahi* showed how Chicanx pop culture and activism was connected to music, poetry, and Indigenous rights around the world. It highlighted how performance, travel, and ethnography illuminated the intersections between the Chicanx experience and movements against neoliberalism since the turn of the twentieth century. Building on previous chapters, it puts Chicanx communities in dialogue with others to highlight the labor, places, collaboration, and aesthetics central to contemporary visions of utopia.

A note on terminology to close this introduction: Throughout the chapters that follow, I use several terms to refer to the people and communities I write about. These include "Mexican American," "Chicanx," "Latinx," "Chicana/o," and "Latina/o." The terms "Chicanx" and "Latinx," in particular, are crucial for their gender inclusivity and refusal to reproduce binary conceptions of gender. As such, they have gained widespread use among scholars and students as a self-referent and as a descriptor of Chicanx and Latinx studies as fields of inquiry. Most of the figures and moments in this book, however, populated time periods before the terms "Chicanx" and "Latinx" entered common usage. For many, more common terms were "Mexican American," "Chicana/o," or "Latina/o." Recognizing the perils of anachronism, I do my best to use each of these terms in its pertinent historical context. This means I use "Mexican American" or "Chicana/o" more when covering the Chicano and civil rights movement eras, while "Chicanx" and "Latinx" appear with additional frequency when discussing the 1990s and 2000s. This is, I recognize, an imperfect practice.

Perhaps more importantly, the signifiers "a/o" and "x" often fail to adequately encompass the Chicanx or Latinx history explored in this book. They are inadequate because some people preferred one over others, and each emerged from unique historical struggles, but also because they do not always explain the relational and transnational dimensions of Latinidad. Nor do they capture the tension and multiplicity within and between such categories. The identities, politics, and pop cultural expressions I uncover here transcend the "a/o" and "x" by mixing and extending the ethnoracial, geopolitical, and geographic expanses of Chicanx and Latinx history. While many of the people and places in this book may not fit neatly into existing Chicanx or Latinx narratives, they do highlight their generative and multiple possibilities. My hope is that this book will help open roads—both those less and well traveled—for making sense of the who and where in Chicanx and Latinx history.

CHAPTER 1

Salt of the Earth

On March 3, 1953, the small town of Silver City, New Mexico, was anything but a utopian scene. An angry throng of more than 150 Anglo residents violently confronted the mixed-race cast and crew of *Salt of the Earth*, the epic film based on the true story of a miners' strike in nearby Bayard, New Mexico. Led by a local druggist, the mob kicked cameras, assaulted crewmembers, and demanded, "All you communists better get out of here or you'll go out in black boxes." They paraded across town for more than two hours while singing "America the Beautiful."[1] The near-riot followed weeks of friction when Silver City was aflutter with rumors that *Salt of the Earth* was communist inspired and employed a multiracial production crew. Threats against the filmmakers came to a head after a local radio station broadcast California congressman Donald Jackson's February 24 address to the House of Representatives. Jackson railed against the still unfinished film as a "new weapon for Russia" in its attempt to "succeed in taking over the free countries of the world."[2] The *El Paso Herald* captured popular sentiment when it congratulated the vigilantes on their "determination to clear away the pink overcast from their beautiful country." The *Herald* concluded, "The air will be sweeter and the climate better when the self-styled movie makers are gone."[3] The storm around *Salt* conjured fear and visions of catastrophe more than any utopian future.

After its premiere in 1954, many wondered why the film sparked such controversy. *Variety* magazine surmised that "one would have to become quite analytical to read the alleged 'Red' line into this . . . production. It certainly isn't on the surface." The *New York Times* called *Salt* a universal story of "conflict that broadly embraces the love of struggling parents for their young, the dignity of some of these poor people and their longings to see their children's lot improved."⁴ Far from danger and disaster, reviewers saw in *Salt* a message of hope, humanity, and togetherness. The story concentrated on marital tensions between Esperanza Quintero and her husband, Ramon, in "Zinc Town," New Mexico, during a miners' strike. The largely Mexican American workforce, joined by fellow Anglo miners, went on strike to protest low wages, dangerous working conditions, and dilapidated housing in the company town. When the company secured a legal injunction prohibiting the miners from picketing, the Ladies Auxiliary of the union took over the picket line. Esperanza emerged as a leader of the strike, and Ramon, along with the other miners, felt his masculinity was being threatened. While the women kept the strike alive, the men were left to cook, clean, and care for children at home. Ramon and the other men gradually came to respect the women's role in the strike and understand that their exploitation in the mines was analogous to women's exploitation at home. Though it may have fallen short of being communist propaganda, *Salt of the Earth* glimmered with challenges to the rigid color line, the cult of domesticity, and the abuse of labor in the 1950s. Some might have even called it utopian.

Divergent responses to *Salt* stemmed from more than the film's content. Detractors like Congressman Jackson and the Silver City mob viewed it as a threat even before it was finished, in part because of several key figures in its production. Prior to launching *Salt*, its director, Herbert Biberman, and producer, Paul Jarrico, were called to testify before the House Un-American Activities Committee (HUAC). Biberman spent six months in prison as an infamous member of the so-called Hollywood Ten and, after being blacklisted, joined with Jarrico to start the International Production Company (IPC). The IPC was their channel to continue making films without the support of Hollywood studios and to employ fellow blacklisted writers and technicians, including African Americans who were excluded from the International Alliance of Theatrical and Stage Employees (IATSE).⁵ *Salt* would become the IPC's first completed project, cosponsored by the International Union of Mine, Mill, and Smelter Workers (Mine-Mill). Dozens of the miners and their wives from the real-life strike the movie was based on were recruited as actors and consultants. During production, the IATSE refused to provide crew members, the female lead Rosaura Revueltas was deported to Mexico, and politicians and the press condemned the film as subversive and un-American. Following the controversy, *Salt* was blacklisted by the motion picture industry after its release in 1954, banned by most theaters, and boycotted by much of the viewing public. It later found renewed life as a pro-feminist, pro-labor, pro–civil rights classic during and after the 1960s.

This extraordinary history of *Salt of the Earth* has been told before, most often as a case study in Cold War censorship or resistance to the era's cultural suppression.[6] It has been rightfully celebrated as a gripping tale of working-class struggle, women's empowerment, and interracial organizing and continues to animate the study of Mexican American, labor, and film history. Recent treatments by Alicia Schmidt Camacho and Ellen Baker, for instance, provided novel and rich readings of the film, the associated labor movement, and the lives of the union families involved.[7]

Less has been said about the making of *Salt* as a utopian project. Accentuating people's hopes for the future was at stake in the Cold War as much as the fate of capitalism, democracy, or communism, and this chapter considers the extent to which anti-racist, feminist, and anti-imperialist visions guided filmmakers and under what circumstances those visions were sacrificed for cinematic success. I am more interested in *Salt* as a collaborative project and social movement of its own accord than as cultural text. This means recognizing the labor of utopia, in this case filmmaking, and all of the painstaking hard work, energy, and emotional expense it entailed. *Salt of the Earth*'s utopian visions were the result of the daily grind by Hollywood moviemakers and the Mexican American mining community of Bayard working together. Riddled with triumphs, setbacks, and contradictions, the labor of making *Salt* recalled Davina Cooper's observation that utopia required an "ethos of maintenance, of digging in and getting things done."[8] This perspective on *Salt of the Earth* requires distinguishing between utopia as ongoing struggle and utopia as endgame. To create a final cut worthy of their aspirations, filmmakers and the mining community had to navigate one another's race, gender, and class differences off-screen, not to mention Red-baiting and threats of physical violence. The result was an on-screen vision of racial, gender, and political liberation that diverged from what transpired on the ground among the cast and crew. Despite its remarkable narrative of uplift and ultimate victory for the mining community, the less progressive politics that plagued its production weren't clearly visible on-screen. Shifting our gaze to the off-screen life of *Salt of the Earth* shows that utopia was challenging and difficult, if not impossible, to build, yet still worth investing in. This harkens to Jean Pfaelzer's generative reading of *Salt* as utopian text in which she argued, "*Salt* suggests the possibility of understanding the significance of how we live class, how we narrate it, and how we might change it."[9] I am much less interested in critiques of the film than in probing its racial and gender politics as a means to consider its utopian parameters. I ultimately suggest that *Salt* elucidated the limits of Chicanx utopias in the '50s as much as it did their possibilities.

WHY *SALT OF THE EARTH* MATTERS

Salt of the Earth has achieved iconic status in film, labor, and Chicanx history. It continues to resonate with viewers and critics for its enthralling story and reminder that working folk and their cultural politics can be as essential to understanding the 1950s as nation-states and high-level geopolitical policy. If the film unabashedly conveys a pro-union politics by making heroes of the miners and their wives in their standoff against the tyranny of the mine owners, it also underscores how seemingly disparate class interests worked together in an unorthodox, unique fashion. *Salt*'s production brought Hollywood filmmakers and Bayard miners together through their shared insubordination to capital and the state as much as any shared experience of exploitation.[10] It simultaneously brought white and Black filmmakers, professional actors, and stagehands together with Mexican American miners and white organizers. *Salt*'s creation told a triumphalist story of working-class politics while also relying on collaboration across racial and ethnic lines. Despite being wrought with race and gender conflict, as we see below, the film remains an extraordinary work of unlikely partnership and a powerful affront to Cold War–era suppression.

The making of *Salt* was politicized by the era's Red-baiting, demands for cultural and political conformity, rigid cult of domesticity, and racial segregation. Amid escalating fears of domestic subversion and foreign invasion fueled by Soviet advances, diversity and difference were openly discouraged, attacked, and demonized. Infamous inquiries by Senator Joseph McCarthy's Permanent Subcommittee on Investigations and the House Un-American Activities Committee sought to cleanse the culture industries, labor, and the Left of ideological dissent. Hollywood film and television were besieged by allegations of communist infiltration and foreign influence. Mexicans and other Latinos in the United States were among those targeted by the Immigration and Nationality Act of 1952, known popularly as the McCarran-Walter Act. It set strict new guidelines for legal entry into the United States and naturalization, and greatly expanded the grounds upon which undocumented immigrants could be deported.¹¹ *Salt of the Earth* was not spared the impact of such big-picture political trends and legislation. As we have seen, the entire project was branded as a communist instrument and, in addition, Rosaura Revueltas, the female lead and a Mexican national, was deported in the midst of filming in New Mexico.¹² Those involved in making the film paid a price for being part of a project that refused to fully shed political critique or silence Mexican Americans and women. *Salt of the Earth*, to borrow from James Scott, was one instance when the hidden transcripts of Cold War–era resistance came more fully into public view.¹³

Both the real-life strike on which the film was based and the creative process to make it were an experiment in union, race, and gender politics. The inspiration for *Salt* was the 1950–1951 strike by Mine-Mill Local 890 against the Empire Zinc Company in Bayard, New Mexico. Although Mine-Mill was Red-baited and had its charter revoked by the Congress of Industrial Organizations (CIO) in 1950 for alleged communist infiltration, the largely Mexican American Local 890 in Bayard went on strike for fifteen months. They demanded "collar to collar" pay (remuneration for all time spent underground in the mines), paid holidays, a modest pay raise of five cents an hour, and job classifications that did not relegate Mexican American miners to the lowest positions and less pay for doing the same work as Anglo miners. After the union deployed two picket lines that shut down production for eight months, the company secured an injunction that prohibited further picketing.¹⁴ Facing arrest, jail time, and fines if they continued the strike, the men of Local 890 reluctantly agreed to a proposal by Mine-Mill Ladies Auxiliary 209 that the women of Bayard take over the strike. The idea was initially presented by Virginia Chacón, Aurora Chávez, and Virginia Jencks. All three were married to active Local 890 members or Mine-Mill organizers. The women realized that because they were not actual members of the union, it was not illegal for them to picket. The wives, children, and other women of Bayard went on to conduct picket lines for seven months. During this time, many of the union men were forced to care for children and tend to daily chores at home. The miners eventually returned to work in 1952 and, although they did not win all of their demands, they secured higher wages, a new contract, and hot water plumbing for company-owned homes, a major issue for the women strikers.¹⁵

The Bayard strike was part of a larger landscape of radical Mexican American labor politics during the early Cold War. Mine-Mill militants, for example, had been involved in forming the Left-leaning Asociación Nacional Mexicana Americana (ANMA) in 1949, an organization committed to the defense and promotion of Mexican American rights across the Southwest. A New Mexican chapter of ANMA was born following a contentious police brutality case just months after the Empire Zinc strike began.[16] Along with several additional groups, including the American Committee for the Protection of Foreign Born (ACPFB), ANMA advocated for equality in housing, education, voting, women's rights, and immigration for both documented and undocumented immigrants and Mexican Americans. They saw the plight of Mexican Americans intertwined with that of noncitizen Mexican immigrants because of shared ethnic and class discrimination. In addition to fighting the devastating effects of the 1947 Taft-Hartley Act on organized labor, ANMA encouraged coalitions with African American and Jewish progressive causes, supported the peace movement against the Korean War, and protested the discriminatory application of the McCarran-Walter Act. When Local 890 struck against Empire Zinc in 1950–1951, ANMA provided financial support, food and clothing, and publicity in support of the strikers.[17] This broader political world in which the Bayard strike unfolded helped fuel its interracial, feminist, and internationalist organizing principles.[18]

Given its history, it is not surprising that the story of the Bayard strike appealed to Biberman and Jarrico. Both had been called before HUAC in 1951 for their affiliation with the Communist Party and blacklisted by 1952. Along with the screenwriter Michael Wilson, who was also Jarrico's brother-in-law, they perceived their own persecution as similar to that of the Mine-Mill unionists. Around the same time that Mine-Mill was striking in Bayard, Biberman and Jarrico formed IPC with the intent to produce movies about working-class, ethnic, and women's rights. They also made a point to include African Americans, and, in late 1951, Carlton Moss and Frances Williams joined IPC. Moss was a successful writer and producer, having authored productions for the Federal Theater and radio scripts for NBC. He had also produced a 1944 documentary for the War Department called *The Negro Soldier* that was screened for army inductees during World War II. Frances Williams was an accomplished actress who would go on to a distinguished career as both entertainer and civil rights activist.[19] After welcoming Moss and Williams on board, IPC was on the verge of making a feature film about the Scottsboro Boys, nine African American young men in Alabama convicted of raping two white women in the early 1930s, whose case was taken up and publicized by the Communist Party's International Labor Defense. They also considered a film about the African American writer

Paul Robeson and another on the life of Frederick Douglass. When Jarrico learned about the Bayard strike from organizer Clint Jencks while on vacation north of Taos, New Mexico, however, all other existing projects were put on the back burner. Jarrico excitedly told Biberman, "This is a story that's got everything. It's got labor's rights, women's rights, minority rights, all in a dynamic package."[20] The IPC soon came together with Local 890 to form a committee to oversee production of the film, recruit actors from the union and Bayard community to play themselves, and ensure the finished film was something they could all be proud of. The Hollywooders relinquished a fair amount of creative control over the script and production process to ensure that it addressed concerns of the mining community. Although problems and disagreements arose, it is not unfair to say that the IPC sought a filmmaking process that was as democratic and intersectional as the story they were dramatizing.[21]

The making of *Salt of the Earth* was as extraordinary as the film itself. It was something of a social movement and experiment in class, race, and gender politics all its own. It brought together the Hollywood Left with the working-class Mexican American Left. It mobilized film for dissent and opposition when mainstream politics and culture discouraged such activity. Those involved tried to take seriously the ways capitalism in the United States was raced and gendered. It was a utopian project, one that rested on the labor of its creators and their efforts to capture on-screen the glimpses of a better world modeled by working-class struggles off-screen. Such a project was grueling, full of hazards, and a reminder that making utopia was not easy.

RACIAL CROSSINGS

In its coverage of *Salt* in March 1953, the African American *Atlanta Daily World* called it a "Race Film."[22] The *Daily World* argued that branding of the film as un-American by politicians and the public was a response to the racial identity of Mine-Mill unionists and the film crew as much as any alleged communist sympathies. Along with a few other Black and Spanish-language newspapers, the *Daily World* celebrated *Salt*'s message of racial justice and the collaboration of the white filmmakers, Mexican American miners, and multiracial crew who made it. They countered the negative press about *Salt* and recognized that it was chock-full of racial crossings by parties with divergent backgrounds and experiences.²³ While many applauded *Salt*'s declaration of brown-white-Black unity against capitalism's evils, most observers were likely less aware of racial tensions in its off-screen production.

The finished film didn't stress much racial tension either. It was a feel-good version of poor Mexican and Anglo miners working together with white union organizers to fight the evil company. It was a story of old-fashioned class warfare in which the multiracial working-class emerged victorious. Juan Chacón, the president of Local 890, who played the male lead of Ramon Quintero, believed this was the film's greatest achievement. He argued that *Salt* "shows that workers can get along regardless of religion, color and politics." He added that it demonstrated "what we can do when we organized and we [Mexican Americans] and Anglo workers organized together."²⁴ Multiple narrative threads and scenes from the movie reflected this, including white "Okie," "Arkie," and ethnic white unionists being among the striking miners, the amiable working relationship between the white organizer Barnes (played by real-life Mine-Mill organizer Clinton Jencks) and the Mexican American rank and file, and the tight-knit relationship between Barnes's wife (played by Jencks's wife, Virginia) and many of the Mexican American women that eventually took over the picket line.

If racial cooperation was an important storyline in the film, it begs the question of how race shaped the making of *Salt*. Although it was most remembered for bringing together the largely Mexican American union and white filmmakers, the production included a number of African Americans, too. Black participation in *Salt* has been largely overlooked, but it offers a unique sight line into the project. Both Carlton Moss and Frances Williams pushed for additional Black crew to be included, a direction IPC embraced since it aligned with its initial desire to do African American–themed films and create content in support of civil rights. The hiring of Black crew members was important because many were not afforded regular employment from big Hollywood production companies. In his 1965 book, *Salt of the Earth: The Story of a Film*, Biberman nostalgically recalled the African American technicians that worked on the film. He wrote, "We had three Negro crew members who were at long last fulfilling a dream—they were engaged in making a motion picture, and fighting to learn how against a more equitable future for Negroes."²⁵ In another instance, following a meeting between filmmakers and union members early on in production, Biberman recalled that "the men gathered to talk about the crew that had come from Hollywood. The Negro and the Anglo people of the crew worked so well together that the miners had thought they had been working side by side for many years."²⁶ Such snippets about the Black crew on *Salt* are revealing. They suggest that everyone got along, yet raise questions about what Biberman didn't remember and whether the Black crew, Mexican Americans, or women involved might tell another story. If nothing else, Biberman's recollection illustrated how gender shaped his memory of race in the production of *Salt*. For him, it was the men, not the women, who met and discussed the Black crew. This was a clue, as we see below, that the racial dynamics were not as harmonious as Biberman seemed to think they were.

Still, the collaborative spirit required members of IPC and Mine-Mill to deal with one another's differences and design measures to incorporate everyone's ideas into the film. For example, the production committee formed to manage the daily work of shooting in New Mexico included six representatives each from the IPC, Local 890, and the Ladies Auxiliary 209. In addition to scheduling day-to-day logistics, including babysitting to allow the Bayard women time to attend meetings, the committee helped Biberman, Jarrico, and Wilson rewrite the script. Chacón noted that the committee held "meetings in which the union people pointed out to our Hollywood friends that a scene we had just shot was not true in certain details. When that happened we all pitched in to correct the mistake. Most of these mistakes were made because the movie craftsmen had not lived through all our struggles."²⁷ Michael Wilson commented that he would have ordinarily "detested" the collective writing process, "but in this case I didn't mind it [at] all. . . . I welcomed their opinions because in the process of asking questions, of hearing their opinions, I was learning more about them. It made me better qualified to write the story of their lives."²⁸ Biberman and Jarrico remembered fondly the process of collective critique. After Wilson completed the first script, they recalled, he returned to the mining community with his treatment, "where it was read, discussed and criticized by a score of miners and their wives. With this guidance in authenticity[,] he [Wilson] proceeded to write the first draft screenplay. When it was completed, again we followed the procedure of group discussion and collective, constructive criticism. By rough estimate, no less than four hundred people had read, or heard reading of, the screenplay by the time we commenced production."²⁹

This creative process had real results. Union members challenged instances of ethnic or racial stereotyping and inaccuracy. For instance, they objected to story lines that portrayed the white union organizer as rescuing the workers. They challenged scenes that represented Mexican American mining men as womanizers and drunks or depicted Mexican American homes and communities as dirty and unorganized.[30] Clinton Jencks recalled that this process "wasn't all easy. There were people who came in, making the film, [who] had very strong ideas about how the film should be made. . . . We'd have arguments. . . . We'd be working hard all day,. . . and we'd have meetings until late at night, hammering out problems for the next day." He concluded, "It was a beautiful kind of process of interchange."[31] All of this lends support for the claim that the daily labor of making *Salt* reflected a progressive approach to race and was intended to build a working world where everyone's visions of what the film could be were taken seriously.

Dynamics external to *Salt* made the challenge of creating a racially inclusive and equitable moviemaking process more toilsome. In his "Red Movie in Making" speech to Congress in February 1953, Congressman Donald Jackson bashed the film as communist and framed the racial politics of *Salt of the Earth* very differently. Jackson, an active member of HUAC and a fierce anti-communist, argued that the *Salt* project was spreading propaganda that the United States "is against all colored people" and that the film was "deliberately designed to inflame racial hatred." He falsely charged that the film conveyed the idea that safety regulations in the mines were only for Anglo miners and that the IPC imported two carloads of "colored people" for the sole purpose of filming a mob riot scene, which he said was a negative representation of Black people.[32] While his charges were rich with irony, given how Chacón and others described *Salt*'s production, Jackson's views were echoed by many in the entertainment industry, including the Screen Actors Guild (SAG) and IATSE. While it is unlikely that racist hyperbole from Jackson or others drove filmmakers to mute the racial focus of the film, one wonders if racial harmony was highlighted, perhaps even overemphasized, as an antidote to the racist hysteria surrounding the making of the film.

The desire to present a racially unified working class was evident in the film's neglect of tensions between white and Mexican American miners. At its core, the 1951–1952 Bayard strike was about racial inequality between workers. Chacón observed, "The companies around here have always been afraid of Anglo-Mexican unity. For a hundred years our employers have played up the big lie that we Mexicans are 'naturally inferior' and 'different,' in order to justify paying us less and separating us from our brothers."[33] Among the biggest complaints by Mexican American miners was that they were subjected to a two-tier wage system in which they were paid significantly less than Anglo miners for the same job. Jencks recalled that the Mexican American miners' decision to strike was motivated by "just a simple straightforward refusal of the company to follow the wage and working condition patterns . . . already established at the other mines in the district."[34] Once the women of Bayard were more directly involved in the strike, the fact that Mexican Americans did not have indoor plumbing in their company-built homes while Anglo miners did also became a central issue.[35] The result was that the great majority of strikers were Mexican American and only twelve of the initial ninety-two striking miners were Anglo. The real-life strike was based on demands for racial equality *among* the miners and *within* the mining community, a point Jencks emphasized when he claimed the heart of the strike was about fighting the "100 percent, white, Anglo-Saxon supremacy" that determined hierarchy in the mines.[36]

The discrepancies between the real-life strike and the one in *Salt* stemmed in part from preconceived views about race on the part of those in charge. Biberman and Jarrico as much as admitted their ignorance about Mexican Americans. Early on in the production process, Jarrico was concerned that they wouldn't be able to tackle the story of the strike and its people with "sufficient humility, with sufficient awareness of their sensitivity to the most subtle forms of chauvinism."[37] Biberman even had trouble distinguishing Mexican Americans from Mexican nationals, a distinction he began to make more clearly only after casting the Mexican national Revueltas in the female lead.[38]

The challenge of navigating racial differences was further crystallized in the experiences of the African Americans on the set. Despite their omission from most historical accounts of *Salt*, they were an important part of the project. Even with several Black technicians on the production team, the Black presence in *Salt* was most felt in Frances Williams's crucial role as interlocutor between the IPC and Mine-Mill. Williams was credited as an assistant producer, but she was responsible for much of the informal arbitration required to get the Hollywood and Bayard contingents to more effectively communicate with one another. Even before filming began in New Mexico, Williams anticipated that tensions were likely to emerge between the white filmmakers and the Mexican American miners. She recalled a conversation with Jarrico, Biberman, and others from IPC just before leaving for New Mexico.

> At our last meeting in Los Angeles, some of the men questioned whether I should go. My reputation as a fighter was thought to be det-

rimental to the project. "You know, Frances," they said, "the Mexicans are very different from the Blacks. They're very prejudiced. They don't really accept Blacks. They're very docile and take things in stride. They don't protest the way you and your people do." In other words, they wanted to keep me quiet. I held my peace, thinking of the irony in the situation. "We're going down to see mine workers who are mostly Mexican Americans and who are on strike! And they don't fight?"³⁹

Williams's frustration with Jarrico and Biberman was a sign of things to come. It foreshadowed how racial and gender differences among those involved in the project led to competing visions of political liberation. To put it bluntly, while the film was a brilliant achievement in many ways, it may not have come off as it did without Williams laboring to smooth over discrepancies among the parties involved and between its turbulent off-screen politics and on-screen message of equality.

Williams initially joined IPC after mutual acquaintances suggested to Jarrico that she would be a valuable addition to the company. After the two met in New York to discuss the prospect of teaming up, Jarrico was convinced she should join the team. Williams's formidable track record as a performer, steadfast commitment to growing the African American presence in Hollywood, and personal story were exactly what Jarrico and Biberman were looking to bring into IPC. Williams was born in 1905 in New Jersey but grew up in Cleveland, where, at age sixteen, she began acting at the Karamu House, one of the longest-standing African American theaters in the country. At Karamu, she befriended the writer Langston Hughes and the artist Zell Ingram, among others, establishing a network of fellow Black performers that would eventually include Paul Robeson and many others. It was Robeson who suggested that Williams study theater in Russia to see firsthand a socialist revolution. She did so in 1934, encountering communist philosophy and arts training difficult to come by in the racially segregated United States. Williams moved to California in 1941 and jump-started her acting career with a part alongside Ginger Rogers and David Niven in *Magnificent Doll* in 1946. Her long and illustrious career included performances on Broadway, roles in over forty films, and, at its end, a key part in the television sitcom *Frank's Place* in 1987. It was in the early '40s, however, upon arrival in Los Angeles, when Williams began to cultivate a seething critique of the entertainment industry for its lack of Black actors and the appallingly stereotypical roles the few who were afforded opportunities were asked to play. It wasn't long before she helped begin the Minority Actors Committee of the Screen Actors Guild and began breaking down doors for more African Americans to enter Hollywood. This was only the beginning of her political activism. In Los Angeles, she founded the city's first Black theater, the Paul Robeson Community Center, and was the first African American woman to run for the California State Assembly in 1948 as part of the Progressive Party ticket. Around the time she joined IPC in 1951, Williams was also active in the National Negro Labor Council (NNLC), a trade unionist organization targeted by HUAC. Her activist résumé continued to grow long after her stint on *Salt*. Some of this work revolved around entertainment, and some did not. For example, she represented the World Peace Council at the first Angolan Independence celebration in 1975, helped organize Women for Racial and Economic Equality in Chicago, and cofounded Art Against Apartheid in Los Angeles. Williams brought all of her political dynamism and dedication to equality to bear on *Salt of the Earth*.[40]

Williams's recollection of *Salt* was decidedly mixed. She openly recalled the shortcomings of its racial politics and failures of leadership as much as she celebrated the utopian vision of the final version. She recalled, "Oh, it came out a very good film," but "I think there's a whole side of it that they have never said anything about."[41] In her biography of Williams, *Meet It, Greet It, and Defeat It*, Anna Christian highlighted Williams's sometimes rocky relationship with Biberman and Jarrico and her discomfort with their approach to working with the Mexican American unionists.[42] Years after the experience of working on *Salt*, Williams said of Biberman, he was a "good director," but also "a strange fool, . . . an arrogant fool."[43]

Soon after she arrived on set—over protests from Biberman, who initially did not want her on-site—Williams quickly learned that she was not the only one with concerns. "I got to New Mexico on a Saturday night," she recalled, "and they had a gathering on Sunday morning, and these Mexican Americans came to me and said, 'Could you help us? These people [the filmmakers] just don't understand.' This is the first Sunday that I'm there, and I don't mean just one person [came to me], I mean groups."[44] It quickly became clear to Williams that she wasn't the only one who saw that the Hollywood moviemakers were struggling to win over the mining community. Juan Chacón said as much when he recalled that union members were initially in awe of the "movie big shots" and that it took some time before they felt comfortable with "El Biberman," the nickname many of the miners took to calling the director.[45] In another, slightly more malevolent instance, Virginia Jencks remembered a union member named Gonzales. He eventually befriended her husband, Clint, but only after telling him, "I hate you . . . all of you with blue eyes."[46] Despite the best of intentions by organizers and filmmakers, it shouldn't come as a surprise that Mexican American miners were wary of their intrusion into the Bayard community.

It didn't take long for Williams to emerge as the interlocutor between the IPC and Local 890 on a myriad of issues. Upon touching down in New Mexico, for example, she immediately "noticed with some consternation . . . that the [IPC] group had rented a recreation clubhouse with a screened-in porch, and a spectacular view overlooking the city, a resort kind of place that was used for vacationers when they came to New Mexico. I protested. None of us knew enough about the Spanish language, and we didn't know enough about the people. I felt we should be living with the people in their homes so that we could understand them and what their grievances were. That was the first big fight we had."[47] Eventually, the Hollywood crew rented the ranch of a former Mine-Mill miner as headquarters for the duration of the film's production. When she agreed to join IPC and work on *Salt of the Earth*, Williams was the one who insisted on hiring Black technicians. She recalled, "We couldn't find any Black technicians in Los Angeles. I was able to get a young cameraman named Hillburn who was working with a documentary group in New York to come out [to New Mexico] and work with us."[48] There were at least two more Black technicians she helped recruit to join the crew in New Mexico. In his pathbreaking study on the suppression of *Salt of the Earth*, James Lorence cited one specific instance when Williams helped change the trajectory of the film. He wrote that Williams was able to "successfully urge revisions in Wilson's initial emphasis on the role of the film's white union organizer (Barnes)" in order to avoid "the screenplay's portrayal of an Anglo organizer 'saving the Mexican masses.'" Clint Jencks, the real-life Mine-Mill organizer upon whom the Barnes character was based and who played Barnes in the film, agreed wholeheartedly with the changes wrought by Williams and Wilson.[49]

Williams recounted a number of incidents when the IPC's ignorance about working with Mexican Americans left much to be desired and threatened to undermine the project. Her role as assistant director included helping gather the actors, read lines, and making sure everyone "knew what they were doing and why." Because of her role in helping manage the daily schedule, Williams observed, "I was able to build up a rapport with many of the people that I would not otherwise have been able to." Early in production, for instance, a group of miners came to Williams with concerns that the IPC group was oblivious to how participation in the film might jeopardize their already marginalized status in Grant County in New Mexico. They told her, "These men don't know where we are and their attitude is going to cause those of us who are still working and even the ones on strike who are still on payroll to lose our jobs because they don't understand. Will you speak to them?" Williams called a meeting with the production heads and remembered that only Michael Wilson had sympathy for the concerns of the Mexican American miners. Biberman and Jarrico didn't even want to take the meeting, but were eventually persuaded to do so. Things ran more smoothly for a while, until a number of Mine-Mill folk came to Williams again. This time they were incensed that the IPC had run radio ads searching for movie extras, even though it had been agreed the union would provide any additional employees the film needed. According to Williams, the miners were insulted and betrayed, but also at risk because the IPC did not comprehend the tenuous position of the union in local and regional politics. Unionists feared unnecessary advertising of the film might enflame racial tensions in Silver City and the surrounding area. As we've already seen, they weren't wrong. Jarrico told Williams there was no time for another meeting, but she angrily insisted. She recalled, "Despite the fact that we got a number of things straightened out, these foolish men went back to their technique of trying to hire people over the radio. It was disastrous; we almost lost the whole project."[50]

Williams's involvement in *Salt* went largely unrecognized. Her official credit on the film as assistant producer failed to capture her immense contributions as mediator between filmmakers and unionists or thoughtful critic whose insights guarded against the filmmakers' racial ignorance. In his lengthy recollection of the film, Michael Wilson briefly mentioned Williams. He remembered, "Predictably, the members of the Ladies Auxiliary assumed a major share of responsibility for the daily maintenance problems of child care, food, transportation, communication. One of the Hollywood people who worked with them on these tasks was Frances Williams, a black woman from the Hollywood political community. Her presence seems to have been particularly valued by the women of New Mexico, one of whom said, 'Don't forget to talk about Frances, she always gets left out.'"[51] Another union miner, Lorenzo Torrez, who played himself in the movie, observed that if not for Williams, the input of miners on the film would have been far less than it was. He also affirmed that "she was never really accepted" by Biberman, Jarrico, and the IPC. It is not surprising that Williams, the lone African American woman on the Hollywood team, was the most essential ally for many of the Mexican Americans on the project, especially the women. Historians have since begun to acknowledge Williams's participation, yet have likewise not done justice to all the work she did to make *Salt* a success. In hindsight, as she was the person involved in *Salt* most engaged with the racial politics of the film industry, it's not a shock that Williams highlighted the contradictions of its racial messaging. Her role and perspective mattered deeply precisely because she exposed the dissonance between the representation of racial utopia on-screen and the failure to practice it off-screen. Williams's own thoughts on *Salt of the Earth* say a lot about its racial politics. "When I finished, I was all right," she remembered. "I'd gotten the ugly part of *Salt of the Earth* out of my system. The irony is that even with their lack of respect for other people's dignity, it was a landmark picture."[52]

Salt exposed the difficulties of doing an interracial, collaborative movie project during the Cold War. Without discounting the film's success, it is worth appreciating its remarkably taxing challenges. As Shana Bernstein showed in her work on interracial social movements of the era, it was not easy to push aggressively for civil rights while simultaneously navigating racism and anti-communism.[53] *Salt of the Earth* underscored that this was as tricky in popular culture as it was in other political arenas.

FEMINIST VISIONS

Despite the desire by filmmakers to tell a triumphalist story of women's empowerment, *Salt*'s feminism was as frayed as its racial dynamics. Frances Williams's efforts to ensure that union families and Mexican American women had a voice in the project were indicative of such. In her 1977 commentary on *Salt of the Earth*, Deborah Silverton Rosenfelt agreed. On the one hand, she observed that *Salt*'s feminism was rare for 1950s moviemaking and a welcome "vision of growing power through growing sisterhood." On the other hand, she remarked that it "offers no criticism of the nuclear family itself and the basic division of labor along the line of traditional gender roles. Its feminism stops," Rosenfelt concluded, "where feminism stopped in the lives of those who worked on the film and lived the history on which it is based."[54] As in the case of race, the gender politics of making *Salt* were contested and more complicated than they appeared on-screen. In her analysis of the film, Ellen Baker pointed to a useful, if general, notion of feminism for making sense of the discrepancies. She explained feminism as "the recognition that women are subordinate to men, the belief that this subordination is not natural, and the conviction that an end to male domination is both possible and desirable."[55] In each of these aspects, the making of *Salt* revealed competing conceptions and lived experiences of feminism for men and women, Mexican American women and white women, and miners and filmmakers. Gender, race, and class differences ensured that the variant feminisms that informed the film were not always equal, as not all listened like Frances Williams did to the voices of the Mexican American women involved in the project.

Those who viewed *Salt of the Earth* saw a film that prioritized the Ladies Auxiliary's efforts to push the union to expand their strike beyond the mines to include the entire community in a working-class struggle. The film emphasized the positive impact of Mexican American women's collective action on both the immediacy of the strike and the longer-term fate of the mining families. Esperanza and the other women picketers stood up to their husbands, to the male sheriff and his men who tried to break their lines, and to the male heads of the mining company. Viewers are left with the impression that life in Zinc Town after the strike will value women's unpaid labor as much as work in the mines. There is hope that the women's organizing and autonomy will have a lasting effect on the entire community. Such visions were indelibly stamped in iconic scenes, including Ramon stumbling over the "woman question" as he hung laundry while Esperanza led the picket. Or, in another, Esperanza emphatically used her shoe to fend off aggressive attempts by the sheriff to break the women's picket, all while Ramon and the other men sat idly on a nearby hilltop.

The significance of such scenes was conditioned by gender and American life during the early Cold War. As Elaine Tyler May showed, a 1950s cult of domesticity associated the public sphere with masculinity and the private sphere with femininity.[56] This was particularly the case in Mexican American communities like Bayard, where patriarchal constructs of family and ethnic identity were especially stout. Alicia Camacho Schmidt further noted how the notion of the domestic had double meaning for Mexicans, Mexican Americans, and other Latinos in the age of the McCarran-Walter Act. Their domesticity invoked debate over the lines between citizen and noncitizen or subversive and not-subversive as much as public and private or masculine and feminine.[57]

In the bigger landscape of Cold War domesticity, to put it another way, Mexican American women strikers were simultaneously viewed as un-Mexican and un-American.

Salt was also a collaboration between two heavily male-dominated industries that made it difficult for feminist politics to take hold. New Mexican mining and Hollywood filmmaking featured few women. It's not far-fetched to say that the men from the IPC and the union found common ground in their own political awakening about feminism and struggles for gender equality. Their shared masculinity and gender privilege may have been the shortest way through to a working relationship for these men from vastly different class and occupational positions. The miners of Bayard also shared fraternal bonds sutured by their participation in an almost purely male line of work, hours spent together in the darkness of the underground mines, and collective opposition to the mining bosses. When the women eventually took over the picket lines, a central part of the story in the real-life strike and the movie was the ensuing crisis of manhood among their husbands. Even as their political influence grew as the strike unfolded, the women were viewed more as substitutes or proxies for the male strikers than as autonomous political subjects of their own.

The role of women in the IPC was also open to question. Biberman, Jarrico, and Wilson were the authoritative voices in IPC, but, in addition to Frances Williams, there were other women in the company. Though they were also often overlooked, Sylvia Jarrico (wife of Paul Jarrico) and Sonja Dahl Biberman (sister-in-law of Herbert Biberman) were active in the IPC and on set in New Mexico. Both were associate producers, though not listed in the credits. Like Williams, Sonja Biberman advocated for the needs of the Bayard women in the production committee and worked as a "jack of all trades" throughout the production process. Neither Sonja Biberman nor Sylvia Jarrico was, as Ellen Baker noted, "afforded the same kind of formal recognition as women in a film on the Woman Question that [IPC members] Carlton Moss and Frances Williams received as African Americans in projects on the Negro Question."[58] Nevertheless, it must be noticed that Sylvia Jarrico and Sonja Biberman were "associate" producers, whereas Frances Williams was an "assistant" producer, an indicator of the racialized hierarchy of the production team. Nor, apparently, did it occur to those in charge of *Salt* that Williams may have offered crucial insight on both the "Woman Question" and the "Negro Question." That Williams or the Mexican American women of Bayard were able to impact *Salt* as much as they did is a testament to their strength and ingenuity.

The gender politics of mining and filmmaking helped determine what was and wasn't included in *Salt of the Earth*. One omission, for example, was domestic violence. In her indispensable book *On Strike and on Film*, Baker noted that domestic violence was not uncommon in the mining households of Bayard. Though it was rarely made public, let alone dealt with through legal channels, domestic violence was a known issue among men in the union.[59] In the movie, the physical violence against Mexican American women was by white lawmen or strikebreakers. Among the most memorable scenes, in fact, were those when strikebreakers ran over the women picketers with their cars, and the women stood firm in the face of the sheriff's order to use tear gas to disrupt the lines. The women in the real-life strike also defied gender norms more brazenly than in the film. They threw rocks and used unorthodox weapons like knitting needles and eggs against both strikebreakers and the police. Many dressed in a more masculine or "modern" fashion, but were shown to wear more traditional clothes in the film.[60] *Salt* also failed to acknowledge that no women participated in the final union negotiations with Empire Zinc that settled the strike.[61] Such omissions suggest that the men involved in making *Salt of the Earth* may have experienced far less of a political awakening off-screen than the Mexican American women of *Salt* did on-screen.

It is not surprising that voices of Mexican American women were stifled. Most Mine-Mill unionists viewed the strike in largely patriarchal terms that framed women's politicization as linked to their domesticity. For example, José Fuentes, the president of Local 903 in nearby El Paso, Texas, authored an article for the Mine-Mill newspaper after his visit to the women's picket lines in Bayard. He exhibited the ambivalence and sexism with which many union men viewed the women strikers. He wrote,

> We would have never thought it possible that the wives of the striking brothers would have felt such a sense of responsibility and cooperation or that they would have had such an urge to struggle jointly with their husbands, fighting for a life a little more comfortable for themselves and their children. . . . Jail, clubs, pistols, tear gas, criticism, blows from the deputies, every kind of inhuman treatment—all turned out to be nothing, compared to the happiness of their homes.[62]

In her brilliant reading of the Mine-Mill newspaper, Camacho surmised that the unionists "struck an uneasy balance between promoting women's labor activism and containing their problematic militancy to the domestic front of struggle."[63] The real-life strike and film featured a disruption of gender roles when the women took over the lines and men took over housework and childcare, but even when the gendered division of labor was temporarily inverted, it was ultimately reinforced. As Rosenfelt argued, *Salt* largely failed to disrupt the Cold War cult of domesticity that privileged the nuclear and reproductive family as central to the integrity of the nation.

In the years that followed the completion of *Salt*, the impact of the strike and the film on the women's lives continued to be mixed. Some Bayard women saw their husbands' behavior change for the better, their marriages and homes become more egalitarian, and their self-confidence grow.[64] Others, like Virginia Chacón, wife of Juan, didn't think things changed all that much. She later remarked, "We're still back in the old way. Not the new way.... The movie was made, fine. That's as far as it got. We went back to the old way. And it's still in existence."[65] Not surprisingly, as Rosenfelt described, the Hollywood women affiliated with *Salt* were more active in the extended life of the film. Sonja Biberman was a key figure in its distribution and helped arrange future screenings, including at an international women's film festival in 1975.[66] Gail Sondergaard, the actress and wife of Herbert Biberman, who was initially slated to play the part of Esperanza before the Bayard community objected to a white woman playing the lead, finally got her chance to perform *Salt*. She read excerpts from the film as part of her one-woman show, "Woman, Her Emergence into Fuller Status as a Human Being in Relation to Her Mate."[67] If *Salt of the Earth* foreshadowed the coming of second-wave feminism in the '60s, the divergent trajectories of the women involved also anticipated the racial and class fissures that would come with it.

The story of Rosaura Revueltas was a case in point. While the male lead of Ramon went to a member of the union, Biberman never considered this an option when casting the role of Esperanza. Revueltas was a professional actress from Mexico. Her arrest and deportation under the auspices of the McCarran-Walter Act in the midst of filming in New Mexico prompted outcries in both the Spanish-language press in the United States and in the national press in Mexico. It caught the attention of many in the Mexican film industry, which threatened to protest Revueltas's treatment by prohibiting American actors from appearing in Mexican-made films.[68] In the wider panorama of Latina/o radicalism, Revueltas's deportation placed her and *Salt of the Earth* in the same conversation with other Mexican American women and Latina activists persecuted in the 1950s under the McCarran-Walter Act and other oppressive measures. Revueltas was mentioned alongside women like Luisa Moreno, Josefina Fierro, and Emma Tenayuca, all three of whom were forced to leave the United States or go into hiding after decades of organizing across the US Southwest. Each had long histories of uncompromising advocacy for ethnic Mexican, immigrant, women's, and labor rights dating back to the Great Depression.[69] They organized across lines of citizenship and national borders, linked working-class Mexican American struggles to others fighting racial capitalism, and understood all too well the particular risks for Mexican American women under the domestic containment policies of the Cold War. Despite the association of Revueltas and *Salt* with this extraordinary history of Latina activism and persecution, the film failed to engage this longer tradition of feminism and organizing.

It may not be off the mark to suggest that *Salt of the Earth* was simultaneously behind the times, ahead of its time, and a product of its time when it came to projecting women's rights. To borrow a Cold War–era term, the film and its production process contained Mexican American women's activity as much as it cultivated new possibilities. The Mexican American women involved in *Salt* fought against long odds that included the retrenchment of patriarchy and normative domesticity in the Cold War, the motion picture industry, and everyday life in the Mexican American mining communities of New Mexico.

ANTI-IMPERIALIST ERASURES

Salt of the Earth's utopian visions of race and feminism were curtailed by Cold War politics and the internal dynamics of its production process, but its anti-imperialism fared even worse. When Representative Donald Jackson blasted the film in his February 1953 speech to Congress, he explicitly linked it to a broader communist, geopolitical threat against US democracy and capitalism. Jackson claimed the filming of *Salt of the Earth* so close to the Los Alamos atomic testing grounds amounted to flagrant communist infiltration with intent to destabilize national security. Without having seen the yet unfinished film, he characterized *Salt* as anti–Korean War because it valorized a labor strike against a critical war industry. For Jackson, *Salt* played a potentially instrumental role in the communist plot to "incite minority against the majority and, when the back of the majority has been broken, the Communists will incite minority against minority and, through this division, will succeed in taking over the free countries of the world." Because of its racially charged nature, he argued, *Salt* would cause "incalculable harm not only to the United States but to the cause of free people everywhere" if it were shown in Latin America, Asia, or India.[70] From Jackson's vantage point, the film was another domino in the ongoing propaganda battle crucial to winning the Cold War.

Jackson's outlandish conspiracy theories and partisan propaganda about *Salt* notwithstanding, links did exist between the 1951–1952 Bayard strike and the anti–Korean War movement. Not only was Mine-Mill antiwar, but from the beginning of the dispute between Local 890 and Empire Zinc, the war had put the company at an advantage. Empire Zinc was a subsidiary of New Jersey Zinc, whose profits soared with a surge in wartime demand for zinc. By the early 1950s, the company was as strong as ever. That *Salt* did not mention the Korean War is lost on Jackson but no less glaring. In close readings of different versions of the *Salt* script, Benjamin Balthasar showed that the strike's relationship to the Korean War was strategically omitted from the final cut. In fact, the original script, prior to rounds of collaborative editing by the production committee, contained a much stronger and more explicit critique of US imperialism and Cold War foreign policy.[71]

Salt of the Earth also neglected the political environment along the US-Mexico border in which the Bayard strike grew. In the film, the radicalism of the Bayard community stemmed organically from the immediacy of local union politics. The longer tradition of Mexican American resistance in New Mexico and the borderlands was forgotten or ignored. The legacy of the Mexican American War, cross-border currents of the mining community and industry, and internationalist orientation of Mine-Mill organizing were absent. In his sweeping labor history of Chicanos in the Southwest, the historian Juan Gómez-Quinones argued that the Hollywood filmmakers were unable to comprehend the "complexity of the strike, its context, and its aftermath." Despite his critique, Gómez-Quinones concluded that the film was an "enduring artistic classic testimonial that evokes the travails of struggle."[72] Zaragosa Vargas demonstrated that the anti-communist congressional campaign against Mine-Mill was coordinated with the Immigration and Naturalization Service (INS) in an effort to stamp out cross-border labor solidarity.[73] *Salt* was a feature film, however, not a documentary, and Biberman, Jarrico, and Wilson felt strongly that the film needed a universal and absorbing plot if it were to be successful.

Still, from a historical perspective, the disregard for border life and its impact on Mine-Mill depicted the Bayard community as detached from the place they called home. Strikers and their families came across as more displaced and deterritorialized than deeply rooted in the region where they had lived for generations. While their struggles for racial, gender, and civil rights were important in the film, their contentious past of living through the on-the-ground effects of US imperialism along the border was not. The fate of the Mexican American mining community in 1950s New Mexico, let alone their dreams of a better future, could not be fully grasped without recognizing the preceding century of land loss, political liquidation, and stripping of rights following the Treaty of Guadalupe Hidalgo in 1848.

Although *Salt* was an early instance of what several Cold War historians established as a more expansive pattern in which anti-imperialism was rhetorically delinked from civil rights, it nonetheless stood apart from other 1950s films.[74] Despite painstaking efforts to deal progressively with labor and gender issues, incorporate the mining community, and project a stridently pro-union message, the film decoupled working-class Mexican American life from streams of anti-imperialism that swirled around them. To be fair, most contemporary films that dealt with working-class lives fared even worse. Movies such as *On the Waterfront* and *Viva Zapata!* tended to present unions as evil and immoral, trumpeting the virtues of US democracy and capitalism rather than acknowledging their exploitative and discriminatory underbelly. *Salt* did quite the opposite, but it was far from the threat to US imperialism that Jackson and other anti-communists believed it to be.

A FINAL CUT

Salt of the Earth fell in the middle of what Eric Hobsbawm referred to as the "age of extremes," the period from 1914 to 1991 when catastrophic war, ecological disaster, totalitarianism on the left and right, the deepening poverty of the Global South, and other crises led to dystopian cynicism and unbridled utopianism as diametrically opposed poles of political thought.[75] *Salt* trafficked in visions of a better society that confronted the perils of Cold War persecution and oppression. Its production process shined a light on the possibilities, limits, and contradictions of its anti-racist, feminist, and anti-imperialist visions. It's also fair to say that *Salt* was not shaped alone by white Hollywood elites making a movie about a people, place, and struggle they did not know much about. While Biberman, Jarrico, Wilson, and the IPC had the last word, the Bayard community also bore responsibility for *Salt*. It was a collaborative effort and an arduous process that entailed a complicated race and gender politics from start to finish.

Despite its extraordinary history, many of the utopian visions in *Salt of the Earth* were never fully realized. Tracing these unrealized strands shows the utopian imagination that was embedded in daily cultural labor, difficult decision-making, keeping an open mind, and being resilient. The making of *Salt* was an experiment in utopia not just because of the content of the finished film or because it sought, let alone created, an ever-elusive ideal society. Nor was it utopian because it constituted or facilitated some big moment of political transcendence that solved all of the problems faced by the IPC, Mine-Mill, or the Mexican Americans of Bayard. *Salt*'s utopia was an arduous process and everyday responsibility that required hard work to keep it going. In producing a film that challenged the exploitation of working folk, Mexican Americans, and women during the Cold War, those involved tried to make unequal relations of capital, racism, and sexism unworkable on the ground on- and off-screen. They were not always successful and had plenty of blind spots, but they tried, both in the moment and in the longer run. The IPC and Mine-Mill wanted to cultivate labor solidarity among *Salt*'s viewers and even inspire more union-sponsored films. The men and women of Bayard showed that those without great wealth and power could impact how pop culture told their stories. As the IPC seemed to intuitively realize, those with few resources and little political might had a great deal to say about how to imagine a better world. Still, the film and its production process showed that it was not uncommon for utopia to elide difference and diversity for homogeneity and cohesion. One person's vision of utopia was rife with problems and dystopian pitfalls from the vantage point of another. This was especially the case during the Cold War when the lines between anti-racism and racism, feminism and sexism, and anti-imperialism and Cold War conservatism were not always as clear as they seemed to be. Perhaps because those in the IPC read the Bayard strike through the lens of their own persecution, the possibilities for Mexican American radicalism and feminism were left unfulfilled in the final cut.

Nonetheless, *Salt of the Earth* made a lasting historical mark and not just because it was a remarkable film. It foreshadowed how Mexican American social movements, race relations, and utopian dreams would continue to register in film, music, television, and art. Chapters to come cover people, places, and moments far from *Salt*, but, taken together, form a montage of Chicanx pop culture and its politics of the possible. We turn next to Mexican American music and the brown-eyed soul sound of the 1960s.

CHAPTER 2

Brown-Eyed Soul

In the week of May 23, 1970, the East LA band El Chicano hit number 28 on the Billboard Hot 100 with "Viva Tirado." Its eclectic mix of rock, jazz, and other genres helped make it the first song to hit every Billboard category save country. It may seem odd that El Chicano appealed to such a diverse audience. The group had recently changed their name from the generic-sounding "VIPs" to register alliance with the Chicano movement's radical critique of racism, poverty, and political neglect. The name change resulted in confusion over who El Chicano was and how their music should be classified. When on tour in New York, for instance, band member Bobby Espinosa remembers, "They didn't know where to book us. We ended up playing a show at the Apollo Theater with the O'Jays, Jerry Butler, the Last Poets, all these black groups. They didn't know what we were. They'd say, 'What are you guys, Indians? What's a Chicano?'"[1] The longer history of "Viva Tirado" explains a lot, however. The song was originally written by Gerald Wilson, a Black jazz trumpeter and composer. Wilson was born in Mississippi, grew up in Chicago, and made a name for himself as part of the LA jazz scene during the 1940s. His original version of "Viva Tirado" paid homage to a Mexican matador named José Ramón Tirado, a salute inspired by Wilson's affection for Mexican music and culture.[2]

"Viva Tirado" revealed the multiracial roots of the brown-eyed soul music scene that took East LA by storm in the mid-1960s. El Chicano and other Eastside bands were part of an audio and political thicket that grew straight from the city's interracial past. They were Chicanas/os making music with Black and white Angelenos that drew on the history of interracial living and activism in Los Angeles. They blended rock 'n' roll, soul, jazz, R&B, and Mexican and Caribbean rhythms, drawing inspiration from Motown and the British invasion. The author Luis Rodríguez described them as "the heroes and heroines of low-rider car clubs, street gangs and high school teens. Their records were sold as soon as they came out and whenever they made appearances, they crowded dance halls and concerts."[3] In a 1994 retrospective, the *Los Angeles Times* described brown-eyed soul as "black soul music strained through Chicano musical roots. Latin rhythm, melodic phrasing and vocal inflection crossed with proto-punk energy levels."[4] It also came to serve as a soundtrack for the Chicano movement in LA, reverberating with organizing and marches across the city. Like the musicians they listened to, protesters riffed on the city's interracial history, engaging Black, Latin American, and Third World struggles across Los Angeles and beyond. Eddie Serrano, an original member of the ultra-popular band Cannibal and the Headhunters, stated simply, "There was definitely an East LA sound at the time—you couldn't mistake it."[5]

The rock and bluesy riffs with a Chicano flavor weren't just good for cutting rugs. While others plumb the musicology of its notes and beats, I explore more the utopian impulses embedded in the social and political constellations brown-eyed soul stirred between and among Chicanas/os, African Americans, and other groups. Brown-eyed soul pointed toward a more just, less racially segregated society. Although rarely explicit, unrefined, and experimental, the utopian impulses in brown-eyed soul were also uninhibited and unconstrained, lending support to Ruth Levitas and Tom Moylan's claim that "music's capacity for direct human expression produces a capability of expressing the suffering, hope, and desire of oppressed people."[6] Up against the postwar resegregation and deindustrialization of LA, such relationships and encounters pointed toward an alternative lived experience of race, one that, as Alex Chavez notes in another musical context, was conveyed through "sonic enactment and reception."[7] Bringing Chicanas/os together with African Americans and others in the many venues, backyard parties, recording studios, and cruising scenes where it was played, brown-eyed soul prophesied an alternative racial landscape, resonating with Gaye Johnson's declaration that "the history of struggles shared by Black and Brown people in Los Angeles from World War II to the present is a history of shared spaces and shared sounds."[8]

Like "Viva Tirado," brown-eyed soul grew from LA's interracial musical and political past. Utopian impulses didn't randomly appear in the music but stemmed from the fertile mix of the city's racial history and spatial dimensions. Young folk in the brown-eyed soul scene were, to borrow from Natalia Molina, place-makers who interacted "in ways that empower[ed] those who inhabit[ed] the surrounding area."[9] By making music, hanging out, and engaging with the social change unfolding around them, they made the city their own and stamped it with their multiracial imprint. Just as they blended musical categories, they also mixed racial communities and political movements. In her study of religion and utopia in the Chicano movement, Jacqueline Hidalgo asked "how, why, and with what consequences they [Chicanos] have come to remake home, to reclaim space, in and through scriptures."[10] For many in the brown-eyed soul scene, music was their scripture and the means to make sense of surroundings, cultivate relationships with others, and manufacture everyday utopia that, to draw from Alex Zamalin, was "like religion not because of the dogmatic theology or secular truths it postulates, but because it conjures powerful, irrepressible, sometimes ecstatic feelings: of salvation, of being at home in the world, and of reconciliation with strife."[11] While such affect and its interracial dimensions were often temporary or elusive, they also blossomed from previous generations of LA youth. If brown-eyed soul's practitioners had been versed in the queer theory of José Esteban Muñoz, they might have agreed that "hope as a critical methodology can be best described as a backward glance that enacts a future vision."[12]

Tracing and listening for utopia in brown-eyed soul is a slippery enterprise. To follow its tracks, I view the music as a sonic archive of the shared experiences and aspirations of Chicana/o youth. I consider how brown-eyed soul was grounded in three chapters in Los Angeles history. The first is the city's interracial cultural politics after World War II. Second is its overlapping histories of the civil rights and Chicano movements. Third is the legacy of brown-eyed soul's interracialism since the 1990s. These story lines reveal the lasting, if yet unfulfilled, utopian reach of brown-eyed soul. Chicano musicians did not pretend to be historians or claim to be visionaries of a new world. They did, however, generate sounds and experiences that sparked utopian feelings, moments, and possibilities. These are worth considering. While brown-eyed soul doesn't provide an empirical account of postwar conditions in LA, its seemingly apolitical songs acquired deeply political and social meanings. Despite being bought and sold as a commodity, sometimes articulating new forms of misogyny or racism, and rarely meant to be taken literally, brown-eyed soul showed how people's connection to the past shaped their ideas of the present and future.

A LONGER HISTORY OF BROWN-EYED SOUL

The Los Angeles that Gerald Wilson settled in after a stint in the US Navy during World War II was a city undergoing demographic, economic, and political changes.[13] Southern California, especially LA, experienced a population explosion as a result of the wartime economic boom, immigration from Asia and Mexico, and the subsequent birth of first-generation US-born children. One important byproduct of these circumstances was close-knit spatial relations that sprouted from LA's multiracial environment. Sharing residential areas, frequenting the same nightspots, and, in some parts of the city like the Eastside, attending integrated high schools led to a myriad of contacts among Mexican American, African American, Japanese American, Filipino American, and other Angelinos. Although geographic proximity did not always lead to social interaction, the dramatic changes during World War II set the stage for sharing social circles, workplaces, political struggles, and music.[14]

During the 1940s, a unique music scene intertwined with zoot suit fashion and LA youth culture. According to one journalist:

> It was no accident that Los Angeles and Southern California became the birthplace of R&B. People had been migrating there from all over the United States since before the Depression. When they came, they brought along their music. During the War the defense industry concentrated in the area soaked-up thousands of workers, and thousands of blacks moved in from the South and Northeast to get those jobs. Money was plentiful for a while, but leisure time hours were short. The need for entertainment was satisfied by hundreds of nightclubs, juke joints, saloons, and theaters featuring live music and dancing. The blues from the Deep South, brittle New York jazz, hot string jive, and Chicago jump blended into a new music.[15]

Black, Mexican American, Filipino, and Japanese American youth flocked to music hot spots in the heart of LA's African American neighborhood on Central Avenue. Mexican American pachuco artists like Don Tosti and Lalo Guerrero made the Black tradition of scat singing their own by doing it in Spanglish. Cuban composers and musicians influenced sojourners like Dizzy Gillespie. Jazz, mambo, and Mexican rhythms merged to form what Anthony Macías called "Hollywood Latin."[16]

Such cultural borrowing and collaboration mirrored similarly diverse, if uneven and shifting, political coalitions that grew from wartime urban conditions throughout the city. As Scott Kurashige and Kevin Allen Leonard have shown, a range of interracial and multiethnic political coalitions took shape as Angelinos struggled to make sense of an intense public debate about race following the bombing of Pearl Harbor while they simultaneously sought equal participation in the city's war effort. For instance, though the voices protesting Japanese American internment were sporadic, they did include the likes of the African American lawyer Hugh Macbeth Sr. Soon after Executive Order 9066 (which authorized relocation of Japanese Americans and Japanese immigrants to internment camps) was issued, he actively campaigned against the disenfranchisement of Japanese Americans. When Macbeth investigated land loss by Issei farmers in California, he quickly deduced that white agricultural interests sought to profit from the situation, and he penned briefs for cases in conjunction with the Japanese American Citizens League (JACL) and American Civil Liberties Union (ACLU) against internment and the discriminatory California Alien Land Law, which prohibited Asian immigrants from owning land.[17] On the labor front, many African Americans, Mexican Americans, and Jewish Americans came together in efforts spearheaded by the Congress of Industrial Organizations (CIO) and the local Communist Party to fight for worker rights across the city. Leaders in these same communities participated in the Citizens Committee for the Defense of Mexican American Youth, the Sleepy Lagoon Defense Committee (SLDC), and the Council for Civic Unity, which were formed to free a group of young Mexican American boys erroneously convicted of murder and conspiracy in 1942. These groups also responded to the infamous Zoot Suit Riots in 1943.[18] Among the principals were the labor organizer Luisa Moreno and the journalist-activist Charlotta Bass. Moreno was born in Guatemala yet fought tirelessly for the rights of Mexicans and Mexican Americans in Southern California, among other things, by helping organize the first Congress of Spanish-Speaking Peoples. Bass, an African American born in South Carolina, owned and published the *California Eagle*, one of LA's longest-running Black newspapers. As Gaye Johnson argued, Bass and Moreno, like Macbeth and so many others, were part of far-reaching "constellations of struggle" and a "common framework of World War II–era interracial, anti-racist struggle."[19]

During the decade after World War II, efforts to advance racial justice in Southern California were inevitably and increasingly linked with spatial and cultural issues. Led by the former Marine officer William Parker, a reorganized Los Angeles Police Department busily tried to prevent white patrons from visiting nightclubs in the predominantly Black Central Avenue area at precisely the moment when white musicians, including Chet Baker, Shorty Rogers, Shelly Manne, and Dave Brubeck, were among those popularizing postbop "cool jazz" as a form of more or less improvised music shorn of its previous associations with Blackness and vice. To the northeast of Central Avenue, Brooklyn's perennially underachieving baseball team took possession of a stadium erected on the foundations of one of the city's oldest Mexican American neighborhoods. Despite the presence of a thriving local community, municipal leaders used the power of eminent domain—financed by Federal Housing Administration funds—to raze the bungalows of Chavez Ravine. In each case, new freeway construction allowed increasingly suburbanized white populations to pass between points of interest with less direct interpersonal contact with nonwhite people than before. Thus, rather than progress toward desegregation, the interval between the end of the Second World War and the explosion of the 1965 Watts Riots was a time of increasing urban resegregation. This was perhaps exemplified most aptly by California voters' overwhelming approval of a ballot initiative upholding restrictive housing covenants and their subsequent support for the openly racist gubernatorial candidacy of Ronald Reagan.[20]

Unsurprisingly, the same period witnessed new openings for points of contact between communities of color. Organizations like the Mexican American Community Service Organization (CSO) and League of United Latin American Citizens (LULAC) routinely collaborated with the National Association for the Advancement of Colored People (NAACP), the JACL, and the Jewish Community Relations Committee (CRC). As Shana Bernstein showed, these groups struck a delicate balance between their collective push for civil rights and the rigid anti-communism of the era.[21] In the early 1950s, for example, building on an earlier event sponsored by the Nisei Student Club of Los Angeles City College, more than two thousand people attended a four-day festival of ethnic culture held at the Soto-Michigan Jewish Community Center in East Los Angeles. Jointly sponsored by the NAACP, JACL, and the Jewish Centers Association, the festival showcased presentations of "traditional" Japanese, African American, Jewish, and Mexican cultures in an effort to "establish lasting bonds of friendship and understanding through the democratic American way of greater equality." Flanked by the NAACP chairman E. I. Robinson and JACL regional director Tats Kushida, City Councilman Ed Roybal presided over the event.²² These cultural galas helped cement the growing bonds between the NAACP, the JACL, and predominantly Mexican American organizations. On the surface, these events suggest episodic forerunners of what would later be termed "multiculturalism." The relationship between presentations of cultural difference and ongoing political projects, however, illustrated an ongoing relationship between Black, Japanese American, and Mexican American civic groups that extended to the NAACP, the American Jewish Congress, and the JACL's participation in the landmark school segregation lawsuit brought by Mexican American families to desegregate schools in Westminster, Orange County, in 1946.²³

The interracial sensibility present in postwar politics found novel aural outlets as well. On the heels of the Mexican American pachuco songs of the late 1940s, a number of Black jazz artists in the early '50s generated huge followings among Mexican Americans on the Eastside, including the trio of saxophonists Joe Houston, Big Jay McNeely, and Chuck Higgins. Higgins had citywide hits with "Pancho Villa," "Wetback Hop," and "Pachuko Hop," the last in honor of Mexican American zoot-suiters from World War II years. He remembered that "Pachuko Hop" "didn't have a Spanish flavor, but when we released the record, all the [Mexican American] gangs around here [Los Angeles] would just follow us around, wherever we played."²⁴ After the legendary deejay Hunter Hancock, whose show featured Black music but was wildly popular among Mexican Americans, played the song on the radio, Higgins began to play live versions of the song for Mexican American audiences that lasted close to two hours.²⁵ Big Jay McNeely's steady gigs included playing with Johnny Otis at Angeles Hall on First Street in Boyle Heights, the Million Dollar Theater downtown, and El Monte Legion Stadium, where Mexican American fans flocked to see him play. His connection with Mexican Americans, McNeely recalled, went back to his youth when he "was raised with Mexican Americans in Watts. It was nothing," he said, "for me to be acquainted with Mexican Americans."²⁶ Little Julian Herrera also had a big hit in 1956 among East LA Mexican Americans with his Johnny Otis–produced "Lonely Lonely Nights," an early Chicano rock record sung in the style of Black soul singers. Otis, who considered himself "black by persuasion" despite being the son of a Greek immigrant, figured Herrera to be Mexican American but soon learned that he was a Hungarian Jewish runaway from New Jersey who had been taken in and raised by a Mexican American woman in Boyle Heights. In a scenario emblematic of the diverse roots of brown-eyed soul, a Greek American who considered himself African American produced a pop hit sung by a Hungarian Jew who considered himself Mexican American.[27]

Aspects of what would become brown-eyed soul also pervaded the outlying areas of Los Angeles. Matt Garcia noted in the 1950s and early '60s that the rural outskirts of LA were home to music hot spots near where many Mexicans worked in the citrus groves. Venues like El Monte Legion Stadium and clubs like Rainbow Gardens, where the house band was a multiracial group called the Mixtures, drew fans to see performances by McNeely and other Black and Mexican American artists like Ritchie Valens who were central to the birth of rock 'n' roll in Los Angeles.[28] These more rural venues drew large crowds in part because they faced fewer restrictions on underage gatherings and segregation than those in LA proper.

At the same time, the Mexican American generation was jamming in venues across the breadth of Los Angeles. The historian Anthony Macías provided an exhaustive archaeology of the musical interactions between African American and Mexican American musicians and fans, "from the zoot suit and the jitterbug to neighborhood jazz instructors and high schools, from boogie woogie and jump blues to doo wop, Motown and Afro-Latin music."[29] Significantly, jazz musicians formed a crucial part of this musical moment, whether in the guise of mixed Black and brown school bands like the Jordan High Junior Hep Cats; or the big band swing competitions that pitted the Sal Cervantes Orchestra against the George Brown Orchestra; or as in the case of the avant-garde saxophonist and composer Anthony Ortega, who studied music alongside Eric Dolphy, Buddy Collette, Horace Tapscott, Charles Mingus, and other burgeoning local African American jazz artists in the private classes of the legendary local music teacher Lloyd Reese. These figures—and Macías found many—point to the existence of an intersecting jazz world alongside the rhythm and blues and pre–rock 'n' roll worlds that would give rise to brown-eyed soul.

Such links only hint at the mutuality of Chicano and Black connections. Brothers Coney, William, and Britt Woodman all recalled family musical gigs for Mexican neighbors in Watts, as did the trumpeter Art Farmer and the saxophonist Buddy Collette.[30] Gerald Wilson summarized his feelings by noting, "I have been into the Mexican culture for a long time. Just listening can get you somewhere, but you have to be exposed to the people."[31] Personal exposure formed part and parcel of the jazz composer Charles Mingus's experience as well. Like Big Jay

McNeely, Mingus was raised in a multiethnic Watts community populated by Blacks, Latinos, Japanese Americans, and a smattering of whites. He would make repeated efforts to develop interpretive fusions of African American and Latino sounds, including his 1957 recording *Tijuana Moods*. A conceptual album based on his impressions of the border city, the record begins with an adaptation of a Dizzy Gillespie tune Mingus reshaped during the car ride from LA to the border. The record then moves through a number of impressionistic sketches of border life, including a nightclub, a gift shop, and a bevy of street musicians. In one tune, "Los Mariachis," Mingus sought to capture the sensibility of musicians forced to anticipate the tastes of prospective clients by linking a series of stylistically divergent sections through a recurring melody meant as a Mexican riff on the blues. Imagining a young Carlos Santana (then a recent arrival in Tijuana) as a busker playing B. B. King and Little Richard tunes in the streets of Tijuas gives a good sense of the back-and-forth of musical interaction during this time. Music from LA, as Josh Kun reminded us, "grew out of a bi-national audio thicket, balancing African American voices with Mexican voices, and to grow up in this was to learn some of the most basic lessons of border life: how to speak in forked tongues, how to import and appropriate and combine and reinvent, how to be who you are using somebody else's stuff."[32] Of course, Ramón Ruiz pointed out that African Americans drawn to Tijuana by advertisements published in LA's Black newspaper, the *California Eagle*, often encountered incidents of bigotry and patterns of segregation.[33] Still, by the time of Mingus's sojourn, African Americans had been traveling to Tijuana for at least three decades, and the city was familiar to figures like Jack Johnson, Sonny Clay, and Jelly Roll Morton.[34]

Back in Los Angeles, the sound of the 1950s was grounded in the spatial parameters of daily life.[35] One such place was Phillips Music Company on Brooklyn Avenue in Boyle Heights. William Phillips was a Jew from Rochester, New York, who ran away from home and joined the navy before he turned eighteen. He eventually settled in East Los Angeles, where he married, started a family, and opened a music store in the 1930s. While Phillips never assumed a Mexican American identity as did Little Julian Herrera, his two sons remember that "he felt more comfortable with Mexican Americans."[36] Despite moving his family to Beverly Hills, Phillips kept his business in Boyle Heights, where, by the 1950s, the store had become a kind of "community melting pot."[37] It was a local hangout where youth of all racial stripes from across the Eastside could buy or just listen to the Latin jazz, rock, cumbia, and Yiddish swing records that helped make up the multinational mix of the Eastside scene. Phillips, who learned to play the drums in the navy and had performed across LA, permitted local kids with an interest in music to jam in the store after hours. He also had an eye for talent and introduced young Mexican American musicians to his industry contacts in Hollywood and the music joints along Central Avenue.[38] A retrospective on Boyle Heights noted that Phillips's customers, including some who went on to form bands like Thee Midniters, Los Lobos, and Ollin, "provided a soundtrack to the social and cultural transformations that defined the Eastside."[39] In a gesture reflective of the kind of place Phillips Music Company was, Phillips gave a corner of his store to Kenji Taniguchi upon his return to Boyle Heights from the internment camps following World War II. Taniguchi sold sporting goods equipment, soon opened his own store down the street, and became the biggest provider of sporting goods on the Eastside. Nor should it be surprising that Bill Phillips sat on the Soto-Michigan board of directors or that he campaigned for Ed Roybal, the Mexican American US congressional representative for the district from 1949 to 1963.

These linkages help us recall that the brown-eyed soul sound of the 1960s and '70s stood on cultural foundations built during a time when Chicano and African American urban cultures were deeply and inextricably linked to one another. Far from pointing to a popular culture that was in any way derivative, the development of an identifiably Chicano music, in particular, during the decades before the full explosion of the Chicano movement, remained contingent upon a complex urban terrain in which borrowing, innovation, and the reworking of extant cultural forms like *rancheras* and *corridos,* as well as boogie-woogie and jump blues, formed an integral part of a citywide search for dignity and fun. This created the conditions for a popular culture capable of extending hundreds of miles, from El Monte to Venice Beach, from Santa Barbara to Tijuana. Back in the day, this geography of sound and dance constantly contested the racist spatial parameters of Southern California; today, it illustrates the limits of scholarly and popular accounts that take unincorporated East Los Angeles as the sine qua non of Mexican American culture in the greater Los Angeles area.

At the same time, successive interracial musical scenes attest to the limited manner in which African American cultural history has yet to grapple fully with what Jelly Roll Morton called "the Latin Tinge." If we are serious in proposing California as a center of Black cultural production—whether in the pioneering jazz of Kid Ory and Morton; the avant-garde jazz of Ornette Coleman, Bobby Bradford, and Horace Tapscott; the boogie-woogie and rock 'n' roll era; or contemporary hip-hop—we must do more to extend Peter Narváez's pathbreaking examination of "the influences of Hispanic music cultures on African American blues musicians" to new places and new musical genres.[40] Here, the pioneering work of Gaye Johnson pointed us toward a new sonic mapping of relational Black and Chicanx studies. In describing the influence of Mexican military bands on the burgeoning jazz and blues music scenes of late nineteenth-century Louisiana, Johnson reminded us that the questioning of ostensible ethnic boundaries often serves as a precursor to the rethinking of stylistic and generic conventions as well.[41] Narváez and Johnson are both pathbreaking and evocative in that their investigations illustrate how the musical crossings of brown-eyed soul possessed antecedents going back more than a century. Perhaps new research will reveal a rhythm and blues equivalent to Lightnin' Hopkins's offhand but serious warning to "always watch out for them Mexicans with the six-string guitar. They can do so much on it they'll kill you with it."[42] Or perhaps groups like Los Lobos from East LA will finally find their way into the blues canon. At the very least, greater attention to the possibilities of interethnic musical milieus along the US-Mexico borderlands would reveal a fuller picture of the earlier links that underscore the undeniably common aesthetic and political sensibilities that have arisen time and again.

THE SIXTIES SCENE

El Chicano's "Viva Tirado" not only helps excavate the roots of brown-eyed soul but also reveals the complexity of the 1960s scene.[43] When they shed the moniker "VIPs" and renamed themselves El Chicano, the band mirrored the thousands of young people who increasingly self-identified with the Chicano movement of the late 1960s and early '70s. Chicanas/os rejected assimilation, whiteness, and a status quo long associated with the term "Mexican American" in favor of the political empowerment, Indigeneity, radicalism, and cultural expression encapsulated by the label "Chicano." On the one hand, then, the Eastside music scene reflected the hardening of racial and ethnic divisions in the city that, along with growing racial violence and rebellion in Watts and urban areas across the country, fueled deep-seated cultural nationalism and often divisive gender relations that bifurcated interracial and intraracial interactions. On the other hand, brown-eyed soul combined new sounds, styles, and rhythms in ways that articulated a Chicano and Black politics that drew from one another and cultivated connections between the two.

The brown-eyed soul scene of the 1960s was a realm nourished by social ingenuity and political inventiveness and conditioned by the world around it, and, in turn, it shaped the lives of people in its orbit.[44] The scene built upon the interracial past of the Mexican American generation while also being home to utopian impulses that showed music's capacity to "signal temporary moments when something quite new and potentially transformative might be glimpsed."[45] Its utopianism, as embryonic as it may have been, rested on its interracial foundations in a time of increasing spatial resegregation and rising ethnic nationalism in LA and beyond. Brown-eyed soul was utopian, to borrow from Jill Dolan, "not in a didactic, descriptive way as in traditional 'utopian' literature," but "through the communication of an alternative experience."[46] Chicana/o youth mixed social and political geographies as they did musical genres, echoing José Esteban Muñoz's reflection that utopias are "relational to historically situated struggles" and "can also be daydreamlike, but they are the hopes of a collective, emergent group, or even the solitary oddball who is the one who dreams for many."[47]

By the mid-1960s, brown-eyed soul sowed the dreams of many Chicana/o youth in Los Angeles. Bands such as Thee Midniters, Cannibal and the Headhunters, the Jaguars, the Premiers, and the Village Callers remained popular among Mexican Americans and African Americans in the city, but also increasingly experienced national success. Part of this growing reach of the LA Chicano sound stemmed from the intensified commercialization of popular music, the phenomenal growth in the popularity of rock 'n' roll, and the diverse urban experiences that marked LA and other cities in the sixties. Led by Little Willie G (for Garcia), for example, Thee Midniters, whose many influences included the Temptations, Smokey Robinson and the Miracles, and the Beatles, had citywide hits with "Land of a Thousand Dances" in 1964 and their first studio single, "Whittier Boulevard," in 1965. "Whittier Boulevard," an ode to the most popular cruising spot for Mexican American youth, signaled brown-eyed soul's reclamation of urban space for young Chicanas/os. The song was mostly instrumental, but it began with Little Willie G shouting "Let's take a trip down Whittier Boulevard!" Ronnie Figueroa chimed in with a celebratory "Arriba, arriba!" The Chicano music historian and deejay Ruben Molina noted, "That kind of sets it off and says,

'This is Mexicano.' But then, it goes into the surf guitars." In the song, he continued, "You'll hear influences from surf music to rhythm and blues to Mexican music. It's basically what the Chicano is: We're a mixture of Mexican heritage but living in America. It kind of signified: We are here. This is who we are."[48] Little Willie G similarly recalled "Whittier Boulevard" as a kind of call to action "because it was us. And it gave us a voice. You know, sort of like a rallying cry for us to kind of assemble and say, 'Hey. Are we on the same page?' And most of us said, 'Yeah.'"[49] Cannibal and the Headhunters re-covered "Whittier Boulevard" to national acclaim a year later in 1966. It became—and remains—an anthem among young Mexican Americans on the Eastside and across the city. Though "Whittier Boulevard" was more of an up-tempo rock tune, Thee Midniters blended rhythm and blues, soul, funk, salsa, and more traditional Mexican forms of music in their repertoire and in the countless live performances they gave across Southern California during the 1960s. David Rando might have described the growing reach of brown-eyed soul as a "musical moment [that] teems with cultural expressions of a fleeting but repressed desire for social reorganization and collectivity."[50]

Other Mexican American bands similarly found a measure of national success in 1964 and 1965, a period one critic noted as a watershed year in East LA music.[51] The Premiers, who hailed from San Gabriel, climbed to number 19 on the national charts with their 1964 hit, "Farmer John." They followed with an album for Warner Bros. Records and tours through the Midwest and East Coast that included sharing the bill with Diana Ross and the Supremes.[52] Around the same time, the Blendells hit number 62 on the charts with their cover of a young Stevie Wonder's relatively unknown song "La La La La La." The Blendells were originally known as the Blenders but changed their name in a nod to the 1950s Black R&B group the Dells.[53]

Not only did numerous Mexican American bands draw heavily from African American music, but, as with Chuck Higgins, Big Jay McNeely, and others from a decade prior, some Black artists had massive followings among Mexican Americans as well. One such singer in the 1960s was Brenton Wood, who had his own local hits with the likes of "Gimme Little Sign" and "The Oogum Boogum Song." Both were on his 1967 *Oogum Boogum* LP released on LA-based Double Shot Records. The former hit the Top 10 on the Billboard Hot 100 chart and also had success in the UK, France, Germany, and Australia. The song helped earn him a three-week tour across Europe in 1968.[54] His "Baby You Got It," "Can You Dig It," and many others were LA classics with citywide recognition. Wood was born in Louisiana but grew up in San Pedro, Long Beach, Compton, and South Central LA, modeling his silky vocals after Sam Cooke and crooning about love and heartbreak. Mexican Americans from East LA helped drive him to stardom, and Wood later noted that "they've [Mexican Americans] kind of picked me out of the whole batch and they keep me going."[55] His popularity on the Eastside was also lasting, as evidenced in 1992, the same year the legendary deejay and producer Art Laboe released a collection called *Brenton Wood's 18 Best*, when Wood was chosen to headline the Latino Rock 'n' Soul concert at the Greek Theater in LA. As it was in the '60s, the *Los Angeles Times* exclaimed, "These days the veteran performer's fortunes rest in East LA and other Mexican-American strongholds." For his part, Wood acknowledged his Eastside fans, stating: "They're [Mexican Americans] very loyal. This is like the third generation of kids that have been following me. The kids like my music. It's timeless music I think, because everyone that grows up is bound to go through this at one time or another—break up, get back together, boyfriend-girlfriend type stuff." Laboe added that "Latinos like to dedicate songs[,] and his songs are good for that."[56] As much as any other in the brown-eyed soul scene, Wood was a reminder of the affective power of music to cross racial lines, acknowledging that it "can express lament and consolation, restlessness and lack, and unrestrained desire and striving" that existed on the Chicana/o Eastside as it did elsewhere.[57]

Perhaps the biggest smash on the Eastside in the 1960s was Cannibal and the Headhunters' 1965 remake of "Land of a Thousand Dances," which was originally written and recorded by Chris Kenner and successfully recorded by Thee Midniters. It was Cannibal and the Headhunters' version, however, that went to number 30 on the national charts. Wilson Pickett took his own version into the Top 10 in 1966, but it was Frankie "Cannibal" Garcia, lead singer for the Headhunters, who made the song catch fire. As legend had it, when Garcia forgot sections of the lyrics, he covered for his memory lapse by singing, "Na-na-na-na-na." The altered lyrics became the song's catchy hook, evoking Fischlin, Heble, and Lipsitz's observation that "improvised musicking is a critical form of agency, of embodied potential that is inseparable from other social practices" and can teach "people to enact the possibilities they envision."[58] It was such a hit that the band was booked to open for the Beatles 1965 tour in the United States. Before their rise to stardom, Garcia was reluctant to have his picture taken, and without an image to put to the sound and name of the band, many promoters assumed they were African American. This led to them getting gigs to open for several of the Motown acts that had influenced their music. Garcia recalled, "We were so young a lot of groups took us under their wings. The Temptations and Miracles used to do routines in the backroom, you know, 'I'll show you this move and we'll show you that one.' It was like our training, our school."[59]

One of the few women-led bands was the Sisters. Ersi, Rosella, and Mary Arvizu were, in fact, sisters who grew up in East LA and have been referred to as "the Chicana Supremes of the Eastside." In 1965, when Ersi was thirteen years old, she and her sisters had an LA hit with "Gee Baby Gee," a song originally recorded by the Dixie Cups. As he did for other Eastside bands, their manager Billy Cardenas identified obscure B-sides of existing records for the Sisters to remake.[60] Within a few years, the group broke up, but Ersi went on to sing with the Village Callers and, perhaps most famously, with El Chicano. She was the lead singer for El Chicano on their first album and sang vocals for their classic version of the Mexican ballad "Sabor a Mí." The Sisters begat Deborah Vargas's study of "dissonant divas" in the history of Chicano music in Texas, in which many women artists "do not easily fit the normative parameters of subjectivity in dominant academic and public cultural narratives of Chicano music and have been literally and discursively unheard, misheard, or overheard."[61] Arvizu's presence in the Eastside scene revealed a California version of "dissonance—as chaos, cacophony, disharmony, commotion, static"—that disrupted "the heteronormative and culturalnationalist limits of la onda."[62] Arvizu's presence in the '60s scene and her reemergence as an iconic Eastside recording artist in the 2000s showed that a disharmony with brown-eyed soul's normative gender roles was uncommon but possible.

Independent record labels were key to the growth of brown-eyed soul and its multiracial reach. One key figure was the producer Eddie Davis, known as the "musical godfather of East LA." Davis was born in 1926 to a mixed Jewish and Catholic family in Boyle Heights and, after a career as a child actor and singer, became a restauranteur. He recalled, "That's how I got into the record business. I wanted to be a singer. I kept trying to get a deal and nobody would ever give me a deal. And I couldn't get anything going. I got in the restaurant business, made a lot of money, and decided, if nobody will record me, I'll record myself."[63] Davis was famous for saying, "Let's make this clear right now! If anybody thinks I got rich over my East Los Angeles music[,] they're very wrong. I cooked a lot of hamburgers to make those records."[64] Davis went on to own and operate seven different record labels, including Rampart, Faro, Linda,

Gordo, Valhalla, Boomerang, and Prospect Records. Davis worked with a who's who of the Mexican American Eastside sound, including producing the biggest national hits by the Premiers, the Blendells, and Cannibal and the Headhunters. He also produced a lineup of African American artists that included the Atlantics with eighteen-year-old Barry White in 1961, the Four Tempos, the Soul-Jers, and the pianist Sarah James. Billy Cardenas, who was also born in Boyle Heights, collaborated throughout the 1960s with Davis, managing and promoting many of the groups that appeared on Davis's labels.[65]

Brown-eyed soul's popularity grew among Black and brown audiences when bands played across the city. Posters and flyers for live performances revealed a plethora of venues like concert halls, high school gymnasiums, community college campuses, hotels, and even parking lots. Flyers and posters were easily produced, sometimes handwritten, and placed where Eastside music enthusiasts would see them. Spots like Belvedere Park Auditorium, the Paramount, Big Union Hall, Belair Rollerdrome, Salesian High School, East LA College, and many more were home to live shows.[66] Popular white deejays like Dick "Huggy Boy" Hugg and Art Laboe spread the Eastside sound via their popular radio shows and, in Laboe's case, promotion of concerts.[67] The live circuit was a way for bands to grow their fan base, but it also stamped brown-eyed soul's more open, emancipated interracial mingling and socializing on the city. Their performances in venues across LA evoked everyday utopias that, according to Davina Cooper, "don't focus on campaigning or advocacy. They don't place their energy on pressuring mainstream institutions to change, on winning votes, or on taking over dominant social structures. Rather they work by creating the change they wish to encounter, building and forging new ways of experiencing social and political life."[68] Little Willie G of Thee Midniters recalled what a busy evening of playing multiple gigs might be like. "We'd start off in San Bernardino, then go out to the San Fernando Valley, then down to Torrance and end up here in East Los Angeles at the Union Hall on a Saturday night. We could set up Thee Midniters, an eight-piece band, in fifteen minutes and tear it down and be in the van in eight minutes."[69] With its urban mobility, musical fusion, and racial blending, brown-eyed soul exhibited what Alex Chávez described, in another musical context, as the "dialogic interplay between embodiment and aesthetics."[70]

Brown-eyed soul shared qualities with other regional and international music scenes that together formed a civil rights movement-era soundscape that stretched from Los Angeles to San Antonio to Detroit to Kingston, Jamaica, and many points in between. As Manuel Peña showed for San Antonio and across South Texas, for example, from the late 1940s on, the influence of Black jazz and blues artists like T-Bone Walker and Clarence "Gatemouth" Brown mixed with the western swing of the German-influenced Adolph Hofner and his San Antonians to shape the 1950s and '60s music of Tejano groups such as Freddy Fender, Sunny Ozuna and the Sunliners, Charlie and the Jives, and the Lyrics. Tejano artists mixed R&B, jazz, blues, doo-wop, and soul and, in many instances, borrowed from Black vocal styles.[71] Once Motown began cranking out hits, the Black American soul and R&B sound found eager listeners in Kingston, Jamaica, where ska, rock steady, and then reggae crooners like Ken Boothe and Alton Ellis borrowed style, lyrics, and music from Sam Cooke, Otis Redding, Marvin Gaye, and countless others after listening to their hits via radio from Miami and New Orleans. Along with the Tex-Mex scene, the rocksteady/reggae scene, and the Motown scene, the brown-eyed soul scene in LA demonstrated that interracial and cross-cultural flows were local, regional, and even transnational. Its expressions were unique to LA, but also spoke across time and space to musical traditions in other urban areas where racialized groups similarly struggled to endure life at the bottom of the social order.

Just as the music of the Chicano and African American generation of 1960s Los Angeles was a piece of a much broader soundscape, so too did politics in the city increasingly engage what Cynthia Young and Laura Pulido called the US "third world left."[72] Some Black, Chicana/o, Latina/o, Asian American, and Native American groups saw their communities as "internal colonies" and claimed third world identities that merged critiques of racism and poverty in the United States with internationalist streams of leftist and anti-imperialist politics. Pulido made evident the cross-cutting organizing efforts in Los Angeles and Southern California during the era by Black Panthers, the predominantly Japanese American East Wind, and the Centro de Acción Social Autónomo (CASA), groups with distinct racial or ethnic identities that traversed shared activist terrains and political principles. Lorena Oropeza and Ernesto Chávez detailed how the biggest protest of the Chicano movement occurred when tens of thousands of anti–Vietnam War protesters turned out for the Chicano Moratorium in East Los Angeles on August 29, 1970.[73] George Mariscal elucidated that in San Diego, as in LA and elsewhere, the Cuban Revolution dramatically shaped how local Chicana/o and Black university students constructed a transcendent internationalist political imaginary.⁷⁴ We might also point to the Black Panther support of the Chicano high school blowouts in LA in 1968 and the ongoing links between the Black Panther Party (BPP) and the United Farm Workers of America (UFW) as outlined by Lauren Araiza.⁷⁵ Abigail Rosas demonstrated that African Americans, Mexican Americans, and other Latinos came together during the war on poverty to establish community health clinics and school readiness programs in LA.⁷⁶ On the "cultural front," to paraphrase Michael Denning, George Lipsitz noted the internationalist sensibilities of Chicano poster art, while Cynthia Young suggested pushing the periodization of the '60s forward into the next decade to include the revolutionary third cinema developed by Black, Latino, Asian American, and Middle Eastern student filmmakers affiliated with the ethnocommunications program at UCLA.⁷⁷ Such events and activities not only revealed the extent of the worlds in which many Los Angeles Black and Chicana/o activists saw themselves, but reminds us that Cold War ideologies never fully contained the interracial and oppositional vibe of politics in the postwar period, especially when it came to cultural expression and music.

Still, the Cold War could short-circuit the interracial and utopian impulses of brown-eyed soul. The Vietnam War, in particular, disrupted the flow of the music when many young Chicano musicians were drafted and left their bands behind. Jimmie Meza, the guitarist for the Atlantics, for example, was drafted into the army just a month after performing on television and hearing his records on the radio. He bluntly recalled, "Getting drafted, really, put an end to my music." Other cases abounded. Mike Rincon, the leader and bass player for the Blendells, was inducted in 1967 and went on to serve in the military police in Panama for his two-year tour of duty. Another former member of the Blendells, Rudy Valona, was drafted in 1966 and, he recalled, "that blew everything" just as he and a few friends started playing studio gigs as part of a new band called Los Vaqueros. The Premiers lost their lead guitarist Lawrence Perez when he was drafted in 1967. Bandmate George Delgado remembered, "We just put everything on hold," since Perez had been "spearheading the whole musical arrangements" and "had a lot to do with the drive of the songs we did." One especially poignant story was that of Andy Tesso, a guitarist for Cannibal and the Headhunters. He was drafted and went to Vietnam just two months before the band went on tour with the Beatles. "When I came back," he said, "I didn't want to play anymore."⁷⁸ Little Willie G of Thee Midniters summed up by saying that "Vietnam really just tore everything apart. Not everybody was willing to run to Canada or fight the draft. It was the American thing to do. 'Hey, I'm going. I'll see you guys in two years.'"[79]

If we listen carefully to the shifting nature of brown-eyed soul in the late 1960s and early '70s, we can hear and feel in the music the same range of political and cultural exchange that animated the period's activism. By the late 1960s, several groups on the LA scene, including El Chicano, Tierra, Mark Guerrero, and War, increasingly politicized the brown-eyed soul sound by engaging on-the-ground peace and protest movements, anticolonial struggles, and US-based third world organizing in their music. Many of these late 1960s and early '70s bands consciously made politics a more central feature in their music in ways that did not simply echo popular notions of cultural nationalism and ethnic solidarity, but embraced the longer scope of LA's interracial history. Thus, Chicano and Black cultural politics drew much from one another and the relational and internationalist impulses of the Chicano and larger civil rights movements, providing a soundtrack to political change unbounded by race, culture, or nationalism.

Brown-eyed soul registered the political changes of the era at the same time it indexed the interracial history of Los Angeles. Around the time the civil rights and Chicano movements—and urban life more generally—in Los Angeles began to be eclipsed by the grim realities of economic restructuring, deindustrialization, failure to enforce new civil rights laws, and deliberate abandonment of inner cities and their inhabitants, brown-eyed soul continued to regenerate the interracial and multicultural relationships of years past. El Chicano, Mark Guerrero, Tierra, Yeska, and other bands continued the tradition of combining sounds, aesthetics, and influences from everything from Black jazz to cumbias while also responding to the constricting racial policies of the Nixon, Ford, and Carter administrations. They reversed the trend of Mexican American bands from the Eastside claiming English-language names, sang more in Spanish, and performed songs about overtly politicized topics. Of course, they still sang about love, sex, and good times, but also about the Chicano movement's demands for equal education and protests against police brutality or the Vietnam War. Songs like "Chicano Power" and "The Ballad of Cesar Chavez" by Thee Midniters and Mark Guerrero's "Radio Aztlan," "The Streets of East L.A.," "Pre-Columbian Dream," or "I'm Brown" (which told the story of a down-on-his-luck Chicano who hijacked a plane with a toy gun to bring attention to the plight of Chicanos); El Chicano's and Tierra's rock covers of Mexican classics like "Sabor a Mí" and "Gema"; Tierra's involvement in a Chicano-led boycott against the Coors beer company for discriminatory hiring practices in the early 1970s; and the emergence of Chicano-controlled production companies like Brown Bag Productions that promoted many of the Eastside bands at Cinco de Mayo and Mexican Independence Day celebrations at Cal State Los Angeles and other venues across the city after 1970 all demonstrate that music became more politicized because of the Chicano and civil rights movements' focus on ethnic pride and cultural nationalism.[80] As much as this politicization drew from commitments to ethnic revitalization and nationalism, it was also part of brown-eyed soul's organic connection to the history of Mexican Americans and African Americans sharing public space, politics, culture, and music in Los Angeles. The bassist Freddie Sanchez, as if conjuring up the longer history of brown-eyed soul, put it like this: "We're Chicanos. That means American as well as Mexican. Our music is a combination of everything we've heard and felt."[81]

Just as Big Jay McNeely and Brenton Wood in earlier years had borrowed from Mexican American musicians, African American artists in the post-1968 era continued to connect with Chicana/o music fans in Los Angeles. Perhaps the best example of this continuing phenomenon was War, a group initiated by the British pop star Eric Burdon when he joined the largely African American ensemble Nightshift, the former backup band of Deacon Jones, a football star in the 1960s and early 1970s as a defensive end with the Los Angeles Rams.[82] After parting ways with Burdon, War, with its fusion of Latin jazz, soul, and rhythm and blues, cemented their popularity among Chicanas/os in LA. Cuts such as "The World Is a Ghetto," "Fidel's Fantasy," and "Why Can't We Be Friends?" explored the economic and political conditions of early 1970s urban America and the possibilities of hemispheric revolution. Others, such as "Spill the Wine" and their now classic tribute to car customizers, "Low Rider," made heavy use of Latin rhythms. War's interracial appeal and variant influences, recalled the guitarist Howard Scott, grew from coming of age in mixed Black and Latino neighborhoods, getting their "Latin thing" from playing with lots of different groups and musicians, and, according to one journalist, a "mood of cultural exchange common during the late 1960s and early 1970s."[83] War further strengthened their relationship to Chicana/o audiences by playing legendary free Cinco de Mayo shows in downtown LA, participating in *Low Rider Magazine*'s Fiesta Tours, and playing regularly at car shows. War's popularity fit well with their all-encompassing, if slightly romantic and utopic, approach to their music, a music defined by the conga player Pappa Dee as a "universal fight against 'Unlove.'"⁸⁴

Brown-eyed soul did not just reflect the politics of the Chicano and civil rights movements after 1968. Rather, bands like Tierra and War constituted a critical element of a novel conception of Chicanismo and Blackness, one not circumscribed by singular notions of race or ethnicity and one integrally tied to both the long history of African American/Mexican American relations in LA and the transregional and internationalist segments of 1960s leftist politics. These artists and many of their fans turned on its head the typical identity politics of the day by not getting their politics simply from their race or ethnic identity, but by crafting their own identity from complicated and interconnected political struggles and cultural expressions. Herein lay brown-eyed soul's utopian impulse, reverberating with John Storey's musing that "radical utopianism offers a form of resistance to dominant constructions of reality and our complicity with them."⁸⁵ In its multiracial and musical "mash-up," the scene offered a vision of Movimiento-era Chicanismo unbounded by ethnicity or nationalism. As much as experiences of being Chicana/o from East Los Angeles generated the music, it was integrally connected to other people and places.

MORE UTOPIAN RHYTHMS

On a July Saturday in 1992, more than twenty years after the heyday of the brown-eyed soul scene, War played an afternoon concert in MacArthur Park in Los Angeles. The hundreds of people in attendance, many of them African American and Latina/o, enjoyed what were by then considered the "oldies" for which War was so well known. Songs such as the aforementioned "Why Can't We Be Friends?," "The World Is a Ghetto," and the anthemic "Low Rider" with its ubiquitous twelve-note hook offered a testament to the longevity and continuing resonance of brown-eyed soul. Beyond this, the event showcased a number of much younger Latino rappers who had together contributed to a recent compilation CD entitled *Rap Declares War*, in which LA-area Chicano hip-hop artists, including Kid Frost, A Lighter Shade of Brown, and Proper Dos, and African American artists De La Soul, 2Pac Shakur, and Ice-T, put forth a call for social justice expressed by new lyrics set within a medley of beats based around samples of classic War songs.

The timing and location of the *Rap Declares War* event were significant. The concert took place three short months after the explosion of popular rage that followed the police acquittals in the Rodney King case. The most serious urban disturbance since the US Civil War, the riots were described by the historian Mike Davis as "a postmodern bread riot" that simultaneously encompassed a radical democratic protest of aggrieved African Americans, an interethnic conflict between African Americans and Korean and Korean Americans, and an explosion among the city's multiracial poor. As a formerly elegant urban oasis that demarcated the intersection of Koreatown, the northernmost fingers of predominantly "Black" Vermont and Hoover Avenue corridors, and the overwhelmingly Central American and immigrant Mexican Pico-Union district, the city blocks surrounding MacArthur Park were a polyglot area that saw widespread looting—often of food staples, consumer goods, and other basic necessities—and large numbers of arrests during the riots. With the memory of National Guard armored cars fresh in the minds of many Los Angelenos, including those whose homes were invaded by soldiers searching for stolen articles, it takes little imagination to see the selection of MacArthur Park as a site for the concert as part of a continuing contest over public space that pitted soldiers and police against the Black and brown youth of Southern California.[86]

In the subsequent interval between the Rodney King riots and the present day, MacArthur Park has emerged as an important center within the musical and political renaissance that has helped reshape Los Angeles into one of the most important sites of labor, immigration, racial justice, and youth organizing in the United States. MacArthur Park served as the site for an annual May 1 march coordinated by the Multi-ethnic Immigrant Worker Organizing Network (MIWON).[87] Pre-dating the larger immigrant rights mobilizations that spread during the spring of 2006, the May 1 rallies continue despite a vicious police riot in 2007 and notwithstanding the demise of larger political coalitions led by popular radio personalities, the Democratic Party, Latino elected officials, and the Catholic Church. In another illustration of the park's central place in the city's recent political history, visitors today can take a short walk from the park's eastern edge to a building that served as the main coordination point for the protests that accompanied the 2000 Democratic Party Convention held in downtown LA. Moreover, as was the case with the anti–World Trade Organization protests in Seattle in 1999, the 2000 protests against the Democratic National Committee (DNC) were accompanied and shaped by the contributions of musicians and cultural activists who helped provide the energy, momentum, and context for the strength of the movement.[88]

The efforts of these Chicana/o and African American artists and activists have been far from episodic. Across a wide sweep of Northeast Los Angeles, from MacArthur Park through Echo Park/Silverlake and East Hollywood and over the hills into Highland Park and El Sereno, one finds an archipelago of cafés, bookstores, and performance spaces, all of which speak to a broad structure of feeling that suggests a present-day incarnation of the sorts of musical configurations present in brown-eyed soul. Although Chicanx and Latinx studies scholars have tended to assess this moment and cultural geography using the language of a "greater Eastside" that accompanies the demographic expansion of diverse locales linked by the predominance of Spanish-speaking populations, I argue that the musical production of groups like Quetzal, Burning Star, East L.A. Sabor Factory, and Ozomatli speaks to a Left-inflected, sonic blending that represents a profound coming together of African American and Latin music. Furthermore, as with brown-eyed soul, members and collaborators with these bands have included Chicanos, Latinos, Japanese Americans, and African Americans.[89]

As was the case during World War II and again during the Vietnam era, the contemporary incarnation of brown-eyed soul emerges from a particular political, demographic, and cultural milieu. After 1992, Latinos emerged as a diverse majority within a city that counted nearly a million African Americans and Asians. Los Angeles became poorer during this time as well, despite the efforts of a resurgent, immigrant-led labor movement. On a wider level, new activists confronted a bevy of racist ballot initiatives, the economic dislocation of NAFTA, and two American wars in the Near East. On the local level, then, Josh Kun's description of Ozomatli as "a band synonymous with a post-urban-uprising Los Angeles, justice-seeking-janitors-striking-down-Westside-Wilshire Los Angeles, MTA bus-strike Los Angeles, DNC-rubber-bullets Los Angeles, Rampart-frame-ups-that-put-innocent-bodies-in-jail-and-in-hillside-Tijuana-*dompes* Los Angeles" seems on the mark.[90] As Victor Viesca noted, the band's genesis was political. Core members of Ozomatli coalesced around a struggle to unionize the Los Angeles Conservation Corps. Although their organizing drive failed, activists managed to occupy the headquarters of their work site for more than a year, founding a Peace and Justice Center that served as an activist clearinghouse and performance space for a generation-in-formation of young radicals.[91]

In the decade since the closure of the Peace and Justice Center, groups like Quetzal, Quinto Sol, and Ozomatli have become fixtures at demonstrations, benefits, and fundraising events. In addition, several of the bands formerly affiliated with the Peace and Justice Center have regenerated the international flavor of brown-eyed soul's cultural politics by reestablishing the connection to Mexico made evident by previous generations of LA-area musicians. The music of Quetzal and others, for instance, is profoundly shaped by the Zapatista uprising in Chiapas, Mexico. Group members have pursued the possibilities of Zapatismo-influenced organizing for labor and immigrant rights in Los Angeles and south of the border. This was most evident in their support for and participation in Afro-Mexican cultural and political struggles in Veracruz and elsewhere.[92] In a manner not unlike El Chicano a generation earlier, musician/activists like Quetzal Flores and Martha Gonzalez are part of a new urban landscape defined less by a politics of identity than by an identity of politics. This is not a music that represents radical politics as much as it is a terrain of political activity in its own right.

As was true for their predecessors, the political and cultural tapestry of these more recent musicians and artists can be seen in the transformative aesthetics of the music. Much as War, Santana, and El Chicano obliterated distinctions between jazz, rock, and R&B, Ozomatli and their ilk offer sonic variations that cross ostensibly national, ethnic, and racial music styles. Audiences at Ozomatli concerts may hear as many musical styles as they do songs, and "Mexican" *rancheras*, "Dominican" merengues, "Brazilian" sambas, and "African American" hip-hop may be included on a given track.[93] Quetzal's music, beyond combining a dizzying array of regional Mexican styles grounded foremost in the coastal *son jarocho*, incorporates hip-hop and Lucumí sacred music, while the ska/funk/reggae offerings of Quinto Sol and Burning Star lack a generic name but have been called "Razteca reggae" among many other labels. This is a musical milieu that stitches together Robert Fogelson's famously "fragmented metropolis," most particularly through the coming together of the nominally separate categories of "Black" and "Latino."[94] This, ultimately, is both the lesson and the promise of the brown-eyed soul moment, a kind of Baraka-esque "changing same" in which Black and Chicano communities created and re-created musical forms that speak to the dialectic between the porous nature of ethnic affiliation and the ongoing reality of external and internal racialization within efforts to ensure not just that they survive, but that they live.[95]

The legacy of brown-eyed soul echoed beyond Los Angeles as well.

In 1999, Shin Miyata, a Chicano "oldies" fan from Tokyo, paid an unannounced visit to Hector Gonzalez, who had inherited Rampart Records from Eddie Davis in 1994. Dressed in his Pendleton-style shirt, with goatee and dark shades, Miyata "looked like a homeboy from the Eastside barrios," Gonzalez recalled.[96] Miyata tracked down Gonzalez at his East LA home because he wanted to release Rampart Records songs back in Japan where there was a growing fascination with Chicano lowrider culture. By 2002, Miyata had rereleased the first Rampart Records album by the Village Callers in Japan on his Barrio Gold label, a subsidiary of his new venture, Music Camp, Inc. He went on to release dozens of brown-eyed soul records in Japan from Rampart and other LA-based labels, incorporated Chicano rap and new Eastside bands like Quetzal into his repertoire, and helped grow a niche market for Chicano culture and music in Tokyo. For its part, Rampart Records rereleased its songs in as many as fifty other countries and inked a deal with a Sony Music–affiliated global digital distributor.[97] Miyata first encountered Chicanos when he watched 1970s American television shows like *CHiPs*, starring Erik Estrada as a Mexican American motorcycle highway patrolman named "Ponch," and *Chico and the Man*, set in a fictional mechanics garage in East LA. When Miyata decided to study Spanish while at university in Japan, he passed on going to Spain or Latin America to study abroad like many of his fellow Japanese Spanish-language students. Instead, Miyata took a year off from school to live in East LA. He landed in Boyle Heights in 1984 and immersed himself in Chicano life and culture, taking classes in Chicano Studies at East Los Angeles College, cruising with lowriders along Whittier Boulevard, and catching as much live music by East LA bands like Los Lobos as he possibly could. When he returned to Japan, he began writing pieces on Chicano music and culture for Japanese media outlets, including *Lowrider Japan* with its more than 70,000 readers. After working in the music industry for BMG in Tokyo, Miyata broke out on his own to start Music Camp, Inc., and Barrio Gold. His enterprise has grown over the years, releasing more records, interviewing dozens of musicians, and bringing East LA bands and artists to perform in Japan.[98]

My point is not that Miyata or his fellow Japanese were fascinated simply by the content of brown-eyed soul, but that, to borrow from Walter Benjamin, its history and conditions of production offered new opportunities and possibilities.[99] Like those who came before him, Miyata was a testament to Ruth Levitas's claim that "the power of music as a utopian form rests in its nonverbal, nonrepresentational, abstract character and its consequent capacity to transcend the utterable. It does not merely prefigure a better world but invokes it."[100]

Brown-eyed soul had roots in the longer history of the Eastside sound and struggles for racial justice across the city. Its legacy also lived in the music and new social movements that emerged in the years after its heyday. Through their music, Chicanas/os helped fuel interracial cultural and political worlds that offered different visions of Los Angeles and civil rights. Brown-eyed soul was a reminder that utopian impulses and visions, in their unfinished and transitory form, sprouted from historical conditions and gave meaning to the places and spaces where people found themselves.

CHAPTER 3

Chico *and* Kotter

When network executives rolled out the 1974 television season, Chicana/o activists fervently protested the new NBC sitcom *Chico and the Man*. Set in a rundown mechanic's garage in East Los Angeles, it featured a young, enterprising Chicano Vietnam vet named Chico who worked for Ed Brown, an old, white, curmudgeonly Archie Bunker type. Their generational and cultural clash, mixed with a blossoming affection for one another, made for laughs based on Ed's racist sense of humor and Chico's witty, endearing jokes in return. Protests ignited as soon as the pilot aired. Among the complaints was that Freddie Prinze, the actor who played Chico, wasn't Chicano. He only played one on television. Prinze was of Puerto Rican and Hungarian descent and referred to himself as a "Hungarican" from New York. Activists further lambasted the show as racist and degrading for casting Prinze as Chico (meaning "boy" in Spanish) and the older, white Brown—played by Jack Albertson—as the "Man." Threats of advertiser boycotts and a picket of KNBC's Burbank studios where the series was taped engulfed its first season, although the uproar quieted down after *Chico*'s early ratings success and minor tweaks to its story line.[1]

A year later, in 1975, the ABC affiliate in Boston refused to air another new sitcom. Billed as a smash hit-to-be, *Welcome Back, Kotter* starred the comedian Gabe Kaplan as a teacher of a multiracial group of remedial students in a Brooklyn high school. The "Sweathogs," as the students were known, included Juan Epstein, a Puerto Rican–Jewish "tough guy" known for forging his mother's signature on absentee notes and his uncommon ethnic mix. *Kotter* was slapstick at its best, but following the court-ordered busing of Black students into predominantly white high schools in Boston for the 1974–1975 school year, WCVB-

TV officials feared the show would enflame racial tension. Busing had sparked violence in schools, protests against integration by white Bostonians armed with baseball bats and hockey sticks, and corresponding anti-racist marches. When white parents threatened to hold their kids out of school if busing wasn't eliminated, WCVB banned *Kotter*.[2] "In view of the incredible troubles the city has had," surmised station management, "it would be in bad taste to run the program." In what appeared to be a thinly veiled cover for fear of the show's interracial premise, WCVB argued it was a "badly handled classroom comedy" that "advocated the kind of bad attitudes that are not proper behavior in the classroom." Despite the concerns, *Kotter* soon aired in Boston after initial episodes were positively reviewed and deemed unthreatening.[3]

Kotter and *Chico* were filters through which upward of forty million viewers a week made sense of life in America following the heyday of the civil rights movement. Part of an ethnic and racial revival in prime time, they signaled Herman Gray's observation that television was a decisive arena of symbolic struggle over the meaning of race in national debates over social policies, citizenship, and rights.[4] The two shows registered people's hopes for racial harmony, their lingering frustration over the failure of the movement to fully deliver on its promise, and resentment over the diminishing overrepresentation of white privilege. Along with other sitcoms with racial themes, *Kotter* and *Chico* revealed which narratives, trajectories, and versions of racial reconciliation were most palatable in a country still rocking from the racial violence and social movements of preceding years. They also made known which renderings of post-movement life failed to reel in ratings and big bucks from advertisers. In the high stakes game of network television, *Kotter*, *Chico*, and other sitcoms indexed the possibilities and limits of what race relations might look like in a moment when the racial future was unsettled.

Both programs illustrated the seductive promise and unyielding constraints of pop cultural utopias in the 1970s. Their story lines stretched the Black-white binary to include Chicanos and Latinos in a multiracial representation of life in the United States. Generous critics might have suggested that *Chico* and *Kotter* envisioned a future of racial harmony and reconciliation, serving as widely watched, weekly prognostications of the society the United States could and should have become after the civil rights movement. From this point of view, sitcoms fostered the "social dreaming, longing, and desire for change" that, as Davina Cooper noted, scholars have described as "key dimensions of the utopian, along with the hope—or perhaps more accurately, the belief—that more egalitarian, freer ways of living are possible."⁵ Yet their on-screen narratives and production muzzled voices in the conversation about the racial future, especially those in the Chicano, Latino, and racialized communities the shows purportedly depicted. Production staff and crews rarely included Chicana/o or Latina/o producers, writers, or actors; story lines privileged working-class men, often only including whites marked as "ethnic"; and both shows largely failed to engage the feminist and Third Worldist proclivities of the era's social movements. *Chico* and *Kotter*'s idealist tendencies were entangled with a realism that recalled Ruth Levitas's warning: "Among the difficulties of envisioning utopia are the limits placed by our historical circumstances on what is possible for us to imagine and articulate. Every representation falls short."⁶ Despite the romantic visions of an interracial future portrayed in these shows, prudent observers might have concluded that *Kotter*, *Chico*, and other sitcoms of their ilk reinforced the cultural logic of white supremacy and curbed the cultural reach of movements for racial justice.

Chico and *Kotter* also showed that utopia was elusive and illusory, not always what it seemed, especially for Chicano and Latino communities. From one point of view, Chico and Epstein signaled a new presence for Chicanos and Latinos on television. Chico, for instance, announced his Chicano identity in the pilot episode with an electric retort to two white police officers who called him "Pancho" and "beaner," asked if he had papers to prove he was born in the United States, and pegged him as a suspect in a robbery. He replied, "Why? You got papers to prove where you were born? I'm a Chicano, man! I was born in this country! And, what's more, we had it first. You people are the outsiders! I *habla* your English. Why can't you *habla* a little of my *español*?" Epstein's introduction in the *Kotter* pilot was no less rousing. In almost regal fashion, he told Mr. Kotter his full name was "Juan Luis Pedro Felipo de Huevos Epstein from San Juan," citing his father's Puerto Rican background and that his mother's name was Biberman. Later in the episode, Epstein explained, "I'm gonna do a report on the implications of the socializations of Puerto Rican Jews." Chico and Epstein raised the prospect that sitcoms could challenge racist representations and cultivate progressive discourse about race, lending support to Edward Chan and Patricia Ventura's claim that "the seemingly endless thirst for imagining the bad place of racism with its cruelty requires us to present alternatives that seek racial justice."⁷ Unfortunately, *Chico* and *Kotter* often failed to deliver. Despite their iconic entrances into prime time, Freddie Prinze was not the only one of the two that performed his character's ethnicity. Robert Hegyes, who played Epstein, was neither Puerto Rican nor Jewish. Like Prinze, Hegyes was of Hungarian ancestry. What did it mean that both actors had more Hungarian in common than Chicano or Latino? Cloaking exclusion in a shroud of inclusion, the illusion undermined the utopian, romantic visions of interracial living at the heart of *Chico* and *Kotter*.

TELEVISION AND CIVIL RIGHTS

Chico and *Kotter* were part of a racial awakening in 1970s television. New programming dealt with African American life in shows like *Good Times, Sanford and Son,* and *What's Happening!!*; interracial settings in *Barney Miller, Welcome Back, Kotter,* and *The White Shadow*; and racial reconciliation in *All in the Family, The Jeffersons,* and *Chico and the Man*. Race on television drew phenomenal ratings, and the networks cashed in. *All in the Family*, with everyone's favorite cantankerous racist, Archie Bunker, was number 1 in the Nielsen ratings for five years running from 1971 to 1976. During that same stretch, *Sanford and Son* was in the top 10 every year and twice finished second; *Good Times* was consistently in the top 30 and placed number 7 in 1974–1975; and *The Jeffersons*, a spin-off about Archie Bunker's Black neighbor George, was number 4 in its debut season of 1974–1975. Other sitcoms with racial themes and characters dotted the top 30, too, including *Welcome Back, Kotter, Barney Miller*, and *What's Happening!!*.[8]

The surge in shows about race and, by extension, the working-class lives of Black and brown folk was the result of a nation still in turmoil. Gut-wrenching economic shifts, political crises, and ongoing racial violence rocked the United States into the 1970s. The continuing decline in Keynesian economics, rise of neoliberalism, and escalating deindustrialization saw family income stagnate, unions fall under attack, and the energy crisis make for difficult times, especially for urban communities of color. Watergate, spiraling involvement in Vietnam, and weakened faith in leaders and institutions further scrambled American political sensibilities and helped mark a hard right turn to conservatism. At the same time, as Dan Berger noted, the 1970s were "the '60s' second decade," full of radical possibilities signaled by enduring political unrest in incidents like the Chicano Moratorium antiwar protest in Los Angeles in 1970, the Attica Prison Riot in 1971, the occupation of Wounded Knee in 1973, and ever-maturing movements demanding Puerto Rican independence, women's rights, and gay rights.[9] The drive for social change persisted at a time when optimism gave way to frustration, political exhaustion, and rage that years of civil rights struggle had not produced more results. During the same period, politicians from Nixon to Reagan garnered support by mobilizing white ethnicity, while brown and Black urbanites suffered the brunt of economic and political policies that prioritized profit over people.

Although sitcoms were not immune to the world around them, they were also divorced enough from the real world to reel in viewers with a muted and nonthreatening, if not warped, vision of race in America. They reminded us of Arlene Dávila's musings that "marketable ethnicity" relied on the idea that "manifestations of ethnicity and cultural difference within a given state are never entirely free of its dominant ideological canons."[10] Most sitcoms were filmed in Hollywood or Burbank, but set in big cities where economic and political crisis was most acute. LA was home to *Chico, Sanford and Son, What's Happening!!,* and *The White Shadow*; New York was the setting for *Kotter, All in the Family, The Jeffersons,* and *Barney Miller*; and *Good Times* took place on Chicago's Southside. Place figured prominently, and to the extent that the '70s witnessed a series of political experiments, as Berger noted, sitcoms took the big-city metropolis as their testing ground for stories about Chicanos, Latinos, and African Americans.[11] They were designed to attract viewers and make profits, conjuring David Rando's reflection that pop cultural technologies "allowed for the expression of certain social utopian impulses before they were pressed into the exclusive and proprietary service of capitalism."[12]

Sitcoms, however, largely failed to reflect layered patterns of racialization and struggles for racial liberation in the United States. Black and brown characters were often portrayed as nonthreatening, immature, and disaffected by the more radical politics of the day. Race relations were relegated to domestic spaces like the Evans's living room in *Good Times*, easily controlled venues like *Kotter*'s classroom, or private businesses like Ed Brown's garage in *Chico*. Characters and episodes were estranged and disconnected from insurgent movements for Chicano, Puerto Rican, African American, Cuban, or Latin American independence and solidarity that continued to simmer throughout the 1970s. As in the cases of *Kotter, Barney Miller,* and *The White Shadow*, it was not uncommon for white, male, and ethnically unmarked characters to play the moral and authoritative role over groups of mixed-race and ethnic subordinates. Shows also accentuated gender and class as shortcuts to multiracial coalition and reconciliation. The shared masculinity and working-class milieu in *Chico*'s garage, *Kotter*'s classroom, *The White Shadow*'s high school locker room, or *Barney Miller*'s twelfth precinct for NYPD detectives, for instance, brought characters and their story lines together across racial lines.[13]

Common racial sensibilities across sitcoms were, in part, an effect of the insular nature of the television industry and its faith in previously successful formulas.[14] It is not surprising that the same creators, showrunners, and writers had a hand in multiple shows and that most were liberal, progressive-leaning white men. Norman Lear, for example, who produced *Good Times*, *All in the Family*, and *Sanford and Son*, among others, was the kingpin of 1970s sitcoms.[15] *Chico* and *Kotter* were powered by Jimmie Komack, Dave Wolper, and the partnering of their formidable outfits, the Komack Company and Wolper Productions. Komack created *Chico* and produced *Kotter*, while Wolper brought his muscle as marquee producer and distributor best known for his work on the epic television miniseries *Roots*. Komack, in particular, had a heavy hand in both shows, insisting that his brand of "ethnic comedy" emphasized "seeking audience love and projecting love," all in the hopes that "love will dilute racial strife."[16] Despite his romantic spin, not everyone saw it the same way. As the initial response to *Chico* by Chicana/o activists indicated, many were none too happy that such a select and homogeneous cohort was responsible for crafting much of television's narrative about race in the years following the civil rights movement. Many observers, especially in Latino and African American circles, understood television as a pop cultural battleground where racial representation mattered for creating opportunities in the entertainment industry and for shaping viewer outlooks on race relations.[17] This extended from the public to those on set, including Black actors like Esther Rolle and John Amos of *Good Times* fame, who had high-profile disagreements with showrunners over the depiction of Black people on their show. From this vantage point, prime-time sitcoms were home to a high-stakes culture war over who told the story of race in the post–civil rights era.[18]

Chico and *Kotter* injected Chicano and Latino experiences into the nexus of television and civil rights.[19] Both tracked how Chicanos and Latinos were imagined to be a part—or not—of visions of US life and culture after the civil rights movement. This was especially the case with the recognition of how the Latino presence transformed urban areas like the ones in which both shows were set, a phenomenon that scholars have more recently referred to as Latinization.[20] *Chico* situated Chicanos in the thorny grove of racial and generational reconciliation, while *Kotter* positioned Latinos as pivotal players in its portrait of interracial solidarity. If they gestured toward a kind of racial utopia, however, both shows, like other sitcoms, accentuated how the boundaries of such a project were policed. As the casting of Prinze and Hegyes suggested, Chicano and Latino communities and themes were simultaneously included and erased or obscured. Black and brown writers, let alone directors or producers, were few and far between. On-screen narratives spotlighted the success or failure of individual characters or their ethnic group to coexist with others or assimilate into the mainstream. Little attention was paid to the Chicano or Puerto Rican independence movements that had thrust Chicanos and Latinos into the racial lexicon of the nation and helped explain their new presence on prime-time television. In a way, *Chico* and *Kotter* prefigured debates over multiculturalism in the 1980s and were home to the culture wars before they were declared. Exalted by some as evidence of racial unity, they were soundly blasted by others as blindly celebrating diversity without attention to inequities in representation, resources, and the impact of such ideological discourse on the communities most impacted by policies and ideas about race. Utopia is fleeting under any circumstances, and 1970s sitcoms were no exception.

CHICO, THE MAN, AND THE MOVIMIENTO

Chico and the Man enjoyed a meteoric rise, ending its first season as the third most-watched show on television, behind only *All in the Family* and *Sanford and Son*.[21] Its appeal rested on the peculiar relationship between Chico and Ed Brown, their uproarious exchanges, and the exceptional chemistry between Freddie Prinze and Jack Albertson on-screen. Chico was a young, energetic, and resourceful Chicano who had won a Silver Star in Vietnam and was eager to work hard and make a life for himself. Ed was an old, white, grumpy widower with bigoted views of Mexicans who drank too much, and he grew increasingly agitated as he watched his East LA neighborhood and clientele become increasingly Mexican. Their relationship blossomed after Chico convinced a reluctant Ed to bring him on as a business partner, and Chico moved into the abandoned van in the mechanic's garage underneath Ed's upstairs apartment. Chico's upbeat optimism and willingness to always see the good in Ed clashed with Ed's racist and negative outlook on life. The discord between the two resonated with viewers, especially as the series developed and focused on Ed and Chico's growing affection and respect for each other. *Chico* struck a chord with millions of other Americans facing the upshot of racial grievances in the aftermath of the civil rights movement. It offered a utopian vision of racial reconciliation that included multiple generations, identities, and points of view. Chico was youthful, enlightened, and buoyed by the demands of the movement, whereas Ed, with the parochial mindset of a bygone era, eschewed change. Ed's travails with Chico were not unlike Archie Bunker's with his daughter and son-in-law in *All in the Family*. Just as Archie berated anyone who was different from him or inspired by civil rights, including his Black neighbor George Jefferson and racially mixed coworkers, as a loading dock foreman in the Corona neighborhood of Queens, New York, Ed did the same to Chico and the Mexican American Eastside. Yet, Ed and Chico forged a real affection for one another despite their differences, offering viewers an alluring and rollickingly sidesplitting vision of how racial reconciliation could unfold.

If *Chico's* hopeful vision for life after the civil rights era hastened the show's success, it didn't last long. The show ran four seasons but never fully capitalized on its first campaign, falling to number 25 in year two and plummeting thereafter.[22] Its collapse hinted that conviction for racial reconciliation crumbled as the 1970s progressed and that the utopian vision of Ed and Chico's relationship concealed fissures behind and beyond the cameras. One need not look any further than when tragedy struck and Freddie Prinze committed suicide in the midst of *Chico's* third season. Like the show, Prinze had experienced a remarkable ascent. As *Time* magazine told it, he went from "disarming his foes with switch-blade one liners" in the Latino neighborhoods of Manhattan's Upper West Side to doing the same on New York's stand-up comedy circuit and *The Johnny Carson Show*. When Jimmie Komack saw his act, it wasn't long before Prinze was cast as Chico, signed a multiyear million-dollar deal with Caesar's Palace in Las Vegas, and had his choice of movie roles. Those close to him observed that his fame came perhaps too quickly. The burden of stardom, mixed with drug abuse and marriage problems, drove Prinze to shoot himself when he was only twenty-two years old. The show continued without him through the 1977–1978 season but had lost its magic.[23]

Despite its brief run, *Chico and the Man* introduced barrio life to a mainstream audience, conjuring hopes that it would positively impact perceptions of Chicanos and remind viewers that civil rights were not just Black and white. For instance, Justice for Chicanos in the Motion

Picture and Television Industry (also known as Justicia), a group that included *Chico* associate producer Ray Andrade among its most vocal members, gave Jimmie Komack a public stamp of approval in a January 1974 press release. They said he was "a long-time friend of the Spanish surname communities" and believed television "was handicapping itself by excluding the entertainment of 'LA RAZA' from any top network programs." Justicia prophesied that Ed and Chico would "bring harmony" between "the young and the aged, Latin and Anglo" and that Komack would "inevitably affect many Americans in their distorted preconceptions of Chicanos" by eliminating "erroneous stereotyping," providing opportunities in television to Chicanos, and promulgating "a brotherhood between Chicanos and Anglos." Citing the millions of Mexican-descent folks living in the United States and their negligible voice in Nielsen ratings, Justicia concluded that "it is imperative that Chicanos, along with other minorities, get their fair share of the television and radio public service industry. Justicia and *Chico and the Man* will hopefully be the start of the beginning of this."[24]

Such aspirations were hardly met in reality, however, and it didn't take long for activists to condemn the show as inauthentic and exclusionary. With a catalogue of complaints at the ready, Chicano activists corroborated Alex Zamalin's observation about Black pop cultural utopias, realizing they "needed to seize a space of imagination from which they were barred and imagine a new humanity from which they were excluded."[25] Topping the list of objections was that Freddie Prinze wasn't Chicano.[26] In the tradition of protests against Hollywood's casting of non-Chicanos to play Chicano or Mexican parts by the League of United Latin American Citizens (LULAC), Mexican American Legal Defense and Education Fund (MALDEF), and National Council of La Raza (NCLR), complaints poured in. Groups like the Teatro Nacional de Aztlán (TENAZ), an organization of more than eighty-five Chicano theater groups, lambasted *Chico* for advancing a fraudulent portrayal of Chicano life. This history was not lost on activists from Cal State, Los Angeles, who argued that NBC "has never had the guts to cast a Chicano in a substantial role, much less a starring role, in spite of the fact that Chicanos have repeatedly petitioned them to change their sick and racist policies."[27] Prinze's Spanish, critics argued, sounded too Puerto Rican, and "even his gestures and body movements are not convincingly Chicano."[28] TENAZ member Alicia Sandoval noted, "It's a cute trick. A Chicano show with no Chicanos."[29] *Lowrider Magazine* summed up the anger felt by many. "From the get-go," it argued, "Chicanos knew the program was a phony, Chicanos didn't act like that around Chicano Barrios. NBC started getting protests from the Chicano community. The Chicano community said that first, that was a wrong picture of how Chicanos live and second, that wasn't a Chicano playing the role of a Chicano."[30] Despite its groovy rhythm, even the show's theme song by the Puerto Rican singer José Feliciano was panned by activists for its "distinctly Caribbean flavor."[31]

Critics further scorned Komack's brand of humor as "degrading and racist" for negatively stereotyping Chico; featuring jokes about Mexicans as lazy, dirty, and stupid; and subordinating Chico to Ed Brown. In a letter to NBC president Robert Howard, for example, the Los Angeles Hispanic Urban Center argued that *Chico and the Man* "is a sad continuation of the racist history of the media that has made us almost invisible." It accused the program and NBC of presenting Chico in a "demeaning, 'serf-master' relation to 'The Man,'" ridiculing his "language, speech, habits, and overall presence," and reinforcing overused stereotypes of "simplistic" and dishonest Mexicans that were a "great disservice to the Mexican-American population."[32] Another viewer summarized much of the outcry when he said that the "show portrays a Chicano in a subservient role; demeans the Chicano character and gives Chico little opportunity to demonstrate pride in himself and his ethnic origin. The humor utilized is dangerously close to the Step 'n Fetchit portrayals."[33] Among the most vocal critics, according to an *LA Times* article by two LA-area media activists, were the Brown Beret David Sanchez, the television executive Gil Avila, and the education activist Vahaac Mardirosian.[34] Much of this criticism took on a thinly veiled gender bent, too. Mirroring the masculinist ethos of the Chicano movement, some argued that the show denied Chico his manhood when he was juxtaposed to Ed Brown as the "Man." Brown's paternalism toward Chico, evident, for example, in one episode when Chico chose Ed over his own Mexican immigrant father, led Chon Noriega to claim that it advanced "an oedipalized masculinity."[35]

Discontent with *Chico* was nourished by the paltry number of Chicanos involved in its production and Komack and Wolper's unfamiliarity with Mexican America. As the *Baltimore Sun* asked in late 1974, "What in the world does New York's Jimmie Komack, a talent who learned his trade by bombing in night clubs, know about Chicanos? It's a good question."[36] Caesar Cantu, chairman of the Mexican Heritage Cultural Board in Columbus, Ohio, asked much the same: "Who made them [Komack and Wolper] experts on culture, traditions, music, folklore and ways of life of the Mexican people?"[37] Komack did himself no favors, revealing his naivete by associating *Chico* with a short visit he made to Mexico in the early 1970s. He recalled,

> When I returned to Los Angeles, I discovered I could use my Spanish all over town. I had never realized how strong the Mexican heritage was here; after all, they arrived here first. I began to feel that perhaps the country was ready for something I was enjoying, that maybe the '70s would mark the emergence of the Hispanic people in America just as the '60s had brought the emergence of the blacks.[38]

Detractors pounced. In a press release lambasting the show, one group of activists pulled no punches, charging, "[Komack] is a con man, a narrow-minded bigot and a manipulator of Chicano vendidos [sell outs]."[39] Sandoval from TENAZ noted that "all the writers for 'Chico and the Man' are white and Jewish plugging Catskill humor. I have nothing against such humor, but it has no place in a Chicano program."[40]

The Cuban-born screenwriter and director Migdia Varela echoed such concerns, reminding readers that television narratives of racial utopia left Chicano and Latino writers on the outside looking in. In a letter to the FCC's Complaints and Compliance Department, she wrote, "Komack probably knew as much about Mexican-American culture as I know about the culture of Lithuanian Aborigines." She hammered *Chico*'s lack of Chicano or Latino writers and technical advisers, even questioning whether Ray Andrade was involved in the show. "Their reply of 'we have Ray Andrade here as our technical advisor, and he's presently working on whatever problems arise,'" she believed, "became a copout." Varela contended that Komack and Wolper perpetuated the myth that he was deeply involved, noting that Andrade himself said he had "nothing whatsoever to do with the creative aspect of the show" and that he was merely a "go-between" for the network and producers. Despite public calls by Komack and Wolper to attract Latino writers, moreover, Varela alleged that they privately dismissed "with the barest of explanations all the materials and ideas submitted by Latinos." Varela herself applied to be a show writer, ultimately concluding,

> I don't think that they ever intended to give Latin writers a chance. I don't think that my ideas are the best in the world, but compared to the ideas that have been used, I think mine are pretty darned good. It just appears to me that it's a lot more comfortable to use and reuse the same

old writers, the majority of them being of Jewish background. The ones who have been perpetuating the image of the broken-English Mexican throughout the years. Using denigrating gags; the ones who don't know what the heck is going on—Latin writers can see this. I know other Latin writers who have gone through the same condescending and non-committal 'let-them-waste-their-time-they-have-nothing-better-to-do-anyway' attitude from *Chico* in particular and from others; and perhaps this letter is not meant solely for me. I must arrive at the conclusion that there exists racial, cultural, and even sexual discrimination toward Latinos, particularly and ironically in the *Chico and the Man* show where they are most sorely needed.[41]

Varela was not the only one to make Ray Andrade a focal point. He appeared regularly in the press as "the Chicano whom the character [Chico] was patterned" after and "the fellow who was hired to ride shotgun on the ethnic content on the weekly offerings."[42] Like Chico, Andrade was a Vietnam vet and born in East Los Angeles. He was active in Justicia and, for Komack and Wolper, noted one journalist, was a "trouble shooter/public relation expert/interpreter and fall guy for the numerous ethnic organizations that presumably represent the opinions and interests of America's barrios."[43] As the storm around *Chico* grew, Andrade was increasingly critical of Prinze. In December 1974, he declared, "Freddie isn't putting his heart into learning the Chicano ways. He has the wrong accent. I've offered to take him to the barrio, but he doesn't want to go." He maintained, "I'm for the kid, but he should get down to earth. I blame the producer, his manager." Andrade echoed concerns of others, stating that many problems on the show stemmed from its paucity of Chicano writers.[44] Despite his public posture, Andrade was vilified by critics. They pulled no punches, charging, as the Cal State LA group claimed, that Komack, Wolper, and NBC "took unfair advantage of this clown because of his inability to think. He is being used."[45] Andrade was also accused of undermining opportunities for other Chicanos on the show and exploiting the Chicano movement for his own professional gain.[46]

Protesters demanded cancellation of the show, threatened to boycott advertisers, and called on producers to poll the Chicano community for reactions.[47] This last point, argued Paul Macías of TENAZ, was crucial, since the industry's standard Nielsen ratings "overlooked the Chicano community[,] which can't afford advertisers' products."[48] A group of more than fifty organizations came together as the Chicano Coalition and petitioned the FCC to deny the renewal of KNBC's television license because, in their eyes, it discriminated against Chicanos in employment and programming. In his affidavit as part of the petition, Cal State Northridge assistant professor of journalism Felix Gutierrez argued, "KNBC-TV perpetuates vicious stereotypes by airing controversial network program shows such as *Chico and the Man*. Research shows that programs of this type reinforce negative stereotypes and are detrimental to the self-image of Chicano children who watch it."[49] The social worker and Coalition chairman John Serrano further claimed that "Chicano children need to have positive role models in order to develop a positive self-image," and the petition concluded that "Chico and the Man presented a stereotypic view of Chicano youth that reinforces Anglo American feelings of racial or ethnic superiority over Chicanos."[50]

Komack and Wolper predictably countered their critics. Komack initially distanced himself from criticism, professing, "My feeling is that they're not attacking me, they're attacking the network. I've made my position very clear with the network, with the community—I'm not a qualified social arbiter, I'm interested in the entertainment aspect."[51] He argued that he "never sought out to do a Chicano show" and only wanted "to do a comedy show with an Hispanic character as one of the leads. We had not thought about portraying Chicanos and their lifestyle."[52] Wolper had a slightly more pragmatic approach dating back to the summer before *Chico* premiered, when he told Komack, "I think it is very important that we try to get some other socially significant themes into *Chico and the Man* other than just the Chicano experience."[53] Wolper continued to think practically once criticism intensified, writing to the production team in the midst of season one that "we should discuss a joint policy about what we say about the Chicanos so that everybody isn't saying something different."[54]

The NBC executive John McMahon likely overstated the case when he said, "The most important thing is that we listened," but Komack, Wolper, and the network did make changes. Measures were taken to address complaints that the show's humor was racist and insulting, including pulling already taped shows for touch-ups, such as fewer racial jokes in new scripts and aiming for a more "father-son flavor" between Ed and Chico. Other minor adjustments were also made. The curtains on Chico's van, which were green, white, and red for the colors of the Mexican flag in early episodes, were made more neutral. Isaac Ruiz, a Chicano actor who was second choice to play Chico, was brought on to play Chico's best friend, Mando. In one episode, Mando addressed Chico's Spanish accent, telling him, "You talk funny—not like us." Drawing on Prinze's own background, Chico replied that he had a Puerto Rican mother, a Hungarian grandmother, and had lived in New York for five years. Throughout the fall 1974 season, show creators also carefully documented the number of Chicanos employed on staff, hired several additional Chicano stagehands and technicians, and publicly praised their contributions—all in an effort, as one critic observed, to "chill the beef."[55] By October, for instance, ten Chicanos were employed on the show, including several production assistants, property masters, and Ray Andrade as the lone Chicano associate producer. Komack agreed to marginal modifications, but he ultimately rejected any criticism over casting Prinze to play a Chicano. "I don't really buy that complaint at all," he said.[56] "In a way, I'm glad it happened. What I always wanted the show to be, basically, was a story of son-father-type love between an inventive younger man and a crotchety and resistive older man. We were heading in that direction anyway, but this hassle speeded up the process."[57] Once the air had cleared, Komack trumpeted that "the uniqueness of the Latino humor has hit the whole nation," "hitting No. 1 has made it worth all the trouble,"[58] and, in sum, "I know what makes people laugh, I know people, I know love, I understand souls."[59]

Freddie Prinze did not shy away from the controversy either. He called out the most vocal activists publicly, exclaiming, "The Chicanos are a warm people. They're dynamite friends. I don't think it's the majority making the fuss. It's a few radicals. I was radical when I was 16. Then I realized it's a one-way street. No radical wants the problem solved because he'd be out of a job. I could go out and do exactly as they say and they'd still knock it."[60] Prinze stuck up for his own performance and, as for the charges a Puerto Rican should not play a Chicano, retorted, "When the show first started I went to a Chicano rally and made a speech. I told the people if it was a Chicano playing a Puerto Rican I would want him to give the best image he could of my people. And in my position, I am doing the same."[61] In his trademark fashion, he opined, "If I can't play a Chicano because I'm Puerto Rican, then God's really gonna be mad when he finds out Charlton Heston played Moses [in the classic motion picture *The Ten Commandments*]."[62] He also pointed out that Isaac Ruiz had auditioned for the part of Chico. "Isaac's a Chicano and he tried out for the part of Chico. I'd have more sympathy if no Chicano actor had a shot at the part. But they all auditioned, they had the same chance I did."[63] Prinze further bristled, "I wish I knew what they wanted. They say Chicanos talk a certain way, walk a certain way. I know lots of Chicanos. All different. They don't want an actor. They want a stereotype, a wind-up Chicano."[64]

Neither did Prinze believe his Chico character was demeaning. "Even in the first show," he reasoned, "Chico was the smart one. He came out ahead of the old man." Like Komack, he claimed the show was never meant to be about Chicanos, let alone make fun of them. "We only did the Chicano thing—spick jokes—in the first show and a little bit in the second. Now, we're doing what the show is really about—youth and age and what we can learn from each other. It's the original game plan; it was never intended to be a show about minorities."[65] Albertson said much the same about his own character, Ed Brown. "It isn't really a series about a bigot," he argued. "I play Ed Brown as just a bitter old man who hates everybody because he's alone in the world." Prinze later recalled, "We expected some objection from Chicanos that a New York Puerto Rican would be playing the role, but we speak the same language, Spanish. And we're going through the same social changes." He even went as far as to say, "Chicanos have it harder than Puerto Ricans because there is more prejudice against them, and because they have been struggling longer. And this land was once theirs. That's tough."[66] Prinze's bottom line was the show was a net positive for Chicanos. "The message we're saying to 40 million people," he avowed, "college lecturers couldn't get across in 10 years. There are people out there who don't know what a Chicano is."[67]

Chico and the Man showed that Chicanx utopias were contested, never guaranteed to be progressive, and always susceptible to being hijacked by commercial interests. It simultaneously signaled television's influence in public conversations about Chicano life and the dissonance between the television industry and Chicano communities. On one front, it was a serious matter whether or not Chicanos had a hand in the representation of their community and Movimiento at a moment when their place in an unsettled racial landscape was ambiguous at best. Some Chicanos claimed victory in this fight. Alfonso Tafoya of Nosotros, for example, called the protests against *Chico* "a great triple victory for us. We finally did get the networks to listen, which was a long time in coming. Secondly, we have a hit show now in which there will be a lot of work for Hispanic actors and actresses. And, finally, we have our own Hispanic hero, a good guy in a white hat, and most of our people don't care anymore whether Freddie Prinze is Mexican or Puerto Rican or what."[68] While such an assessment was open to question, it was not debatable that *Chico* was intended to generate ratings and profits, not address the political plight of Chicanos. As a result, it delivered a mangled picture of Chicanos and fell well short of any racial utopia. If anything, it showed that Komack and Wolper's vision of race in America was at odds with many in the Chicano community.

However legitimate the claims that *Chico* was racist and inauthentic, the dispute between creators and critics obscured the interracial and internationalist tides in which the show existed. Prinze and Chico's mixed backgrounds, for instance, might have been pitched as part of the evolving pan-Latino politics of the day, perhaps in conversation with the Chicana artist Linda Lucero's *Lolita Lebrón*, a poster honoring the Puerto Rican nationalist who led the 1954 armed attack on the US House of Representatives in the name of Puerto Rican independence.[69] Others may have found in *Chico and the Man* echoes of brown-eyed soul's interracial tradition at precisely the moment when El Chicano, Tierra, War, and Mark Guerrero politicized the Movimiento-era Eastside sound. Putting *Chico* in this pop cultural milieu suggests it had more to offer beyond a derivative call for brown power. Despite noble intentions of show runners and earnest calls for change by activists, any hopes for *Chico* to "dilute racial strife" ultimately went unfulfilled.

KOTTER AND THE "SWEATHOGS"

The year after *Chico and the Man* debuted, another Komack and Wolper production hit the airwaves. *Welcome Back, Kotter* told tales of teacher Gabe Kotter and his multiracial, remedial homeroom class at James Buchanan High in Bensonhurst, Brooklyn. The "Sweathogs," as Kotter's students were known, included Italian American Vinnie Barbarino; African American Freddie "Boom Boom" Washington; Puerto Rican Jew Juan Epstein; and Arnold Horshack, a white working-class kid of ambiguous ethnic background. Not unlike *Chico*, it emphasized the generational and racial differences between teacher and students after Kotter returned to the school where he had been a student and Sweathog himself. Laughs ensued from Kotter's humor and hip 1970s attitude, and together with the Sweathogs, he tendered a utopian vision of racial harmony, one in which aggrieved groups healed their wounds to tackle the challenges of post–civil rights movement life together. Like *Chico*, *Kotter* recalled Davina Cooper's observation that utopia "can take a conservative or reactionary form," even when intentions are largely "tuned to the possibility of more egalitarian, democratic, and emancipatory ways of living."[70]

For a second year running, Komack and Wolper caught lightning in a bottle. Along with the comedian Gabe Kaplan, who played the role of Kotter, the writers Alan Sacks and Peter Meyerson were instrumental in making *Kotter*, but it was the Komack Company and Wolper Organization that drove the show. Kaplan's stand-up routines, which drew on his own days as a tuned-out high school student in Brooklyn, inspired the episode story lines and appealed to Komack, who was a high school dropout himself.[71] Airing on ABC, *Kotter* became a hit, coming in at 18 on the Nielsen charts for 1975–1976 and 13 the next year, before settling further down the charts in its final two seasons.[72] Although the show lasted only four years, Mr. Kotter and his Sweathogs struck a chord with viewers. Described as "embryonic mafia members" and "loveable hoodlums," the Sweathogs, according to Kaplan, charmed viewers because they were "universal." "Sweathogs are nothing new," he said; "they've been around for nearly forever in every high school in the country. If it wasn't for the colorful kids that we all grew up with, 'Welcome Back, Kotter' wouldn't be such a success."[73] Komack agreed, making the Sweathogs an iconic combination of silly, laugh-out-loud antics and endearing love and unity. Just as he argued that *Chico* was "a love story," he claimed that the central theme of *Kotter* "is about four kids who you love and care about" and that *Kotter*'s "ballgame" was "seeking audience love and projecting love."[74] The interracial love angle worked, and in addition to its very good ratings, *Kotter* was positively reviewed and landed sundry merchandising licenses, including for T-shirts, a board game, lunch boxes, comic books, TOPPS chewing gum trading cards, a children's game with Mattel Toys, "ladies and girls' panties," and many more items.[75]

Kotter's success had much to do with Kaplan's comedy and his own experience as a student at New Utrecht High School in Brooklyn. The Sweathogs were based in part on kids he knew growing up, his humor and love of Groucho Marx shaped every episode, and each episode began and ended with Kotter telling his wife Julie a joke. According to Kaplan, Kotter attended Brooklyn College, faced the "Brooklyn-Jewish decision" of becoming a "pharmacist, an accountant, lawyer or teacher," and ended up "a dreamer and a romantic" caught in a "Kafkaesque nightmare" as "a prisoner of his own roots."[76] Haunted by his past, Kotter was also politically enlightened from the civil rights movement. Although his students were never quite sure whether he was "one of them" (as teacher) or "one of us" (as former Sweathog), Kotter found ways to connect with them and serve as a surrogate father figure. As Komack's original pitch affirmed, "sometimes within the chaos the students listen to what Mr. Kotter has to teach."[77] Kotter was a precursor to subsequent white male saviors of racialized "at-risk" youth, a formula that continued to find prime-time success in *The White Shadow* and *Different Strokes* just a few years after *Kotter*.

If Kaplan's Kotter propelled the show's narrative, its real stars were the Sweathogs. Their racial and ethnic medley was at the heart of their charm, with one critic noting that they included "your Italian American lothario, your hip black kid, a one-man melting pot in Juan Epstein, and the Jewish kid."[78] A young John Travolta played the part of Vinnie Barbarino, the lead Sweathog known for his rugged good looks, "blue eyes and tight jeans."[79] He also played the dozens as well as anyone at Buchanan High, and nary an episode passed without his signature line, "Up your nose with a rubber hose!" Travolta, of course, went on to superstardom, including leading roles in *Carrie* and *Saturday Night Fever* while still part of the *Kotter* cast. Freddie "Boom Boom" Washington, the African American Sweathog, was celebrated for his suave wisecracking and baritone voice. He was played by Lawrence Hilton-Jacobs, a native New Yorker whose career was launched by his appearance in the 1975 film *Cooley High* and his tenure with the famous Negro Ensemble Company, the African American theater company established with Ford Foundation funding in 1967 and boasting a long list of notable alumni that included fellow 1970s sitcom stars John Amos (who played James Evans in *Good Times*) and Sherman Hemsley (who played George Jefferson in *All in the Family* and *The Jeffersons*).[80] Juan Epstein, played by Robert Hegyes, was the Latino of the crew and also the most Jewish. Beyond his ethnic mix, he was known for being the toughest kid in school, originally described by Komack as "the animal who is voted to 'most likely take a life.'"[81] Rounding out the Sweathogs was Arnold Horshack, played by the Italian American actor Ron Palillo. His background was not explicit, but Komack identified him as Polish American, and viewers often assumed he was Jewish, leading the *Jewish Press* to note in their 2012 obituary of Palillo that he "played the obviously Jewish" character of Horshack.[82] Horshack was famed for his obnoxious laugh, goofy mannerisms, and love of Broadway musicals, but his sexuality was somewhat ambiguous, too, although co-creator Alan Sacks claimed that his being gay "was never in our minds."[83] Nonetheless, after Palillo's death, one critic remarked that Horshack "was an important point in the timeline of how LGBT people are depicted on TV."[84]

Despite their differences, the Sweathogs shared a sense of working-class masculinity that knit them together while also sullying them as troublemakers and outsiders to the rest of Buchannan High. In Komack and Sacks's vision, should they ever graduate, the Sweathogs were "guaranteed to wind up as boxers, construction workers, dock workers, teachers, or in jail."[85] Their poverty, lack of social mobility, and segregation from kids in academically gifted classes led one critic to observe, "Exclusion could be a powerful bond and a useful marker of identity that transcended class, ethnicity, and religion. It gave the Sweathogs cohesion on *Welcome Back, Kotter*, bringing Italians, blacks, and (Puerto Rican) Jews together."[86] Their gender—as diverse as it may have been, performed from character to character—united them and distinguished their interracial social scene as unique to young men. The women in *Kotter* were not Sweathogs nor were they part of the same interracial milieu or pivotal to most episodes. Marcia Strassman played Kotter's wife, Julie, and was the primary recurring female character, initially cast as a "long hair, pretty 1968 bohemian" type who was always there to comfort Gabe after long days of teaching. Season one included Debralee Scott as Rosalie "Hotsy Totsy" Totzie, a student in Kotter's class who was one of Barbarino's many girlfriends. She returned briefly in season three for an episode entitled "The Return of Hotsy Totsy" when the Sweathogs snuck out to a strip club, only to find her employed as a dancer.[87] Season three also introduced a new student, Angie Globagoski, played by Melanie Haller, who tried to join the Sweathogs, only to be summarily rejected.[88] Juxtaposed to the few women characters on the show—all of whom were white—it was unmistakable that the racial diversity of the Sweathogs was hastened by their masculinity. *Kotter* was hardly the only 1970s television show to emphasize gender as a shortcut to interracial coalition. Many others did much the same, including *Chico and the Man, Barney Miller, Sanford and Son*, and *The White Shadow*. What *Kotter* and its peer shows failed to acknowledge is that such storytelling erased women, especially women of color, from television's utopian visions about race after the civil rights movement.

If the Sweathogs were racial and ethnic border crossers, Robert Hegyes's Juan Epstein was a case in point. He joined Prinze's Chico and Gregory Sierra's Detective Chano (*Barney Miller*) and Julio Fuentes (*Sanford and Son*) in the small circle of Latino characters on prime time, yet he was also one of television's most outwardly Jewish characters. In season one, Epstein elucidated his unusual background. "You think it's easy being a Puerto Rican Jew? Huh?" he asked. "You think it's easy growin' up in a house with nine other Puerto Rican Jews? Half my brothers were out stealin' pants, the other half were alterin' them!"[89] While his mixed identity generated laughs, it also exemplified what made the Sweathogs and *Kotter* succeed. As Jarrod Tanny explained, "Epstein is defined (and defines himself) as a tough, cool 'ethnic,' comfortable among blacks, Hispanics, Italians and Jews, culturally distinct communities, but ones whose boundaries are permeable."[90] One critic described Epstein as "his own walking-around United Nations."[91] The Sweathogs bonded, Tanny argued, "because they share an alienation from the ideals and morality of white Christian America; most of them are not Jewish, but they are certainly not the proverbial *goyim* of Jewish comedy."[92] As David Zurawik argued, Epstein's rough-and-tough gender disposition affirmed stereotypes of Latinos as violent at the same time as it challenged "the dominant pattern of neurotic, weak, timid, or even effeminate depictions of Jewish men on television."[93] Epstein's Jewish identity likely made his Puerto Ricanness more agreeable to viewers unfamiliar with Latinos, while his Puerto Rican identity made his Jewishness more palatable to others. To put it another way, his mixed identity surreptitiously included and excluded Latinos and Jews in *Kotter*'s vision of racial harmony.

Despite the number of Jewish writers, producers, and directors, Epstein's Jewishness stood out, and not just because of its Latino spin. In 1975, one critic observed, "There are lots of Jews on TV, but no one is emphasizing it," leading some to suggest that Jews self-censored their own on-air presence.[94] Because Gabe Kaplan was Jewish and his comedy reflected as much, *Kotter* was welcomed as a new Jewish addition to prime time. If Mr. Kotter was Jewish, however, allusions to it were downplayed and rarely made explicit. A single exception was a season-one fight with his wife, Julie, when Kotter yelled, "I married a yutz from Nebraska!" only to have Julie retort, "And I married a Jewish prince! Who still sends his laundry to his mother!"[95] Mr. Kotter's "Jew or not a Jew" mystery was not uncommon and was likened to Hal Linden's portrayal of Barney on *Barney Miller*. In the pilot, Miller, who was captain of the NYPD's twelfth precinct in Greenwich Village, was clearly Jewish and married to a non-Jewish wife. His Jewish identity quickly ceased to be part of the show, however, because, as co-creator Danny Arnold recalled, ABC executives believed Linden, who was born to Jewish parents, looked "too Jewish." All references to Miller's background were dropped, and he became a deliberately "non-ethnic" character. Epstein, the Puerto Rican Jew played by the Hungarian-Italian American Robert Hegyes, never lost his Jewishness and ironically exposed the racial and ethnic boundaries showrunners and networks were unwilling to cross for fear of losing viewers.

Although Epstein arrived with less hype and controversy, he joined Chico as the most visible Latino characters on television. It's hard not to associate the two, particularly since they crossed paths off-air, too. Komack recalled, "Bobby plays exactly the kind of spirited street kid I was looking for," leading *татіш TV Guide* to intimate that Hegyes might have played the lead in *Chico* had he met Komack sooner. Despite the potential for rivalry, Hegyes and Prinze became friends when *Kotter* and *Chico* rehearsed and recorded in adjoining studios. Komack teased Prinze, joking, "If I'd seen Bobby first, you wouldn't be here." Prinze played along by replying, "I don't feel like working. Let Bobby do it." On a more serious note, Hegyes was one of the first to notice that Prinze had trouble dealing with his newfound stardom, commenting, "Freddie's highs kept getting higher and his lows lower. He made it big almost overnight and he got to asking, 'Is this it? Doesn't it get any better?'"[96] Linked through their Hungarian roots and relationship with Komack rather than any shared sense of Latinidad, Hegyes and Prinze exemplified how far Chicano and Latino representation on television still had to go and that the illusion of inclusion, perhaps more than any utopian vision, best described *Chico* and *Kotter*'s treatment of race.

Epstein's unique ethnic mix reminded viewers of *Kotter*'s New York essence and that place mattered in the show's vision of racial harmony. That the city sprouted interracial contact not always possible elsewhere was not lost on Gabe Kaplan. He noted, "New York is such a flavorful city. It's a very good place to base a TV show because there is such a large ethnic mix that you get all types of people represented. That's why there are so many shows with a New York locale: 'Rhoda,' 'All in the Family,' 'The Jeffersons,' etc."[97] *Kotter* and *Barney Miller*, in particular, reflected the city's diverse population and, because both were on ABC, were jointly marketed. One ad for *Kotter* and *Miller* included Barney and his multiracial group of detectives with the Sweathogs locked up in the twelfth precinct jail cell.[98] Like Kaplan, *Kotter* producer Alan Sacks was from Brooklyn, and the show drew from their experiences, even if it meant likely turning off some viewers.[99] At a press conference to kick off the 1975 television season, critics from Boston and the Midwest reacted negatively to a sneak-peek of the pilot. They protested that viewers from their regions "couldn't identify with the students in the mythical Brooklyn high school and saw no need for a show about losers and delinquents." One observer noted that the test audience "never overcame the initial undercurrent of hostility, which was apparently enough to cause Komack to have second thoughts about the controversial pilot episode."[100] Nonetheless, he stuck with it and trusted that Mr. Kotter and the Sweathogs would win over viewers.

If the multiracial aspects of *Kotter* were a potential turnoff, Komack, Sacks, and Wolper worked to make the show more palatable to white and middle America while still featuring racial themes. A number of episode concepts were dropped, presumably because they may have been too controversial. The original pitch, for example, included Kotter and Vice Principal Woodman preventing a "near race riot between the blacks vs. the Jews vs. the Italians vs. the Puerto Ricans." In what was likely the creators' thinly veiled metaphor for society at large, the point of the episode was that "everybody loves each other and hates each other." Another story line featured Freddy, the lone African American Sweathog, refusing to be in the Honor Guard for political reasons.[101] As the series developed, however, strikingly few episodes were explicitly about race. Although the Sweathogs occasionally joked about one another's racial or ethnic identities, episodes focused more on class, gender, delinquency, or social issues. *Kotter* was a show with racialized characters without overtly racial themes or story lines. As a result, race and ethnicity were conflated with poverty, hypermasculinity, and misbehavior, leaving open to question if warped views of race and stereotyping drove the show's success as much as any vision of racial harmony. If, as Mark Featherstone and Malcolm Miles suggested, utopian visions could "derange, or denormalize, the present in order to better react and to rethink the ways in which we might transform the world for the sake of the future to come," *Kotter* showed that the opposite was sometimes true, too.[102] Instead of "deranging" and "denormalizing," it "arranged" and "normalized" race in ways that capped any transformative potential.

Viewers and critics reinforced the notion that *Kotter* failed to dig very deeply into racial issues, habitually emphasizing other strengths in the show. *TV Guide* reckoned viewers "could do a lot worse than *Welcome Back, Kotter*," since "most of the time it's very funny" and Kaplan brought an "infectious fun" and "enthusiasm" to the show.[103] A 1978 ABC marketing report of *Kotter* viewers failed to explicitly mention race or ethnicity. Instead, viewers focused on the Sweathogs as "likeable" and "captivating," each a "maturing individual with distinct qualities of his own." Mr. Kotter was seen as the "establishment" figure charged with reining in his unruly students, while also caring deeply for them in his role as a "father to Sweathogs." Audiences characterized the show as "contemporary," "light," and "offering its audience clean humor," as well as "different," "bridges all age groups," and "takes one's mind off things." It was "cute," "not too serious," and "no sex or dope—good clean humor."[104] Viewers seemed to affirm that Komack and Wolper successfully made *Kotter* a show with racialized characters that wasn't about race. By including aggrieved groups in its narrative without amplifying the voices or experiences of their communities, *Kotter* reflected a much less utopian vision of race than the harmonious multiculturalism Komack and Wolper may have intended.

A different unfavorable reading of *Kotter* drove WCVB's decision to ban *Kotter* in Boston. Management feared the show was excessively racial and would exacerbate tensions already at a peak from anti-busing riots. Against the city's history of deeply segregated neighborhoods and schools, the June 1974 court-ordered busing of students to bring more racial balance to public high schools set Boston aflame. The 1974–1975 school year brought parent protests, nearly daily fights between white and Black students, and a heavy police presence on campuses. Tensions boiled over in May of 1975 following several high-profile incidents, including a citywide march against racism that led to skirmishes between anti-busing protesters and the city's Progressive Labor Party (PLP); angry crowds gathering at Hyde Park High to threaten Black students; and anti-busing enthusiasts forming the group Restore Our Alienated Rights (ROAR), which subsequently conducted a sleep-in at Mayor Kevin White's penthouse suite at the Sheraton Hotel and picketed the *Boston Globe*, which they deemed to be pro-busing.[105]

Little changed when the new school year and television season kicked off in fall 1975, bolstering WCVB's belief that airing *Kotter* on the heels of such friction would only make matters worse. Phase II of the city's plan called for more busing, and following new protests in late summer, only 58 percent of students showed up for the first day of school. *Screen Stars* described the scene.

> Kids were hanging out in front of the high school, talking, jiving, smoking cigarettes—a normal scene, you might say. But it wasn't; if you looked hard enough, interspersed in the crowd were angry parents who felt it necessary to keep their kids out of school. When the buses arrived carrying more school children, mostly blacks, the crowd erupted into a howling militant mob! The police who were lined up around the school yard had to restrain the more violent ones, but they

couldn't stop the verbal insults hurled at the kids getting off the buses. A movie scene? No, it was an actual full-fledged race riot—just one of many that have tormented the city of Boston.[106]

The beginning of the school year saw buses carrying Black students stoned, South Boston High put into federal receivership, and Boston's NAACP headquarters firebombed. Violence in the schools carried into 1976, including when more than a thousand Black and white students squared off in a massive rumble at Hyde Park High in late January, a Black lawyer named Theodore Landsmark was beaten with the staff of an American flag by a group of anti-busing protesters, and, in a high-profile case, thirty-four-year-old Richard Poleet was beaten by Black youth in Roxbury after they dragged him from his vehicle. Violence subsided by the beginning of the 1976–1977 school year, but not before WCVB decided the interracial Sweathogs were too volatile a bunch for a Boston on edge.

Despite ABC's high hopes for *Kotter*, the station refused to air the pilot. They justified their decision without overtly mentioning race, but the subtext was clear. Bob Bennett, a WCVB executive, explained.

> We felt that with the problems in the city, in the classrooms, *Kotter*, although it was designed to be a comedy, dealt with very sensitive classroom situations where the principal, among other things, was made to look like a dummy and the classroom itself was made up of incorrigibles, Dead End-type kids. Our feeling was that, at this time in this market, to make fun of the classroom and to do anything other than to try to show it in some kind of constructive way would have been poor responsibility on this station's part. That was on the basis of the pilot.[107]

If WCVB viewed the Sweathogs as "incorrigibles" and "Dead End–type kids" in part because of their racial and ethnic mixing, they never said so and soon changed their tune. Bennett recalled, "Afterwards—I like to think we had something to do with it—the show took a turn to a much lighter form of comedy. The show that's now running [on channel 38 in Boston] is quite a different show from the pilot. Perhaps they had similar problems elsewhere."[108] After WCVB refused to air the pilot and initial episodes, Boston's independent channel 38 picked up *Kotter*; it later made its way back to WCVB after it was judged not to be a threat.[109]

Many educators followed suit, walking a fine line between fearing

Kotter glorified delinquency and stereotyping poor, racialized students as hoodlums. Concerns ranged from Kotter's unruly classroom being "perhaps too realistic for comfort" to whether the show was partially responsible for a rise in student violence and assaults against teachers.[110] By season three of *Kotter*, the American Federation of Teachers (AFT), with some 500,000 members, offered a slightly more nuanced analysis. AFT Public Affairs director Peter Laarman presented two impressions of the show. First was appreciation for its sensitive approach to the classroom and teaching vocation. "They put emphasis on the human dimension," Laarman argued, "the warmth of teachers, the resilience." At the same time, he expressed frustration that the show failed to convey "the seriousness and the difficulties of teaching, the fact that it is an extremely taxing and demanding responsibility." Laarman continued, "In *Kotter*, the students are portrayed as live wires, not too interested in learning—maybe characteristic of some urban students. What doesn't come through is the amount of pain and anger that New York City and other urban students bring to the classroom."[111]

ABC, Komack, and the cast didn't take kindly to the Boston ban or their critics. According to Bob Bennett of WCVB, ABC tried to convince the station to reverse their decision. "They had the producer call us, and the president of the network," he remembered. "They went off on a campaign on the air, with Gabe Kaplan [the show's star] being interviewed on *The Mike Douglas Show*, *The Johnny Carson Show* where he made reference to the fact that he was 'banned in Boston.' But we didn't bend."[112] After the fact, Bennett did begrudge that "WCVB's moral misgivings may have been misplaced. I missed the pilot, but later programs have not only been inoffensive—they've been quite entertaining."[113] Afraid additional affiliates might follow WCVB, the network also labored to ensure that *Kotter* didn't cross any lines. One journalist noted, "Nervous ABC insists on safe-joke entertainment for family hour consumption. Any scene that might give a poor example of how schools actually operate is verboten."[114] John Travolta—whose acting career skyrocketed after his spell as Vinnie Barbarino on *Kotter*—confirmed that the banning in Boston had an impact on the show's content. "So the scripts get lighter and lighter. Now in every episode, we go into a moral. A lesson learned, not scholastically, of course. If Komack has his way, we could play the show based on reality, and it would be out of sight. It could be a powerful influence in getting schools together. But ABC has chopped away, so Komack compromised. Now 'Kotter' is a lie almost."[115] Gabe Kaplan was stunned when he heard of the decision to ban the pilot and defended its reality-based storytelling. "*Kotter* is based on my real school and neighborhood," he claimed. "There were always tough kids around. I was sort of them in a way. There was a class in each grade for the misfits, the under-achievers, the kids who never got started, the toughest kids. And that's just like the class I teach on my TV show."[116] For his part, Komack responded to the ban by saying, "Whatever I'm doing is right. They [the networks] can't explain it, and I'm not about to articulate it. It's fun because it never happened to me before. I'm all pumped up. I tell myself, 'Better do it now while you can, while you have the energy to do it.'"[117] As for the ban, Komack saw it as an extension of the trouble he encountered with *Chico* the year before. "Every year they pick on me," he said with a wry smile in one interview.[118]

Kotter's vision of racial harmony projected a world, or at least a classroom, that, quite purposefully, did not confront the racial issues of the day. This resulted in a successful four-year run, but it also opened up the show to criticism from all corners. Despite Komack's intent to infuse *Kotter* with "love," Kaplan's hilarity, and the chemistry of the Sweathogs, it fell short of the racial utopia Komack, Wolper, Sacks, or anyone else hoped for. It included Latinos and Jews at the same time it excluded them; like *Chico*, it failed to substantially engage the political moment that helped create it, and it was a tutorial in the gendered and ethnic limits in building interracial coalition. Nonetheless, both shows were a pop cultural flashpoint in the representation of race after the civil rights movement. They were prime-time examples of the economic and social transformations wrought by neoliberalism in neighborhoods like East LA and Bensonhurst, Brooklyn; simultaneously, they showed how the onset of neoliberalism swallowed up the possibility of more radical or even marginally more progressive articulations of race in the 1970s. Cynics might argue that this was the fate guaranteed *Kotter*, *Chico*, and every sitcom seeking laughs and profit in the 1970s. Others might see in such shows a moment, albeit fleeting, in which the television industry missed a golden opportunity to work with Chicanos, Latinos, and other aggrieved groups to envision and put into practice a more racially just society.

AFTER *CHICO* AND *KOTTER*

The racial revival on television continued in altered form after *Chico* and *Kotter* ended their runs, even as the heights of the Chicano and civil rights movements faded. With the success of *Chico* and *Kotter* in his portfolio, Komack tried to make the most of the moment. His next big project was *Mr. T and Tina*, intended to be the first sitcom starring an Asian American, with Pat Morita as a Japanese widower with two kids and a housekeeper. It was panned as "offensive" and "stupid," with one critic observing that the basis of the show "seems to be the conflict of East and West," with Tina the housekeeper teaching Mr. T all about the hip 1970s.[119] The pilot was scrapped because of pervasive ethnic slurs, and in a summary judgment of the show, it was described in the *Baltimore Sun* as "another of the comic-turns-to sitcoms shows out of the perverse mind of a man named James Komack." The review continued, "*Mr. T* is clearly the bottom of Mr. Komack's nasty barrel of tricks. The Japanese cultural stereotypes are fractured by American hip idiom," and "the show sets a new standard for idiotic comedy, even for Mr. Komack."[120] After the controversy in casting for *Chico*, Komack felt the heat from Asian American critics. "Now," he said, "the Asian-American society is after me because I cast Japanese actors to play a Japanese family—Pat Morita's family. I wanted Beaulah Quo for the mother-in-law, but she's Chinese and I wouldn't cast her—not after what I went through with Freddie. Pat Suzuki is playing the part." "Now the Asian-American society is mad at me," he continued, "because I don't cast other Asians in an Asian show. They ask what's the matter with using Chinese or Koreans to play Japanese? Why am I unfair to Hawaiians? I tell you, I can't win."[121] Many in racialized communities likely felt the same way anytime they turned on their televisions.

By 1976–1977, *All in the Family* was no longer number 1. It had been replaced at the top of the charts by *Happy Days* and *Laverne and Shirley* for consecutive years running. These were two mostly white, Midwest-based sitcoms. Although shows with multiracial casts and story lines faded, a few continued to be successful. *The Jeffersons* maintained solid ratings into the 1980s. *The White Shadow*, despite being an hour-long drama and never garnering top ratings, enjoyed critical acclaim for its handling of race and social issues during its three-season run. New programs emerged as the 1980s took hold, including *Different Strokes* and *Webster*, both of which renewed the trope of infantilizing Black masculinity and militancy, harking back to Michael, the youngest child in the Evans family in *Good Times*. *The Cosby Show* introduced American viewers to a successful, upper-class African American family in the Huxtables. Latino characters on television were less common, and the days of Chico and Epstein seemed from a different era. Utopian visions of race were less in demand and not as profitable as the '70s waned. For a moment, however, when the trajectory of race relations after the civil rights movement was still very much in question, television was a testing ground for including Chicanos and Latinos in the racial future of the United States. In the cases of *Chico* and *Kotter*, Chicanos and Latinos weren't permitted full participation in pop culture or its visions of racial harmony and utopia.

CHAPTER 4

No Human Being Is Illegal

In 2007, the Center for the Study of Political Graphics (CSPG) in Los Angeles relaunched the exhibition *No Human Being Is Illegal: Posters on the Myths and Realities of the Immigrant Experience* (*NHBI*). It comprised seventy-eight immigrant rights posters offering a vision of the world in which immigrants were treated with dignity and afforded the right to cross borders in pursuit of a better life.[1] Covering the 1970s to 2000s, *NHBI* scrutinized why people came to the United States and the racism, anti-immigrant legislation, labor conditions, and organizing for justice that shaped their experience. It shined a light on the resilient strength of immigrants and their allies while laying bare the devastating impact of global capital on immigrant communities. It was both an archive of the immigrant rights movement and, as the CSPG remarked, a stark reminder of the power of art to record struggles and victories in ways that communicate history and inspire people to action.[2]

The exhibition marked big moments in US immigration history over forty-plus years, including the Immigration Reform and Control Act (IRCA) in 1986, California's Proposition 187 in 1994, and the May Day Immigrant Rights Marches in 2006. It showed that the immigration "crisis" in the United States was, and continues to be, part of a perpetual debate over how the boundaries of the national polity are continually drawn and redrawn. The posters poignantly captured glimpses of immigrant life, mapped shifts in immigration policy, and showcased the remarkable energy of grassroots mobilization in support of new arrivals and existing immigrant communities in the United States. Showing how immigrant rights dovetailed with other social movements and fostered links between seemingly disparate refugee and migrant communities, *NHBI*'s wide-ranging approach made the case that immigrant rights and global justice were two sides of the same coin.

Like other pop cultural utopias in this book, *NHBI* had a distinctly Chicanx and Latinx flavor. Its 2007 relaunch followed the groundswell for immigration rights and reform highlighted by La Gran Marcha, the series of extraordinary 2006 marches in cities across the United States in support of Mexican, Central American, and other immigrants. Like the marches themselves, *NHBI* included heavy participation by Chicanx and Latinx artists and activists who understood that immigration was fueled by global economic and political conditions, but that, in the United States at least, it especially impacted migrants who crossed the US-Mexico border. The dramatic rise of Mexican and Central American populations in the United States since the late 1980s was a crucial impetus for the exhibition and inspired many of its artists. The Mexican-origin population alone grew from roughly 4.4 million Mexican immigrants and 15 million total Mexican-origin folks in 1990 to 11.7 million and nearly 35 million, respectively, by 2011.[3] At the same time, posters in *NHBI* intuitively argued that immigration debate and policy were fueled by political and economic conditions, not necessarily numbers of immigrants.[4] Against an ever-resurgent tide of restrictive immigration policy targeting Latino immigrants as a threat, grassroots efforts emerged to reclaim and humanize immigrant narratives.[5] *NHBI* was one such venture.

Emerging from a vibrant web of political and cultural networks among artists, the CSPG, and its community allies, *NHBI* was a social movement of its own. *NHBI* was not entangled in the multi-million-dollar entertainment industry but was—and remains—part of a larger marketplace of museum exhibitions and public-oriented resources geared toward political education. It was created and circulated at the grassroots level, drawing on relationships and connections between local artists, activists, educators, and curators in California and beyond. Because the CSPG's archive and offices were located in Los Angeles, and the city was often ground-zero for immigration debate, the exhibition had a prominent California feel. Although it included posters, themes, and artists from around the world to make the case that migrant rights were a crucial cog in efforts for global justice, *NHBI* also showed that movements with roots in local places bloomed with utopian visions under the right conditions. The exhibition was not a one-off, but a living and breathing entity reinvented multiple times to reflect transformations in the world. In each rendition, the CSPG swapped or added posters that spoke to changes in immigration policy, advocacy efforts, and audience, all in an effort to share their vision of a better world.

The exhibition traced the arc of immigrant rights during the ascendancy of neoliberalism. Posters logged the impact of policies that favored deregulation and privatization, free market approaches, and a consumption ethos projected onto people's decisions to migrate, their journey to the United States, and life once they arrived. It chronicled how US foreign policy; militarization of the border; defunding of the public sector; and abandonment, surveillance, and gentrification of urban areas shaped the immigrant experience and growth of what Alex Chávez calls a "brown American 'underclass'" that is not often seen as part of the American cultural legacy. As Chávez argued about Latin American migrants in the United States more broadly, *NHBI* showed that they remain "entrenched in the racialized logics of disposability with little concern for the complex cultural adjustments and adaption processes they live out in their attempts at integrating into the highly stratified American social order."[6] Samuel Byrd similarly stressed that the United States responded to the neoliberal epoch "by erecting a system that oppressed a new working class of immigrants by marginalizing them through racial labeling, policing, social exclusion, and delegitimization of their labor."[7] At the same time, *NHBI* narrated the fortitude, resourcefulness, and struggle of immigrants and their allies to both imagine and build a society that rejected such inhumanity. The exhibition was a testament to Arlene Dávila's rebuke that "people and places are never easily reducible into commodities, even in a heightened privatizing context."[8]

NHBI was, to borrow from John Storey, a "radical utopia," "an invitation to imagine" that "pushes away all the demands that this or that is impossible and discovers that hidden in the here and now, almost in plain sight, are the working possibilities that the world might be a different and better place—a fully human place."[9] The posters didn't change the world, but they helped manufacture a demand for change. They called for direct action against the ill effects of globalization and highlighted the resilience of immigrants. They brought places and people together in art-based community making for immigrant rights rather than community-based art making.[10] *NHBI*'s vision of a world in which "no human being is illegal" sought to upend the dehumanization of immigrants, putting into practice Davina Cooper's notion of everyday utopias that "revitalized progressive and radical politics through their capacity to put everyday concepts such as property, care, markets, work, and equality into practice in counter-normative ways."[11] The posters, to evoke Storey again, "defamiliarized" the racialization and criminalization of immigrants, stressing dignity and belonging in lieu of dehumanization and exclusion. *NHBI* made "strange what currently exists in order to dislodge its taken for grantedness and in so doing [made] possible the production of utopian desire."[12] Without turning a blind eye to the violence, poverty, and vulnerability that defined the immigrant experience, the exhibition was home to utopian impulses dependent on reconciling the present and not simply wishing something different.

The exhibition also showed utopia to be profoundly collaborative and expressive of a unique aesthetics. The content of the posters addressed immigration and related policy or socioeconomic conditions, but their look and feel beckoned horizons of justice. They gave shape to people's desire for an alternative society by deploying visuals, signs, and vocabulary that disrupted and defied convention.[13] Recalling Louis Mendoza's contention about the Chicano poet and activist Raúl Salinas, posters in *NHBI* conjured a "new way of looking at and living in the world" that transformed "aesthetic sensibility into a poetics of resistance that is intended to both 'critique and inspire.'"[14] In a broader culture that demonized and dehumanized immigrants, *NHBI* boldly claimed that "no human being is illegal." Although not designed to fit together, the posters fashioned a colorful mosaic of photography, drawing, satire, and spectacle that advocated for hope, energy, and collaboration between communities and institutions fighting for immigrant rights. The exhibition articulated an aesthetics that emphasized the mobility of immigrants, activists, and artists across borders, movements, and styles. *NHBI*'s vision made its aesthetics political and supported Alex Zamalin's claim that "the utopian imagination has often been expressed through art."[15] Its aesthetics showed empathy and community building to be at the heart of utopia, evident in the way Latinx, Chicanx, and non-Chicanx and non-Latinx artists and activists worked closely with one another, the CSPG, and others to sustain the exhibition and animate the immigrant rights movement.

NHBI, POSTER ART, AND THE CSPG

The exhibition's title is a good place to start. On the one hand, *No Human Being Is Illegal* underscored the deleterious effects of global restructuring and dehumanizing discourse about immigrants.[16] On the other, it called attention to experiential and affecting bonds between immigrants, activists, and the artists that created the posters. The phrase itself is attributed to the Holocaust survivor and 1986 Nobel Peace Prize recipient, Elie Wiesel. Wiesel coined the expression when he entered the immigration debate at the invitation of CARECEN, the nonprofit Central American Resource Center offering legal, housing, and civil rights advocacy for immigrants and refugees.[17] Wiesel famously stated, "You who are so-called illegal aliens know that no human being is illegal. That is a contradiction in terms. Human beings can be beautiful or more beautiful, they can be fat or skinny, they can be right or wrong, but illegal? How can a human being be illegal?"[18] *No Human Being Is Illegal* was not unlike other powerful mantras, such as the more recent "Occupy," that, according to Mark Featherstone and Malcolm Miles, signified "first, a recognition of global inequality and a realization of the dystopic present, and, second, a challenge to reinvent the social form through utopian politics and . . . the utopian imagination."[19]

Several posters in the exhibition made explicit use of the phrase, as, for example, did *Ningún Ser Humano Es Ilegal: No Human Being Is Illegal*, Mark Vallen's 1988 black-and-white poster featuring a youthful Latino and Latina gripping and staring through a cyclone fence with the bilingual title framing the poster at top and bottom. A Los Angeles native and self-taught artist, Vallen was inspired by firsthand experiences in the Chicano movement, the punk rock movement, the antiapartheid movement, and immigrant rights. His 1988 poster was created as part of a campaign by the Los Angeles office of CARECEN to fight for the rights of undocumented Central American war refugees, and it inspired additional posters.[20] Take, for instance, the 2006 poster by the Philadelphia office of the American Friends Service Committee (AFSC), a Quaker organization founded in 1917 and "based on the belief in the worth of every person, and faith in the power of love to overcome violence and injustice."[21] Borrowing the same title as Vallen's 1988 poster, the AFSC poster pictured the Statue of Liberty with a red string of barbed wire across her front and "Ningún Ser Humano Es Ilegal" emblazoned at the top. Using *No Human Being Is Illegal* as the title of its exhibition allied the CSPG with the artists, activists, and immigrant rights movement that popularized the slogan and valued its inspirational reach.

Like the Vallen and CARECEN posters, others in the exhibition unleashed the power of poster art to foment struggles for immigrant rights. The posters were not simply reflective of people's desires for change, but they inspired people and brought them together to organize, build community, and speak back to power. As George Lipsitz reminded us, such "posters functioned as part of the movement itself, as vital mechanisms that performed important tasks in the struggle for social change."[22] Their beautiful and striking images—together with powerful phrases and descriptions of hot-button policy issues—educated communities, solidified links between organizations and activists, and articulated an ideology that valued humanity in the face of dehumanization. Posters were crucial elements in the collective action that created the physical and intellectual space necessary to make social change possible. CultureStrike, a national arts organization with several affiliated artists in *NHBI*, decreed the muscle and might of poster art in its mission statement. "We're not trying to reinvent the wheel," they claimed, "but we want to intentionally up the game by investing in *the power of art as a movement in and of itself*. For us, this rich legacy proves that art doesn't just make politics look prettier; with the right resources, art allows us to explore the root causes of problems and experiment with creative solutions without apology or baggage."[23] The CSPG did much the same with *NHBI*, bringing artists and their posters together to sculpt a historical narrative of immigrant rights while concurrently helping grow the movement.

Part of *NHBI*'s creative force lay in its invitation to imagine a different world. This sprouted from the CSPG's curatorial process, but even before that, from the organic practices of the artists themselves. Favianna Rodriguez, who contributed several posters to *NHBI* and was the executive director of CultureStrike, described how her own practice was grounded in Oakland, where she grew up and was long connected with others in struggles for social justice: "My way of coping was through art, like listening to weird music, reading a lot, and creating—creating ALL the time, because that allowed me to have a voice, to imagine something different, and to process my human condition. Art allowed me to create my own reality in my imagination and that transported me into another world."[24] She continued, "In order to cultivate a revolution of the imagination, I have to do my own work so that I can prune the thoughts that limit me—the thoughts that are the product of a colonialist white male patriarchy—so that I may think expansively about what's possible."[25] Rodriguez was only one artist in *NHBI*, but her approach to art and politics, a kind of "oscillating movement between imagining and actualization," was stamped across the entire exhibition.[26]

Poster art and the ideology behind the "No Human Being Is Illegal" slogan made for a potent match. Posters mobilized community; alerted people to upcoming demonstrations; and connected artists, organizers, and the public while generating visibility for immigrant rights. Lipsitz noted in his study of Chicano movement–era posters that they were "designed for quick, inexpensive production and mass distribution."[27] This was especially the case with the advent of the internet when posters could be circulated as GIFs (graphics interchange format). As easy as it was to photocopy and hang posters on campus kiosks or telephone poles, it was even simpler to send posters to hundreds or thousands of folks with the tap of a key on a keyboard. Jesús Barraza, who cofounded the art collective Taller Tupac Amaru (TTA) with Favianna Rodriguez and was also a contributing artist in *NHBI*, elaborated on the impact of social media.

> With Facebook, Instagram, Tumblr, and Twitter, posters have taken on a digital life; they are no longer tied to physical existence on paper. Now they become people's profile pictures or a status to share; they are a way for people to express how they feel about something happening in society. Sometimes the image has a physical manifestation, a poster that is offset—or screen-printed; sometimes these are given away at rallies or marches. The digital version serves as a way for people to connect their online persona with the issue. Other times the image only lives online and serves as a quick response tool for artists to show solidarity and express their support for a cause.[28]

The relatively low cost and easy distribution of posters was not without problems. Barraza described the pitfalls of their online life, including commodification and appropriation that strips posters of their meaning. On the one hand, he emphasized that "one of the beautiful things about our posters is that they can end up anywhere and infiltrate whatever space they end up in" and that many artists "love to hear from people about how they want to repurpose the art we make." On the other, he observed, "The problem that can arise is that the artwork can go into another market we did not intend it to be a part of." It is not uncommon for poster images to be used without permission of the artist and for purposes or messaging they never intended. Barraza concluded, "I think the best we can hope for is that people who take the images we make have the best intentions in what they are doing and respect the message behind the images."[29]

Although they weren't designed to be hung in museums or galleries, the posters in *NHBI* were injected into the public sphere by artists and the CSPG. The first incarnation of the exhibition in 1988 pre-dated the founding of CSPG by a few months and was initially curated by Carol

Wells, who would become director of the CSPG. She worked with the Committee in Solidarity with the People of El Salvador (CISPES) and the Nicaragua Task Force in Los Angeles during the late 1980s, accumulating posters in her organizing with immigrant rights and solidarity activists. Father Luis Olivares, a Roman Catholic priest who declared his church in downtown Los Angeles a sanctuary for Central American refugees, provided $1,000 to help fund Wells's efforts to organize the initial version of the exhibition. Before his death from AIDS in 1993, Olivares was a staunch supporter of immigrant rights and an outspoken critic of US military aid to El Salvador, prompting federal officials to investigate his church and other church authorities to question his actions.[30] The initial iteration of the exhibition debuted for a nearly two-month run at California Lutheran University in Thousand Oaks under the title *Reflections of Latin America: Myths and Realities of the Refugee Experience*. It was shown again in 1989 under the new title, *The Politics of Immigration*, at the YWCA in Santa Ana, California. These late-1980s versions of the exhibition were motivated in part by the sanctuary movement in support of Central American refugees fleeing political violence in their home countries; organizing against English-only laws in California; and the 1986 Immigration Reform and Control Act, which provided a pathway to legalization for some undocumented immigrants while also imposing stiff legal sanctions intended to deny them employment.[31]

Subsequent versions of the exhibition were organized during key moments of immigrant rights struggles in the years that followed. As the CSPG grew, adaptations increasingly incorporated the input of CSPG staff and curatorial consultants from a range of community partner organizations with expertise in immigrant rights organizing and policy. A second incarnation of the exhibition was released as a work-in-progress in 1994. Presented at elementary and high schools in Santa Monica, California, this version took the heading *No Human Being Is Illegal* and was fueled by the furor against California's anti-immigrant Proposition 187, which sought to drastically limit access by undocumented immigrants to public health, education, and other social services. This was followed by another update in 1999 and yet another following La Gran Marcha in 2006, which was in part a response to a new round of anti-immigrant legislation, especially House Resolution 4437 in 2005. Also known as the Border Protection, Antiterrorism, and Illegal Immigration Control Act, H.R. 4437 further militarized the border and criminalized undocumented immigration. This version of the exhibition toured universities, community centers, and art studios across Southern California and beyond for several years, only to be refreshed yet again in 2015 with posters in support of the latest version of the Development, Relief, and Education for Alien Minors (DREAM) Act for undocumented college students and against new rounds of anti-immigrant hysteria. More recently, the CSPG transformed *No Human Being Is Illegal* into an "exhibition to go." Inspired by the mobility and affordability of the poster art form itself, CSPG produced laminated and easily shippable reproductions of each poster in the collection. Institutions, galleries, and museums are able to receive the exhibition by mail for a small fee and present the posters in their own space.[32]

The artists who contributed posters to *NHBI* and the CSPG were deeply committed to immigrant rights. Their collaboration united brilliant art under the umbrella of a single project and narrated a diffuse movement and history of immigrant rights with a strong bent toward social justice and public education, serving as a crucial resource for communities, activists, artists, and scholars fighting for immigrant rights. It grew from rhizomatic pockets of activist and artist activity in communities where immigrants were most impacted by economic, political, and enforcement policies. *NHBI* amplified the voices of folks that might otherwise have been silenced or muffled, showcasing poster art as a means to advance immigrant rights and articulate visions of a better future.

NHBI AFTER IRCA

The first version of what would become *NHBI* was created soon after Congress passed the Immigration Reform and Control Act (IRCA) in 1986. IRCA made it illegal to knowingly hire or employ undocumented immigrants, authorized a 50 percent increase in border patrol staffing, and provided two groups of undocumented immigrants with a pathway to legal residency: seasonal farmworkers who could show they worked sixty or more days in agriculture between May 1985 and May 1986 and those who had entered the United States prior to January 1, 1982. To attain legal residency, immigrants were required to pay a fine and back taxes; prove they did not have a criminal record; and demonstrate basic knowledge of US history, government, and English. Beyond granting amnesty to nearly three million immigrants, IRCA further militarized the border and generated intense public debate over the impact of legalization on undocumented immigration.[33] It was in this climate that Carol Wells and the CSPG produced the first version of *NHBI* under the working title *Reflections of Latin America: Myths and Realities of the Refugee Experience*. Many of its posters were created in the late 1980s as part of advocacy for Mexican and Central American immigrants impacted by IRCA. The exhibition was especially influenced by the significant numbers of Central American political refugees fleeing civil war, political unrest, and economic instability in El Salvador, Guatemala, and Honduras. The growth of the Central American refugee community in the United States, recorded by the US Census as having increased by almost one million between 1980 and 1990 alone, sparked the sanctuary movement and advocacy efforts on these immigrants' behalf by grassroots groups, religious organizations, and university students across the country.[34] Posters in the CSPG's exhibition captured the moment, yet also helped make the moment.

Take, for example, the 1988–1989 poster, *Illegal? No Human Being Is Illegal*, another that used the slogan that would become the exhibition's title. It was cosponsored by CARECEN, the Central American Refugee Committee (CRECE) and Central American Refugee National Network (CARNET) in Los Angeles and featured a black-and-white image of a grown Latino man squatting to embrace a young boy, both in tears. The image was stamped with the word "Illegal?" and additional text urging "Support Salvadoran refugees," "Stop deportation," "The right to work," "The right to live in our places of origin," and "Stop military operations." "No Human Being Is Illegal," along with Elie Wiesel's name, was tucked in the bottom right-hand corner. The image and words together evoked empathy, a call to support the sanctuary movement, and critique of US foreign policy that many felt contributed to violence and political instability in El Salvador.

Octavio Gomez was credited with the photo, and his own story provided a fascinating backdrop to the poster's powerful message. Born in Mexico, Gomez immigrated to the United States in 1968. Prior to becoming a naturalized citizen in 1994, he made a career as a fearless photographer and cameraman, spending nearly twenty years documenting the United Farm Workers movement and working for Spanish-language station KMEX, Spanish-language newspaper *La Opinión*, and as a freelance journalist. Much of his work centered on civil rights and immigration. He was, for instance, alongside Ruben Salazar when Salazar—another journalist—was infamously killed by the LAPD during the Chicano Moratorium, the largest anti–Vietnam War protest in Southern California in 1970. The peaceful protest by 30,000-plus people at Laguna Park in

East Los Angeles was followed by police violence during which Salazar was killed at a nearby liquor store. Both Salazar's murder and the Moratorium would become iconic moments and rallying cries for the Chicano movement in LA and beyond. A few years later, in 1972, Gomez helped resolve the hijacking of a Frontier Airlines jet at LAX after the hijacker asked to speak with someone from the Spanish-language media. Gomez realized that he knew the hijacker, Ricardo Chávez-Ortiz, and made clear to authorities that Chávez-Ortiz's only demand was that the plight of Chicanos be heard. Later in his career, Gomez was awarded nearly $200,000 in damages as part of a freedom-of-the-press case against immigration authorities for interfering with his ability to take photographs for *La Opinión*. The lawsuit followed two events Gomez photographed in 1985, a protest against refugee deportations and an Immigration and Naturalization Service (INS) roundup of undocumented immigrants. In the second, INS agents confiscated Gomez's camera and press credentials while making threats about his immigration status.[35] Although he died of a heart attack in December 2005 at the age of seventy-one, his photos, including the one featured in the 1988–1989 poster, live on and serve as a reminder that every *NHBI* poster had a story behind it of artists and activists laboring for immigrant rights.

Several posters exposed US political and military interventions as chief reasons why migrants fled north. A 1980s poster by an unknown artist, for example, pictured soldiers standing triumphantly over five dead immigrant bodies on a rural dirt road. The caption above and below the black-and-white image simply stated: "No US $$ for Death Squad Government in El Salvador." Another Mark Vallen poster movingly depicted a group of Guatemalan migrants holding a fellow migrant, dead in their arms. It was a powerful declaration for "Voices of Justice and Solidarity for Guatemala," a human rights tribunal and protest held at Los Angeles City Hall in October of 1989. These and other posters elucidated that utopia consisted of more than dreaming about the future; it was also built on "concrete practices through which historically situated actors seek to reimagine their present and transform it into a plausible future."[36]

Other posters emphasized mobilization and advocacy on behalf of refugees and immigrants. Take Mariona Barkus's 1985 poster, *U.S. Sanctuary Movement*. It focused on an image of the Statue of Liberty surrounded by construction scaffolding and a sign stating "Under renovation." Underneath was the celebrated poem by Emma Lazarus etched on the statue, "Give me your tired, your poor, your huddled masses yearning to breathe free." "U.S. Sanctuary Movement" was bolded in large print with the following explanation:

> In protest against Reagan administration refugee policies, cities across the country are declaring themselves Cities of Refuge. City employees are told not to cooperate with Immigration and Naturalization Service officers investigating Guatemalan and Salvadoran refugees who are denied refugee status and deported to their war-torn countries. Berkeley, Ca. and St. Paul, Minn. were the first to take action. Cities across the United States have followed suit: New York City, Chicago, Takoma Park, Md., Madison, Wis., Olympia, Wash., Ithaca, N.Y., Burlington, Vt., Cambridge, Mass., among others. Supporters of the City of Refuge Movement compare their stance of civil disobedience to that of the Underground Railroad during the Civil War.

If they had had a crystal ball, City of Refuge would likely have seen allies in the Sanctuary City movement of the 2000s and recognized eerily similar backlash against those supporting refugees, including revisionist interpretations of the Statue of Liberty and the quote invoked on Barkus's poster. In August of 2019, for instance, Ken Cuccinelli, acting director of US Citizenship and Immigration Services in the Trump administration, altered the Lazarus poem to very different effect. When asked in an interview if Lazarus's words were part of the American ethos, Cuccinelli responded: "They certainly are: 'Give me your tired and your poor who can stand on their own two feet and who will not become a public charge,'" he said. "That plaque was put on the Statue of Liberty at almost the same time as the first public charge was passed—very interesting timing."[37] The comment was made amid efforts to make it easier to reject immigrant visa applications based on income or education level.

The 1987 poster *English Only/Whites Only* was another instance when the IRCA moment forecast the future. Created by an unknown artist from Los Angeles, the poster was deceptively simple. It asked in block letters on red background, "What's the Difference Between English Only and Whites Only?" The CSPG's exhibition card for the poster explained that the English-only movement in the late 1980s was part of growing patterns of xenophobia in the aftermath of IRCA, and though much of the hostility targeted Spanish speakers, many different communities were attacked, including the Chinese community in Monterey Park, California. The CSPG observed that in 1986, the same year the IRCA was enacted, California voters passed Proposition 63, mandating "English as the Official Language" of the state. Many viewed this as a slap in the face to immigrants from Mexico and Central America and to the Spanish-speaking community as a whole, as well as a white supremacist attack on bilingual education.

A number of posters in the exhibition shined a light on immigrant and labor rights as two sides of the same coin during the 1980s. For artists of these posters, the immigrant experience was inescapably linked to shifts in hemispheric and global capital and related employment patterns. *L.A. Should Work . . . for Everyone*," the 1989 poster in support of Justice for Janitors, was one example. A far-reaching movement to unionize custodial workers in Los Angeles and beyond, Justice for Janitors brought together immigrant laborers and activists from many different nations and backgrounds through the Service Employees International Union (SEIU).³⁸ Boldly demanding that no immigrant worker be exploited or excluded from efforts to improve labor conditions, the poster centered the drawing of a muscular arm hoisting a broom high into the sky.

Two members of the Australian-based Redback Graphix collective expressed similar sentiments in their poster, *La Unidad Es la Vida/Unity Is Life*, inspired by a cultural exchange visit to Los Angeles when IRCA legislation was being crafted and debated. The poster included green, pink, yellow, and purple neon-inflected prints of Latinos with the words "LEGAL" and "ILLEGAL" mirrored on opposite sides of the page. "La Unidad Es La Vida; Sin Ella, No Hay Vida" (Unity Is Life; Without It, There Is No Life) was embossed across the top. The lengthy quote at the bottom read: "We put food on the table and clothing on people's backs and do the work most Americans don't want to do for less money than Americans will work for, and now they want me to say I'm thankful because they're giving me amnesty, even though most of the people I know won't get it. Just because I'm legal all of a sudden doesn't mean I'll forget those who aren't."

No Human Being Is Illegal captured the intensity of the sanctuary movement and IRCA moment. As the CSPG noted in its catalogue overview, it covered the reasons people came to the United States, including to escape war, repression, and violence and to seek new economic opportunities. *NHBI* posters marked the late 1980s as a watershed moment, both for immigrants and for those who mobilized on their behalf. It also cemented links between art and politics, giving shape to Naomi Klein's observation that imagining a better future "requires a reclaiming of the utopian tradition that animated so many transcendental social movements in the past. It means having the courage to paint a picture of a different world, one which, even if it exists only in our minds, can fuel us as we engage in winnable battles."[39] These earliest editions of the exhibition reminded viewers that utopian visions of a better world depended on grappling with the ill effects of the past and present. As it rejected the demonization of immigrants and embraced their humanity, *NHBI* continued to harbor dreams of a society that prioritized immigrant rights.

NHBI AFTER PROPOSITION 187

Just eight years after IRCA, California was ground zero for immigrant rights in the wake of its statewide Proposition 187. The eventuality of "majority-minority" status and fears of "Latinoization" led to new anti-immigrant legislation stemming from concerns that growing numbers of immigrants put undue strain on California's infrastructure, institutions, and resources. Passed during the November 1994 statewide election, Proposition 187 was the most visible piece of legislation. It sought "cooperation between [the] agencies of state and local government with the federal government" in order to "prevent illegal aliens in the United States from receiving benefits or public services in the State of California."[40] In practice, Proposition 187 intended to deny undocumented immigrants access to health care and education and aimed to "require police, health care professionals and teachers to verify and report the immigration status of all individuals, including children."[41] It was introduced by Republican assemblyman Richard Mountjoy and was opportunistically embraced by Governor Pete Wilson to galvanize his reelection campaign and anti-immigrant platform.[42] Although Proposition 187 was eventually found unconstitutional, the fury on both sides of its debate did not soon end.

Proposition 187 was related to changes in hemispheric economic policy, particularly the 1994 North American Free Trade Agreement (NAFTA). NAFTA aimed to generate trade between the United States, Mexico, and Canada and create investment opportunities in Mexico after the 1980s debt crisis resulted in millions of dollars in loans to North American banks going unpaid. Miguel López-Lozano described the agreement's neoliberal approach as "the opening of the economy to allow for the flow of investors, materials, and merchandise, modifying the role of the state from being the promoting agent of modernity to instead being only a partner." In practice, this meant deregulation and less taxes for big business but provided no guarantees for those with less power and pull.⁴³ Unlike the European Union did just a few years later, NAFTA largely failed to address the plight of labor or environmental protections against industrial growth, resulting in the increasing mobility of capital paired with a rise in exploitative maquiladoras along the border; clampdowns on border crossings; and more poverty, fewer social services, and increased surveillance by authorities in many immigrant communities. The fallout included rising numbers of undocumented immigrants moving to the United States and less return migration.⁴⁴ Ironically, as López-Lozano pointed out, NAFTA was a utopia for neoliberals, but "those marginalized by race and class have thus become more disenfranchised as social programs are cut and funding instead is directed to development of international competition and a widening of the industrial base."⁴⁵

The CSPG amended *NHBI* in the wake of NAFTA and Proposition 187. New posters channeled the tension, anger, and energy of the moment to challenge neoliberal thinking by connecting the dots between anti-immigrant legislation and broader economic policy. A series of posters produced by the Los Angeles Organizing Committee to Defeat Proposition 187 was a case in point. In the lead-up to the 1994 election, the committee used posters to stress the vital role immigrant labor played in the health of the US and California economies, utilizing simple designs with bold colors and slogans. Examples included several with black block print that stated, "These Hands Sew Your Clothes"; "These Hands Care for Your Children"; "These Hands Pick Your Food"; and "These Hands Pay Taxes." Each poster foregrounded a picture of a needle and thread, teddy bear, strawberry, or dollar sign at the top, while the bottom was adorned with the committee's hotline phone number and "No on Proposition 187." The flip side of the neoliberal conditions that drove NAFTA and Proposition 187 were clear in another poster by the Common Threads Artist Group. Their 1995 black-and-white poster asked, "Guess who pockets the difference?" The question was bracketed by the image of a Latina seamstress on a sewing machine with "$3.50 an hour" stamped across her image on one side and "$75 a pair" in front of a male model displaying a pair of blue jeans on the other side.

Nor were the political implications of Proposition 187 lost on artists in *NHBI*. The cartoonist Lalo Alcaraz's 1994 poster *FRAID*, for instance, denuded the strategy of pitting California voters against undocumented

FIGURE 1. *El Chicano*

El Chicano band members, including Rudy Regalado (right on the bottom), Bobby Espinosa (second from right on top), Andre Baeza (top), and Mickey Lesperon (second from left on the bottom), pose for a portrait circa 1971. Photo courtesy of Michael Ochs Archives/Getty Images.

FIGURE 2. *Cannibal and the Headhunters*

Cannibal and the Headhunters band members circa 1965 in Los Angeles. Clockwise from top left: Jo "Yo Yo" Jaramillo, Frankie "Cannibal" Garcia, Robert "Rabbit" Jaramillo, and Richard "Scar" Lopez. Photo courtesy of Michael Ochs Archives/Getty Images.

FIGURE 3. *The cast of* Welcome Back, Kotter, *circa 1975*

Gabe Kaplan (center) played Gabe Kotter, a teacher who returned to his former inner-city high school to teach a class of remedial students called the Sweathogs, played by John Travolta (bottom left, as Vinnie Barbarino), Ron Palillo (top left, as Arnold Horshack), Robert Hegyes (top right, as Juan Epstein), and Lawrence-Hilton Jacobs (as Freddie "Boom Boom" Washington). Photo courtesy of Walt Disney Television/Getty Images.

FIGURE 4. Being Undocumented Is Not a Crime

Favianna Rodriguez's print *Being Undocumented Is Not a Crime*, circa 2008. © Favianna Rodriguez. Courtesy of Favianna Rodriguez and the Center for the Study of Political Graphics.

FIGURE 5. *FRAID: Anti-Immigrant Border Spray*

Lalo Alcaraz's 1994 poster, *FRAID: Anti-Immigrant Border Spray.* © Lalo Alcaraz. Courtesy of Lalo Alcaraz and the Center for the Study of Political Graphics.

FIGURE 6. *Dream Act*

Originally produced as a woodcut, Raoul Deal's 2012 print, *Dream Act: La Ley Dream*, was included in the *Migration Now* portfolio organized by Favianna Rodriguez and Roger Peet for CultureStrike and Justseeds. © Raoul Deal. Courtesy of Raoul Deal, Migration Now, Just Seeds/CultureStrike Print Portfolio, and the Center for the Study of Political Graphics.

FIGURE 7. *Brown and Proud*

Melanie Cervantes's print, *Brown and Proud*, was produced in 2010 in association with Dignidad Rebelde. © Melanie Cervantes. Courtesy of Melanie Cervantes and the Center for the Study of Political Graphics.

FIGURE 8. No US $$ for Death Squad Government

This poster by an unknown artist captured the political force of the sanctuary movement in support of Central American refugees fleeing civil war, political unrest, and economic instability in El Salvador, Guatemala, and Honduras during the 1980s. Courtesy of the Center for the Study of Political Graphics.

FIGURE 9. Ningún Ser Humano Es Ilegal: No Human Being Is Illegal

Mark Vallen's 1988 poster, *Ningún Ser Humano Es Ilegal: No Human Being Is Illegal*. © Mark Vallen. Courtesy of Mark Vallen and the Center for the Study of Political Graphics.

immigrants. As the CSPG noted, Alcaraz's poster was in the satirical tradition of Jonathan Swift's *A Modest Proposal*, ridiculing "California's Proposition 187 by transforming unwanted immigrants into insects and changing the familiar bug spray from *Raid* to *Fraid*." Alcaraz depicted an older white man in a suit—perhaps meant to mimic Governor Pete Wilson—holding an enlarged aerosol can of "Fraid: Anti-Immigrant Border Spray." With a cartoon bubble, the man claimed, "S.O.S! Spray on Spicks! Keeps on Working for up to 2 Elections!" The poster included the "endorsements" "INS and GOP Approved!" and "9 of 10 Racist Politicians Prefer Fraid." Alcaraz explained the genesis of his poster.

> I was inspired to do this cartoon after reading about a nascent "Border Enforcement Technologies" research program at a Northern California State University. The program was an attempt to get federal research dollars for creating technologies that might deter unauthorized border crossing, but I felt the results sounded literally like a "Roach Motel" for immigrants. One project was a powder developed to stick to "illegals" as they scampered across the kitchen floor—I mean, the US/Mexico border. The powder somehow then lit up the culprit to Border Patrol detection devices.[46]

With his unique brand of humor and political edge, Alcaraz captured both the fear that fueled anti-immigrant policy and the seething critique voiced by opponents of Proposition 187.

It was no surprise that Alcaraz's poster was included in *NHBI*. His art had long advocated for Latino and immigrant rights, and by 1994 he was a vocal critic of conservative politicians in California and beyond. Born in San Diego in 1964 to Mexican parents, he grew up in nearby Lemon Grove, where his father was a gardener and his mother, a house cleaner. Alcaraz recalled how his own background shaped his spin on art and immigrant rights.

> I grew up as the typical first-generation child of immigrants, the translator. So I had to deal with adults at doctors' offices, social service agencies, and school, in English, and I saw firsthand how people talked to my mom and my dad. And what little rights they had. They were exploited by employers, and just kept grinding through. This is why it sickens me to see how immigrants are still treated, especially poor brown immigrants from Mexico and Latin America. It's my life work

to fight back against this injustice. So, yes, it was direct. Foremost, even before I witnessed the cultural whitewashing of American history and nonwhite culture, my conscience was stirred by the immigrant worker's struggle of my own parents.[47]

Alcaraz framed immigrant rights as a pan-Latino experience, observing, "There are many Latinos from Central America who are experiencing the 'pocho' phenomena in their own way, and I try to realize that they are out there too. What we have in common, besides language and our love for pupusas, is immigration. This is the never-ending battle we have to fight."[48] Immigrant rights were core to his belief that his art was "my version of the news, but filtered through my characters" and that "you can show more truth with comics, than with live action, with people, you know."[49] Alcaraz's work was also a reminder that the utopian in the arts sometimes bubbles beneath the surface and can "often imply a mysterious, magical, tantalizing quality—a world that is glimpsed but not fully apparent."[50]

Alcaraz's willingness to take on politicians, corporate interests, and public ignorance on immigration led to professional success, including the first nationally syndicated, politically themed Latino daily comic strip, *La Cucaracha*.[51] It was amid the outcry over Proposition 187 when Alcaraz's character Daniel D. Portado (which in Spanish reads like "deportado," or "deported" in English) helped propel his career. *La Cucaracha* was eventually published in over sixty newspapers nationwide, leading Juan Poblete to argue that Alcaraz "produced excellent early mapping of what today can be called the post-social moment in the history of Latino migrations to, and Latino populations in, the United States."[52] For Poblete, the post-social resulted from neoliberal economic restructuring that increased privatization and socialization in which borders internal to society stewed fear and distrust with mutual interdependence among its denizens and citizens. Poblete noted that for Alcaraz, "Immigrants, and especially undocumented ones, find themselves in the paradoxical position of providing many of the low-paying services demanded by the economic restructuring of the economy and its service sectors while, at the same time, they are the victims of the resentment of the white middle-classes threatened by downward social mobility."[53] Like other artists with posters in *NHBI*, Alcaraz exposed the xenophobia, fear, and contradictory position immigrants faced in society while reminding us that "art should be in our lives, not just on the page."[54]

The artistic and political fury over Proposition 187 inspired more posters for immigrant rights in years after 1994, too. This was, in part, because its legality and enforcement hung in the balance of state and federal courts, but also because artists and activists understood immigrant rights were a perpetual fight. Take, for example, the 1997 poster *La Dignidad No Tiene Fronteras* (Dignity Has No Borders) by an unknown artist for "semana del migrante" (week of the migrant) in Los Angeles. Outlined by a butterfly, it showed colorful scenes of immigrant lives before, during, and after immigrating to the United States, including a village school receiving humanitarian and medical aid; migrants near gravestones and a campfire in the desert crossing the border north; and protesters marching and waving Salvadoran flags and a *Ningún Ser Humano Es Ilegal!* (No Human Being Is Illegal) banner. The poster's title went on to become the stuff of bumper stickers and T-shirts.

The 1999 poster *Welcome to America* by the artist-activist collaborative Think Again was another example of dissecting the repercussions of IRCA and Proposition 187. It featured a movie ticket stub with a silhouette of the Statue of Liberty as background and the words "ADMIT NONE" across the front. Smaller print atop the poster read, "Welcome to America, Wash Our Dishes, Clean Our Clothes, Now Go Home." At the bottom, it argued that immigrants were the motor propelling the California economy, declaring, "California eats because immigrants work. Without farmworkers in Southern California, without janitors in the offices of Century City, without maids in the luxury hotels of San Francisco, the entire economy of California would crumble."

It was no accident Think Again was included in *NHBI*, either. Founded in 1997, their sweeping agenda included viewing "cultural work as essential to affecting social change and engaging people in the political process." Their work took many forms, including "mobile billboards, outdoor projections, guerilla interventions, digital murals, and viral poster campaigns," and their projects engaged multiple causes, "including queer liberation, economic inequality, the ways capitalist culture conspires to jeopardize the outnumbered, undocumented labor and the treatment of immigrants, racism, militarization, gentrification and displacement, and gender parity."[55] Like many others in *NHBI*, Think Again viewed immigrant rights within a nexus of struggles, movements, and communities with art as a central thread between them. Using queer as a conceptual touchstone to move away from identity politics, Think Again deployed their art to wage a "visual war against indifference" and put "artmaking in the service of political action." Like the *NHBI* exhibition as a whole, they viewed "political art as an organizing tool and a method for igniting face-to-face conversations."[56]

NHBI AFTER LA GRAN MARCHA

Legislation aimed at curbing immigrant rights and its related propaganda machine continued after the turn of the millennium. In 2005, the introduction of House Resolution 4437 proved to be an especially dramatic moment, provoking debate and direct action for immigrant rights unlike any other moment in US history. Also known as the Border Protection, Antiterrorism, and Illegal Immigration Control Act, HR 4437 was sponsored by Representative Jim Sensenbrenner from Wisconsin. It passed in the House, stalled in the Senate, and contained several key components, including (1) beefing up border security with new fencing, additional Homeland Security funding, and new military technology to monitor entry ports; (2) an employer verification system for new employees with increased penalties for hiring undocumented workers; (3) further criminalizing violations of immigration law, including extending enforcement to state and local law authorities. In the post-9/11 context, it was not surprising that many argued that HR 4437 conflated illegal immigration with terrorism and subversion of national security. Its controversial measures continued to haunt policy and public debate—and inspire poster art—in the years to come.

The groundswell against HR 4437 in the lead-up to the Senate vote was immense. Community groups, unions, churches, and others mobilized to extraordinary effect, as millions took to streets across the United States in what were the largest marches since the civil rights movement. Culminating in La Gran Marcha on May 1, 2006, the wave of protesters voiced opposition to what many viewed as the most punitive anti-immigrant legislation since Proposition 187. Estimates were that between 3.5 and 5 million people marched for immigrant rights in the spring of 2006 in dozens of cities across the country, all demanding comprehensive immigration reform.[57] Los Angeles and Chicago saw more than half a million people in each city march on May Day alone. More than 100,000 took to streets in San Jose; Phoenix; New York; Washington, DC; and Dallas.[58] The political torrent of the marches was a reminder that it was possible, if only for short intervals, to disrupt the neoliberal epoch, recalling David Rando's observation that "the value of utopia lies not in a completed vision of the future but rather in its capacity to help us imagine a massive disruption."[59] It was a watershed moment, evoking the longer history of immigrant rights and launching what many hoped would be a new chapter moving forward. Observers have since noted that the marches ushered in a new era of civil rights protest, pan-ethnic Latinx identity, awakening of the "sleeping giant" Latinx electorate, and articulations of civic engagement and citizenship that transcended conventional notions of juridical, nation-based citizenship.[60]

Posters were at the heart of organizing efforts and, unsurprisingly, La Gran Marcha held a prominent place in *NHBI*, including several posters produced specifically for marches around the country. Rubén Esparza of Self-Help Graphics, for instance, created his *We Are Not Criminals* poster for the May Day march in Los Angeles. His was one of four posters made by Self-Help Graphics that was distributed on the ground to demonstrators at the march. It was simple yet powerful. Against a bright yellow background, Esparza placed two black helicopters hovering over block-printed words that stated, "We Are Not Criminals." Xico González of the longstanding Royal Chicano Air Force (RCAF) art troupe produced another, *Sitting Bull: No to HR 4437*. It featured a portrait of Sitting Bull above the statement, "If We Must Die, We Die Defending Our Rights: No to HR 4437." Yet another 2006 poster was Mexica Movement's *Don't Run*. It displayed the iconic silhouette of an immigrant family running with the child dragged behind and the words "DON'T RUN!" in huge print across the top. Instead, it encouraged, "Stand Proud! Remember, We are Indigenous to This Continent! We have the right to be EVERYWHERE on our continent." Like other artists, Mexica Movement borrowed the image from CalTrans road signs initially erected in 1990 to warn drivers after dozens of immigrants were killed crossing freeways near the San Diego–Tijuana border.[61]

Several Favianna Rodriguez posters harnessed the energy and hope rekindled in La Gran Marcha. Her 2006 *Legalización Ahora!* displayed protest marchers, highlighting a woman, a man, and a boy with a sign that declared, "Aquí Estamos y No Nos Vamos! Y Si Nos Hechan [sic], Nos Regresamos" (We are here and we are not leaving! And if they throw us out, we will return). The colors and tones, like the individuals in the drawing, were unmistakably brown. Her 2008 *Being Undocumented Is Not a Crime* linked immigrant rights with opposition against the prison industrial complex. It centered an abstract, Indigenous figure with an ankle shackled in an electric monitoring device, asserting "Immigrants are one of the fastest growing segments of the prison population in the

United States today. From the ankle monitoring devices to the detention centers, criminalizing immigrants is BIG business." Her *Nuestro Labor*, also from 2008, juxtaposed sketches and photographs of immigrant women as laborers, stating, "Nuestro Labor Mantiene la Economía del Mundo, Our Labor Drives the World Economy."

As for other artists in *NHBI*, Rodriguez's posters echoed her art and politics beyond the exhibition. She described herself as "an interdisciplinary artist, cultural strategist, and social justice activist" who addresses "migration, gender justice, climate change, racial equity, and sexual freedom."[62] Her devotion to immigrant rights stemmed from being "a first-generation American Latinx artist with Afro-Latinx roots who grew up in working-class Oakland during the birth of the internet, and in the midst of an era of anti-immigrant hate and the war on drugs." Rodriguez is perhaps most known for her Migration Is Beautiful interventions that began in 2012 and used the monarch butterfly as a symbol of freedom and natural migration. Her artistic renditions of the butterfly have since been used for immigrant rights and reform efforts from the halls of the US Congress to grassroots protests across the country.

Rodriguez also served as interim director and cultural strategist for CultureStrike, the national arts outfit that "empowers artists to dream big, disrupt the status quo, and envision a truly just world rooted in shared humanity." Founded in 2011 out of an artist delegation that traveled to the Arizona border to protest the state's anti-immigrant law SB1070, CultureStrike was a network led by migrant artists that, in its own words, "aims not only to change the art of politics, but also the politics of art-making." It included over two hundred artists and spearheaded dozens of events and campaigns in local venues, on social media, and beyond. At its core, CultureStrike believed "cultural work is key to creating systemic change" and wanted to infuse new voices and diverse stories for social justice into the art world. It grew from the history of artists creating at the core of social movements, describing itself as "part lab, activist studio, publisher, think tank, and network." CultureStrike conducted research and workshops; supported fiction, journalism, and poetry on critical issues like migration and climate change; and facilitated visual campaigns and multimedia festivals for similar causes. Its staff and board of directors were a multiracial, multicultural team of artists and activists that worked directly with grassroots campaigns in the United States and around the world. They proudly claimed to be "primarily people of color and first- or second-generation migrants—and our work draws from our unique experiences as women, LGBTQ, working-class, and undocumented people."[63] Along with the Revolutions Per Minute project (RPM) and the Citizen Engagement Laboratory (CEL), CultureStrike gave rise to the Center for Cultural Power, "a women of color, artist-led organization, inspiring artists and culture makers to imagine a world where power is distributed equitably and where we live in harmony with nature." Favianna Rodriguez is President of The Center for Cultural Power, which focuses on content related to migration, climate, gender, and racial justice.[64]

Rodriguez was also part of the Bay Area art collective Taller Tupac Amaru (TTA), which was another object lesson in how *NHBI* included artists with a political edge and an extensive history of immigrant rights work. In addition to Rodriguez, TTA included Jesús Barraza and Melanie Cervantes. Rodriguez and Barraza founded the Taller as a Bay Area screen-printing collective in 2003, with Cervantes joining a few years later. Their aim was to deploy printmaking in the service of social and political change in Northern California and beyond. Immigration rights were among their chief issues, yet they understood them to be linked with other struggles against racism and capitalist exploitation that transcended immigrant communities. Barraza noted that he and Rodriguez "started working together in the mid '90s when we were in college. She was at the University of California, Berkeley, and I was at San Francisco State. We became friends and started working together on a lot of different projects—a lot of stuff that was going on at UC Berkeley, like California Proposition 187, Proposition 209, and, later on, Proposition 21."[65] The political and collaborative nature of their work was paramount. Barraza said,

> Both Favianna and I have done a lot of political organizing, and [working in printmaking] was a way to keep working within the political arena. We're not only making art; we're also working with different people—a lot of the stuff we do as Taller Tupac Amaru really comes from the work that we're doing outside of our work. That's where the politics comes from: the work we do in our daily lives. We really try to reflect the world that we live in.[66]

Even the name Tupac Amaru served a political purpose. It was a signal to Rodriguez's own Peruvian ancestry and the Indigenous leader who led a sixteenth-century insurrection against the Spaniards in what would become Peru. In another nod to their intersectionality, Barraza noted, "Also, being in Oakland, there's Tupac Shakur—that [history] was another thing we were thinking about when we came up with the name."[67]

Like Rodriguez, both Barraza and Cervantes had posters in *NHBI* that drew inspiration from and built upon La Gran Marcha in 2006. Cervantes's 2008 poster urged people to "Keep our families together," framing images of queer Latinx families as targets of discrimination at the hands of anti-immigrant laws and demanding "Family Reunification for All." The poster was part of Cervantes's larger corpus of work that, in her words, was "inspired by the people around her and her communities' desire for radical and social transformation." Her intention was to help "create a visual lexicon of resistance to multiple oppressions that will inspire curiosity, raise consciousness and inspire solidarities among communities of struggle."[68] Barraza's 2008 poster *If Capital Can Cross Borders, So Can We!* was a bilingual call to "Uphold the human rights of migrant workers!" Like Cervantes and Rodriguez, Barraza strove to "create prints that visualize struggles for immigration rights, housing, education, and international solidarity."[69]

Emblematic of the CSPG's and *NHBI's* manifold nodes of artist and activist activity, Rodriguez, Barraza, and Cervantes all participated in additional artist and political collectives in the Bay Area and beyond that advocated for immigrant rights. For example, Barraza and Cervantes began their own enterprise, Dignidad Rebelde (DR), in 2007, just after La Gran Marcha. DR, both explained, grew from the ways "our art practices merged and our shared politics became the guiding principles of our art making."[70] DR brought together their longer histories of activism and socially engaged art making in the Bay Area in new collective and empowering ways. Based in Oakland, DR asserted, "Art can be an empowering reflection of community struggles, dreams and visions. Following principles of Xicanisma and Zapatismo, we create work that amplifies people's stories and create art that can be put back into the hands of the communities who inspire it."[71] Inspired by the Zapatistas and the *indigenista* perspectives by writers, including Ana Castillo, Gloria Anzaldúa, and Cherríe Moraga, who "allowed us to imagine a world where revolution is possible,"[72] DR further explained,

> We recognize that the history of the majority of people worldwide is a history of colonialism, genocide, and exploitation. Our art is grounded in Third World and indigenous movements that build people's power to transform the conditions of fragmentation, displacement and loss

of culture that result from this history. Representing these movements through visual art means connecting struggles through our work and seeking to inspire solidarity among communities of struggle worldwide.[73]

Barraza and Cervantes underscored the versatility of their artistic productions, stressing, "Our art is for museums, collectors' exhibitions, community and cultural centers, individual homes, political rallies and more."[74] In just one example, DR organized popup community workshops where artists and organizations designed and produced posters for protests, rallies, and marches. This included collaborating with the East-Side Arts Alliance (ESAA), a cultural center in East Oakland, to make banners, T-shirts, bandanas, and posters to distribute at the 2010 May Day March for immigrant rights in Oakland. Working together with ESAA, DR "created a visual narrative based on the experiences of those fighting for dignity by creating posters that depict people engaged in the migrant rights struggle."[75] In the spirit of sharing their work far and wide, DR collaborated with dozens of community organizations and institutions, such as other artist groups like the aforementioned Taller Tupac Amaru, Justseeds Artists' Cooperative, and the Consejo Gráfico.[76]

Justseeds Artists' Cooperative was another group with a communal approach to immigrant rights. Along with several dozen other artists from the United States, Mexico, and Canada, Rodriguez, Barraza, and Cervantes were part of the group. They described themselves as a "decentralized network of 41 artists committed to social, environmental, and political engagement." Justseeds, they elaborated,

> operates both as a unified collaboration of similarly minded printmakers and as a loose collection of creative individuals with unique viewpoints and working methods. We believe in the transformative power of personal expression in concert with collective action. To this end, we produce collective portfolios, contribute graphics to grassroots struggles for justice, work collaboratively both in- and outside the co-op, build large sculptural installations in galleries, and wheatpaste on the streets—all while offering each other daily support as allies and friends.[77]

Justseeds was founded in 1998 as the graphics distribution project of Josh MacPhee but transformed into a cooperative in 2007. Based in Pittsburgh, Pennsylvania, since 2010, it operates an online store and wholesale distribution center for art pieces and maintains a blog on art and resistance projects around the world. Their online presence includes dozens of posts and entries on immigrant rights, related exhibitions, and community events.

If La Gran Marcha was a focal point for *NHBI* and, more broadly, wrought a new convergence of poster art with immigrant rights activism, the years after 2006 were equally charged. In 2010, the state of Arizona passed House Bill 1070, reigniting immigration debate across much of the United States. Known by some as the "papers please law," SB 1070 made it a state misdemeanor for immigrants not to carry proper documentation and required local law enforcement to determine immigration status during a "lawful stop, detention, or arrest" where there is "reasonable suspicion" that the detainee is an "illegal immigrant." It also levied penalties and arrest on those "aiding" undocumented immigrants. Immigrant rights activists contended that the bill legalized racial profiling, and they called for boycotts of Arizona after Governor Jan Brewer signed the bill into law, prompting protests around the country. Joe Arpaio, sheriff of Maricopa County and based in the state's capital city, Phoenix, came to symbolize the anti-immigrant posture for his vocal support of SB 1070 and demonization of immigrants. His aggressive enforcement of the bill included the reintroduction of archaic chain gangs and decrepit tent cities for arrested immigrants. SB 1070 spurred copycat legislation in other states, including Alabama House Bill 56, which denied basic social services to undocumented immigrants and made it criminal to hire them or rent apartments to them. HB 56 further outraged activists nationwide because of Alabama's relatively small Latinx community. In places like Montgomery, where they made up only 4 percent of the population, Latinxs were terrorized by law enforcement officers and driven into the shadows for fear of arrest. This law was viewed by some as even harsher than the Arizona version because school administrators were required to report on the immigration status of their students.[78]

NHBI captured the 2010 moment with rage, hope for the future, and beautiful images. Posters included those by Roy Villalobos, from Chicago; Ernesto Yerena, from Los Angeles; Melanie Cervantes, from Oakland; and Favianna Rodriguez, also from Oakland. Villalobos's *Arizona Liberty* centered a portrait of the Statue of Liberty with half of her face depicted as a *calavera* (skull). Just above it were the words, "Arizona Liberty for All SB 1070," with the "All" crossed out. Yerena's poster proclaimed "Alto Arizona" (Stop Arizona), above an outline of the state made to look like a fingerprint. It further noted, "Enough Is Enough.

Stop SB 1070!" Cervantes's *Brown and Proud* displayed a Latina with her fist in the air underneath the words, "Brown and Proud, Todos Somos Arizona" (We Are All Arizona). Before being included in *NHBI*, Cervantes's piece was originally designed to be given away at protests in Oakland and in Arizona. Rodriguez's offering on SB 1070 featured the iconic slogan "Undocumented Unafraid" and "No Tenemos Miedo" (We Are Not Afraid) on a sign held by a young Latina protester wearing a "Legalize Arizona" T-shirt, which became a staple for protesters and organizers in community mobilizations against SB 1070. The posters themselves were also distributed at marches and circulated online as part of fundraising and virtual organizing efforts to challenge the bill. As was the case with other *NHBI* artists, Barraza and Cervantes of Dignidad Rebelde allied with those organizing against SB 1070 by helping organize immigrant rights workshops and sending posters to Arizona groups like Puente Human Rights Movement, Tierra y Libertad Organization (TYLO), and No More Deaths—No Más Muertes. Their aims included supporting immigrant rights and "organizations committed to using art as a tool for social transformation."[79]

Melanie Cervantes's *Brown and Proud* was later acquired by the Smithsonian American Art Museum (SAAM) as part of its exhibition *¡Printing the Revolution! The Rise and Impact of Chicano Graphics, 1965 to Now*.[80] Opened virtually in 2020 during the Covid-19 pandemic, *¡Printing the Revolution!* was organized by E. Carmen Ramos, curator of Latinx art at SAAM, and also included Favianna Rodriguez's *Migration Is Beautiful* butterfly print. Its aim was analogous to that of *NHBI*. "More than reflecting the need for social change," stated its description, "the works in this exhibition project and revise notions of Chicanx identity, spur political activism and school viewers in new understandings of U.S. and international history."[81]

Another wave of post-2006 posters in *NHBI* supported the DREAM Act. Also known as the Development, Relief, and Education Act for Alien Minors, the legislation was initially introduced by Senators Richard Durbin from Illinois and Orrin Hatch from Utah in 2001. It aimed to provide temporary residency to certain immigrants who graduated from US high schools, arrived in the United States as minors, and had lived in the country continuously for at least five years prior. If they completed two years in the military or two years at a four-year college or university, they would obtain residency for six years. In practice, the DREAM Act sought to allow young undocumented immigrants the same access to higher education as legal citizens. It initially failed to pass the Senate and was reintroduced several times. Despite not passing, it continued to be a flashpoint for immigration debate throughout the Obama presidency and into the Trump presidency. Supporters recognized that the Supreme Court's 1982 decision in *Plyler v. Doe* made it illegal to charge undocumented students tuition in public K-12 schools but did not address college students. In the first decade after the DREAM Act was introduced, over 1 million undocumented students could not receive financial aid or normalized immigration status that would have allowed them to more easily access and attend college. The DREAM Act provided safe and sanctuary status to those who had lived in United States for at least five years; entered the country at fifteen years old or younger; were of good moral character; had been accepted to an institution of higher learning or earned a high school diploma; were younger than thirty-five years old; and did not have a criminal record.[82]

The great majority of these students had lived most of their life in the United States after migrating with their parents when they were minors, even infants. Elioenai Santos from Veracruz, Mexico, for example, came to the United States when he was two and grew up in California. He remarked:

> Sometimes people don't understand what being undocumented means. People don't know who we are, and they think of us as criminals. We are more than that. I have friends who call me "wetback" just as a joke and say, "go back to your country." But I'm 22 years old and I have been here for 20. This is my country. If I could talk to politicians, I would say, "Look us in the eye. We are not a faceless people. We love this country."[83]

Though it failed to become law, the DREAM Act energized massive mobilizations by new groups like United We Dream, DreamACTivist, and IDEAS. Ongoing efforts to pass the DREAM Act resulted in the Obama administration's temporary solution, Deferred Action for Childhood Arrivals (DACA), which stopped the deportation of those under thirty-one years of age if they had arrived in the United States younger than sixteen and did not have a criminal record. DACA was eventually rolled back by the Trump administration, revealing anew the precarious status of undocumented immigrants.

In its most recent revision, *NHBI* included several posters urging support for the DREAM Act and the young people and their families most affected. Take, for instance, Raoul Deal's 2012 poster *Dream Act*. It was a black-and-white image of a mother with a young daughter in her arms at a political rally. Behind them, fellow protesters held signs stating, "Stop Breaking Up Families" and "Dream Act Now!" Deal is neither Chicanx nor Latinx, but he went to graduate school in Mexico City, where he worked with the renowned Mexican artist Felipe Ehrenberg and was inspired by the Taller Gráfica Popular. His poster in *NHBI* was originally produced as a 50″ × 68″ woodcut in Milwaukee, Wisconsin, as part of an exhibition called *Ni de Aquí ni de Allá* (Neither from Here nor from There) that involved interviewing members of the city's Latinx community. A smaller version was included in the *Migration Now* portfolio organized by Favianna Rodriguez and Roger Peet for CultureStrike and Justseeds.[84] It noted, in part, that "migration is fundamentally about our right to move freely across planet Earth, in search of our fullest and best selves."[85] Another DREAM Act poster in *NHBI* was Ray Hernandez's 2012 poster with the silhouette of a college graduate in red, white, and blue. It proclaimed, "DREAMERS, Education Is Our Liberation, Access Denied Since 2001," and was also produced with CultureStrike. The Dreamer-themed posters in *NHBI* linked the DREAM Act to the longer history of immigrant rights. Like the Dreamers themselves, the artists and CSPG pointed toward a better future for Latinxs and utilized their art to help get there.

NHBI BEYOND BORDERS

As much as any other in the exhibition, Yahaira Carillo and Julio Salgado's 2013 poster, *Out of the Closets! Out of the Shadows! Into the Streets!*, inextricably linked immigrant rights with other movements for social change. A butterfly outlined six Black and brown youth with "Out of the Closets! Out of the Shadows! Into the Streets!" printed just above. Below it read, "No LGBTQ Exclusion!" and "Migrant Rights. Queer Rights. Human Rights." It also contained the Audre Lorde quote, "There is no such thing as a single-issue struggle because we do not live single-issue lives." As was true for others in *NHBI*, Carillo and Salgado's art and politics were enmeshed. Salgado, for example, was cofounder of the Dreamers Adrift project, a multimedia platform led by undocumented artists with the goal of "taking back the undocumented narrative through videos, arts, music, spoken-word and poetry." It was established in 2010 by four undocumented college graduates, initially focused on bringing attention to the DREAM Act. Dreamers Adrift subsequently expanded its focus but maintained the immigrant experience as its raison d'être. It has produced nearly one hundred short videos and two original series as part of its visual arts catalogue.[86] Not coincidentally, Salgado also served as Artists Projects coordinator for CultureStrike.

Many more posters in *NHBI* shared the intersectional vibe, including many in the exhibition's section on "International Organizing for Justice." These posters drove home the point that immigrant rights was a global movement, one in which Latinx and Chicanx visions of a better world for immigrants in the United States dovetailed with other struggles around the world. *NHBI* included posters from Germany, France, Greece, Netherlands, and Australia dating back to the mid-1980s, many of which touched on themes similar to the US-based posters and framed immigrant rights as part of labor and civil rights. These artists poignantly connected seemingly unrelated immigrant communities in struggles against the shared effects of global capital, ensuring that the slogan "No Human Being Is Illegal" excluded no one. Sandy Kaltenborn's 1999 poster, *Kein Mensch Ist Illegal*, for instance, deployed "No Human Being Is Illegal" in German in support of a benefit for the Caravan for the Rights of Refugees and Migrants, a network of individuals, groups, and organizations in Berlin that advocated for refugee and immigrant rights. As the CSPG explained, Kaltenborn and the Caravan were committed to "the struggle for socio-political justice, equality and respect for the fundamental human rights of everyone. In 1998/99 the Caravan traveled through 28 cities to protest discrimination against refugees and migrants."[87] Another internationally flavored poster, *Danger*, by the Anti-Racist Group of Rethymno Students in Crete, Greece, also adapted the iconic CalTrans immigrant crossing caution image. It was created for their Third Anti-Racist Festival of Rethymno, which was also titled No Human Being Is Illegal. The international reach of *NHBI* showed that its utopian dimensions were, to borrow from Michael Cucher's study of Chicano murals, nourished by using images "to create tangible connections, across time and space, between related aspirations for social justice and community empowerment."[88] The meaning of the phrase "No Human Being Is Illegal" gained strength, as Elie Wiesel argued, in numbers and in its global relevance.

NHBI was and remains a dynamic archive, exhibition, and community nexus rolled into one. It brought together rich materials and connected artists, resources, and activist networks for immigrant rights. It was hopeful and forward looking at the same time that it captured the history of economic and policy impediments to immigrant life. Tracing immigrant rights during the neoliberal epoch, it rejected immigration policy and anti-immigrant xenophobia that fomented border militarization, policing, and surveillance of immigrant communities and racialized Latin American immigrants as a drain on the US economy, a criminal threat, and a danger to US society. The community building and reclaiming of immigrant humanity so central to *NHBI* showed how art and activism powered the imagination of a better world, one that projected a vision of the future born from struggle and circumstances far from utopian, but in which "No Human Being Is Illegal."

CHAPTER 5

Border Reggae

In February 2008, El Foro, one of the premiere live music venues in Tijuana, Baja California, hosted the city's fifth annual Bob Marley Day celebration. Advertised throughout the Tijuana and San Diego areas as the "Tribute to the Legends," the concert and festival was one of many held around the world in honor of reggae's biggest star, his music, and his message of social justice. The show also highlighted the unique reggae scene that had emerged along the US-Mexico border since Marley's death in 1981. While the lineup included internationally known acts Alpha Blondy (Ivory Coast), Cultura Profética (Puerto Rico), Don Carlos (Jamaica), and Midnite (St. Croix), local acts Tribal Seeds (San Diego), Los Astrorumberos (Tijuana), and Cartel de Zion (Tijuana) took to the stage as well. Event promotion was binational, conducted via radio stations and ticket outlets on both sides of the border, including Tijuana's own reggae-themed store, Tijuana Roots and Culture. And, like many reggae events in the San Diego–Tijuana metroplex, concertgoers came from both sides of the international border to join the party. As much as the show was evidence of reggae's global popularity, it illustrated the particular ways race, cultural politics, and the African Diaspora met in the production and consumption of reggae music along the Mexico-US border.

The Tribute to the Legends show in Tijuana is a good way to begin thinking about the complexities of a region that is among the few in the world where the first world meets the third to simultaneously produce deeply rooted interdependence and inequity among the nation-states and people who live there. It begs discussion about the social identities, political possibilities, and utopian impulses of reggae scenes that emerged along both sides of the border from the early 1990s through the

2000s.¹ Though it is difficult to gauge how big the border reggae phenomenon was, and the saliency among its variant participants was inconsistent, the dozens of bands, routine concerts, and festivals with hundreds if not thousands of fans in attendance, and the cultural infrastructure of specialty shops, radio shows, and recording studios that dotted the region, reflected a sizable scene. As I discussed in chapter 4, the interval between the passage of the North American Free Trade Agreement (NAFTA) in 1994 and the uproar over Arizona's Senate Bill 1070 in 2010 was marked by anti-immigrant hysteria and increasing militarization of the border. During these nearly two decades, border reggae generated utopian glimpses of a different society, lending credence to David Rando's observation that "as thoroughly as music is shaped by the social sphere and as well as it can consequently capture history, it is nonetheless able to transcend the given world that gives rise to it."² In this chapter, I look into how communities from along the US-Mexico border came to articulate their hopes and dreams by playing music that was inspired by Afro-Caribbean cultural expression and traditions. I explore how border folk fashioned interracial and transnational social and political configurations through reggae that sought to dilute the toxic impact of neoliberal globalization, border enforcement, and immigration policy.

The utopian impulses in border reggae straddled the line between commercialization and autonomy. The music sprouted from the economic and political foliage along the geopolitical boundary between the United States and Mexico, positioning musicians and their fans to critique the impact of globalization and make use of its far-reaching networks. On the one hand, the music made audible people's desire for a less militarized and less impoverished, more humane and more open border region. Grounded on cultural labor and creative exchange, it gave form to interracial, diasporic, and transnational dimensions of border life that were often obscured or discouraged by policy or popular debate. On the other hand, border reggae was shaped by market forces and sporadic connection to social movements. Border reggae challenged consumer capital—or at least was not fully absorbed by it—at the same time that it was embedded in circuits of consumer capitalism. Its utopian possibilities were unique to its reggae roots but indicative of pop culture and music more broadly. As Rando noted, "despite its near total commodification, music can still attach feeling and experience in ways that potentially break out of the consumerist orbit and can unpredictably fuel the imagination with dreams of other worlds."³ Border reggae's capacity to invoke alternative visions of life and identity along the US-Mexico dividing line called to mind Ernst Bloch's belief that "music, by virtue of its so immediately human capacity of expression, has more than the other arts the quality of incorporating the numerous sufferings, the wishes and spots of light of the oppressed class." Music is, he urged, "seismographic, it reflects cracks under the social surface, expresses wishes for change, bids us to hope."[4]

Utopian impulses in border reggae mushroomed from the junction of life in the US-Mexico borderlands and the African Diaspora. Surveying the "Chicanx" and "Afro-Mexica" genres of border reggae, I investigate how artists fused experiences of being Mexican, Chicanx, and Indigenous with Jamaican reggae and Rastafarianism to create new racial sensibilities and social movements. These linkages gave rise to unique reggae forms that manifested utopia in the music, politics, and identities of its practitioners.[5] Their stories show how reggae's political aesthetics resonated in the borderlands and how "identity, like Diaspora," as Stuart Hall argued, "is never complete, always in process."[6] Chicanx reggae from US border towns like San Diego, El Paso, and even Los Angeles exhibited a cosmopolitan, internationalist, and multiethnic Chicanx identity. "Afro-Mexica" reggae from Tijuana and Mexicali-based bands drew from life experiences south of the line to connect with Indigenous, African Diasporic, and US Chicanx communities as much as with other Mexicans. In both cases, reggae players expressed connections with movements for racial and global justice; embraced a border existence that crisscrossed cultural and political divides; and rebuffed border tropes of nationalism, divisiveness, and segregation. As they made music, they also produced Latinidades that were positioned against and fully embedded in the constraints of poverty, policy, and racial inequity along the border.[7] The music was thus confirmation of the region's longer history of Black-brown interchange, as examined in chapter 2, yet it simultaneously revealed tensions among borderlands residents over access to limited housing, jobs, and social services. This points to Gaye Johnson's observation that in 1990s and 2000s Southern California, in particular, anti-immigrant nativism and anti-Black racism coexisted in ways that made Black and brown communities "more differentially separated and related than ever before."[8] Border reggae thus reverberated with Shana Redmond's claim that music can be "strategically employed to develop identification between people who otherwise may be culturally, ideologically, or spatially separate or distinct from one another."[9]

Border reggae–evinced utopia was deeply rooted in local places along *la frontera*, even as it was caught in economic tides that connected distant people and places left vulnerable and exploited by globalization. The music grew from global connections and networks at the same time as it eloquently broadcast visions by folks whose everyday life was determined by living near and routinely crossing the boundary between the United States and Mexico. Place gave deep meaning to border reggae yet did not curtail the music's growth or circulation. The music cultivated a collaborative social and political spirit that resulted in shared organizing and struggle around issues related to the border, immigrant and Indigenous rights, Zapatismo, and self-determination. There was often an intricate relationship between border reggae and social movements, lending support to George Yúdice's contention that some cultural practices and venues have the potential to be turned into resources that might "be mobilized in the pursuit of social justice under certain circumstances."[10] Border reggae was one example of how globalization operated in the form of everyday cultural and political expression as much as it did in the activity of transnational corporations and nation-states. Rather than assume utopia was abstract, deterritorialized, and disconnected from movements for social change, border reggae showed it was deeply territorialized and concretized in local relationships, cultural politics, and efforts for transformation along the US-Mexico border.[11]

Border reggae further showed that utopia was often entwined with dystopian circumstances. It was created within—and often directed at—global political and economic currents that stripped or devalued the humanity of border dwellers. On both sides of the line, poor life chances were marked by government surveillance, immobility, poverty, alienation, racism, and disenfranchisement. This was especially the case during the neoliberal fallout and militarization described by Miguel López-Lozano as "the dystopian conditions prevalent in the shadow of NAFTA." Writing about Chicano and Mexican novels in the context of the 1994 North American Free Trade Agreement (NAFTA), López-Lozano identified literary dystopias as "negative representations of imagined future societies where the abuse of technology, authoritarianism, and the overall dehumanization of society have created the conditions for the end of humanity as we know it."[12] In the real-life version, border reggae offered alternative revelations on what life could be like. It was part of the longer history of Black and Latinx pop cultural figures who, to borrow from Paul Ortiz, "theorized outside the nation's borders and beyond its mythologies of innocence and exceptionalism to challenge the crises facing them inside the belly of the beast."[13] I ultimately suggest that border reggae helped its participants claim dignity in the face of the dehumanizing effects of capital and political negligence. Border reggae's utopian impulses were sutured to its dystopian context, inseparable yet light years apart from the world it sought, evoking Rebecca Solnit's reflection that utopian visions emerge in the midst of human disasters, what she described as "a paradise built in hell."[14]

BORDER POLITICS AND (IN)DIGNITY

The global economic restructuring of the last several decades shaped the life chances of those in the US-Mexico borderlands, just as it did for those elsewhere. The intensification of deregulation; the favoring of free markets; global flows of capital, ideas, and labor; and the growth of mass technology and communications produced low wages, high unemployment, and devastating declines in social spending all over the map.[15] These conditions were no less stringent for the Chicanx and Mexican communities from which border reggae emerged in the 1990s, fostering a volatile, often hostile, political context in which artists made their music, reminding us that "every utopia always comes with its implied dystopia."[16]

Where the United States meets Mexico, people live the paradox of what Peter Andreas calls a "borderless economy" with a "barricaded border."[17] Andreas described how the contradiction between the free movement of trade and the hypercontrolled movement of people shaped the lives of those who live along and cross the border. More than a simple dichotomy between goods and people, however, globalization elicited a myriad of political, economic, and social relationships and experiences that shaped the creation and flow of culture, reggae music included, along the dividing line between the United States and Mexico. The very presence of Afro-Caribbean-inspired music at the border, with its many sounds and politics, revealed that people generated unexpected cultural relationships and efforts for social transformation amid the seemingly overwhelming forces of global capital.

NAFTA ushered in a new stage of neoliberalism that shaped decades of border economic development, including intensified commercial exchange, the rise in maquiladoras, and a growing disparity between the haves and have-nots, which was often experienced in border *colo-*

nias and barrios as more poverty, fewer social services, and increased violence, particularly against women. It was during the 1990s when hundreds of unresolved kidnappings and murders of women occurred near the Ciudad Juárez–El Paso border and when thousands of immigrants died from exposure, dehydration, or being run over by moving cars while crossing the border.[18] At the same time, we saw the use of low-intensity warfare by Mexican and US authorities against undocumented immigration, the war on drugs, and illegal smuggling bring the deployment of military-inspired and hi-tech fences, technology, and enforcement techniques—all with an aim to control human traffic across the border.[19] The result was government initiatives like Operation Blockade in El Paso (1993), Operation Gatekeeper in San Diego (1994), Operation Safeguard in Nogales, Arizona (1994), and Operation Rio Grande in East Texas (1997). Add to these structural efforts to close the border an impoverished civic discourse about the negative impact of "illegal aliens" on the US economy and democracy led by talking heads like CNN's Lou Dobbs, critics like Samuel Huntington, and self-organized public groups like the Minutemen, and one can understand the forces shaping the lives of border dwellers, crossers, and migrants.[20]

From California to Texas across the US Southwest, the political fallout of such conditions and debate was no less harsh. While efforts by the border patrol, Immigration and Naturalization Service (INS), and, by the 2000s, Immigration and Customs Enforcement (ICE) were applauded by many, others couldn't help but see the violent repression and dehumanization of Latin American immigrants and ethnic Mexicans who had lived in the region for generations. As examined in chapter 4, the angry outcry over undocumented immigration and shifting demographics of California and the Southwest toward "majority-minority" status and "Latinoization" led to a number of anti-immigrant laws and campaigns. California's Proposition 187 in 1994, which sought to limit access by undocumented immigrants to health care and education; late-1990s anti-affirmative action campaigns in California and Texas resulting in Proposition 209 and the Hopwood decision, respectively; the anti-bilingual education Proposition 227 in California; the 2000 antigang Proposition 21 in California; the federal passing of House Resolution 4437 in 2005 that imposed stiff legal sanctions for "aiding" undocumented immigrants; and Arizona's passing of Senate Bill 1070 criminalizing undocumented immigrants in 2010 all stirred up an anti-immigrant, racially tense political climate.[21]

As Victor Viesca noted in his work on contemporary Chicanx music in Los Angeles, such tensions generated new and conflicting forms of political opportunism, social activism, and cultural expression. Some, like former California Governor Pete Wilson, who won reelection in 1994 despite low approval ratings, capitalized on anti-immigrant fear campaigns to protect white privilege. At the same time, many Chicanx, Latinx, and other activists mobilized politically against them, resulting, in part, in renewed articulations of Chicanidad, Mexicanidad, and Latinidad.[22] Anger against draconian measures of border and immigration control and solidarity with new social movements inspired by the Ejército Zapatista Liberación Nacional (EZLN) in Chiapas, Mexico, led to the emergence of political and cultural revolt from the same conditions of global capital that stripped the dignity and life chances of borderlanders. From protests against Proposition 187 in 1994, to the 2006 Gran Marcha May Day mobilizations for immigrant rights, to the groundswell against SB 1070 in 2010, people lashed out at power by reclaiming dignity, crafting new identities and political connections, and imagining a different border experience.

Alongside, and in some ways ahead of, more organized movements, border reggae offered new ways of thinking about challenging times. From the interstices of commercialism and grassroots cultural practices rose alternative spins on border identity, culture, and politics. Loosely affiliated with organized political action, these efforts came with the heavy rhythm, drum, and bass of a reggae beat and were something of a soundtrack to the ways that border communities responded to the debates and policies about the places they called home. Though border reggae and other cultural productions may not have had the power to repel globalization head-on, in part because it was deeply embedded in the circuits of transnational capital itself, it did show, as Roberto Alvarez argued in the context of border commerce and policy by the United States Department of Agriculture, that "the local-level behavior of people illustrates a complex reordering of identities, economies, and political persuasions."[23] Herein lies a most crucial lesson of border reggae. If borderlands culture and identity have routinely been described as either that of northern Mexico, the southwestern United States, or a hybrid mix of the two, border reggae suggested that the complexities and articulations of border identity, culture, and politics may be too great to categorize in such a consistent or overarching fashion. The transnational, interracial, and social movement–inspired reggae music coming from Tijuana, El Paso, and points in between revealed countless ways to embrace and make the border one's own.

CHICANX REGGAE

Amid the intense politics and shifting economy in the US Southwest, a vibrant reggae scene emerged in cities along the northern side of the border in the early 1990s. Mirroring the growth of reggae's popularity in Latin America, East Asia, the Pacific Islands, and Europe, border reggae was unique because of its Chicanx essence. Indeed, while West Coast surf culture, Pueblo and Hopi reggae enthusiasts in New Mexico and Arizona, and college music scenes helped fuel the music's popularity across the Southwest, grow the number of reggae specialty stores, and attract touring international acts, urban Chicanxs embraced the Rasta sound and vibe as much as anyone, putting a new spin on longer histories of Mexicans creating music that mixed sources, styles, and sounds and was inspired by the African Diaspora.

Chicanx reggae bands Quinto Sol from Los Angeles, Big Mountain and Quinazo from San Diego, Rastafarmers from Phoenix, Rising Roots from Calexico, and Border Roots and Radio La Chusma from El Paso created a distinct brand of reggae that articulated a unique interracial and transnational Chicanx sensibility. They showed that, to borrow from David Rando again, "the impulses that surround music can move in different vectors, only some of which can be mapped and exploited in advance."[24] Simultaneously making use of and challenging the cultural nationalism of previous Chicano generations, these artists exhibited a Chicanismo that was neither separatist nor assimilationist, both local and transnational, and fundamentally based on their interactions and identification with other marginalized groups. Chicanx reggae artists imbued long-standing Movimiento iconography and ideas with new meanings, social relationships, and political formations. They also built on the long history of Chicano cultural work that grew from aesthetic, social, and political collaboration with Black artists and other racialized and aggrieved communities. Like other social dreamers and utopians before them, Chicanx reggae artists crafted their identity from their politics rather than drawing their politics from their identity. They made their music and politics in concert with firsthand experiences of globalization, migration, and border crossings and often deep diasporic relationships with the Black practitioners of Jamaican, British, and African reggae. Driven by reggae's universal appeal and messages of peace, social justice, and resistance, these Chicanx musicians interwove their music and political activism to claim dignity in the face of the dehumanizing effects of the anti-immigrant ethos, militarization of the border, poverty, and criminalization that shaped the lives of many Chicanxs and Mexican immigrants in the US Southwest.[25]

The Chicanx sensibility in border reggae included an intricate and, at times, contradictory relationship with Indigenous, Mexican, and Afro-Caribbean iconography, music, history, and cultural traditions. Chicanx reggae acts, for example, often put interracial, transnational, or contemporary spins on Chicano historical claims to a Mexica Indigenous and Mexican identity.[26] Quinto Sol, who formed in the early 1990s as part of East LA's Chicanx activist and underground music scene, is named after the reference in Aztec philosophy to the historical period of the fifth sun, or the contemporary epoch. Evoking what the vocalist Mizraim Leal called a "Razteca" identity, Quinto Sol combined their claims to Indigenous Mexica and Raza identities with deep Rastafarian and reggae influences. For Leal, even reggae's signature "skanking" of the guitar chords "represent[s] the Mexica, always marching forward."[27] El Paso's Radio La Chusma similarly dubbed their music as "Pachuco reggae—puro Razafarian," drawing on El Paso's history as a pre–World War II–era birthplace of the iconic Mexican American zoot suit and pachuco style and their roots in Jamaican music.[28] Accordingly, Radio La Chusma's founder, Ernesto Tinajero, explained the cover art on the band's 2007 album *91.5 MexM*. Of its depiction of an FM radio tower broadcasting from the top of an Aztec temple, he said, "It represents the transmission and communication of our ancient culture.... The youth, especially the Chicanos, need to explore themselves, question the history that was taught to us, and figure out how to utilize our knowledge of our ancestors with today's situations. This album is only a window, it's up to the listener to connect with the past, present, and future and feel proud to be of this Earth."[29] Joaquín "Quino" McWhinney, the Scotch-Irish and Chicano front man for the San Diego reggae outfits Big Mountain and Quinazo, invoked his song "Tierra Indígena" to explain the role of Indigenous history in his evolving notion of being Chicanx. In addition to highlighting the historical links of the Aztecs with the political, spiritual, and imagined Chicano homeland of Aztlán, Quino elaborated that "the song is about Indigenous culture, many struggles, the struggle of African people, the struggles of the Indigenous people of the Americas, about being able to interpret history correctly."[30] Chicanx reggae artists thus attempted to draw on strands of obscured history to create new identities and politics that helped generate visions of a different future.

While many artists understood that their Chicanx reggae, culture, and identity were shaped by both Indigenous and Black histories, struggles, and traditions, it's revealing that claims to Indigeneity were animated through their love and adoption of Afro-Caribbean reggae. While this seemingly circuitous route to claiming Indigenous history and identity might be viewed as contradictory, it may in fact be a result of the border region's complex history of interracial relationships, cross-cultural exchange, and, in the case of ethnic Mexicans in particular, often contentious and alienating history with Indigenous communities. If reggae opened a long way around for Chicanxs to reclaim their Indigenous roots, however, it was equally evident that such a process could invoke both Blackness and Indigeneity as empty, monolithic, and ahistorical signifiers.

The interracial and transnational political spheres from which Chicanx reggae artists crafted their own sense of Indigenous-, Mexican-, and Afro-Caribbean-inspired identity suggested at least an implicit grappling with the pitfalls of cultural nationalism and historical selectivity. As Josefina Saldaña-Portillo astutely warned, claims to Indigeneity by Chicana/o activists have historically been riddled with contradictions. Saldaña-Portillo argued that "the limits of mestizaje as the dominant trope in the formation of Chicana/o identity . . . fetishizes a residual Indian identity to the detriment of contemporary Indians in the United States and Mexico."[31] Influenced by Indigenous political struggles around the world and, particularly, by the emergence of the Zapatistas in Chiapas and Zapatismo's powerful tenets of popular participation, radical democracy, and collective struggle, some Chicanx reggae artists addressed these concerns. Big Mountain, for instance, explained the meaning and symbolism of their group's name by stating:

> Special recognition goes to the Dine' People [Navajo] of the Big Mountain region of Northern Arizona. It was their struggle that inspired us to name ourselves Big Mountain. They are involved in a bitter fight with various forces, including the US government, that conspire to remove them from their ancestral lands, and turn their lands over to mining interests. This could only lead to the destruction of their sacred land, their culture, and the only way of life they've ever known.[32]

As did Quinto Sol and other Chicanx reggae artists, Big Mountain continued to draw links between the struggles of Indigenous populations around the globe, claiming they "are dedicated to bringing awareness to the struggles of indigenous peoples everywhere." Big Mountain continued: "Whether it be the sovereignty movement of the Hawaiian people, the Zapatista freedom fighters in Chiapas, or the incidents at Oglala, we are all bound in the common fight for the survival of our native cultures. We must recognize the solidarity, we all must share against injustice."[33]

The reggae of El Paso's Border Roots further revealed a Chicanx identity based on its fluid, multiple, and intersecting character. The lead singer and guitarist Mark Moses Alvarado, who began his music career as a member of the Santa Barbara band Soul Force while a student and deejay at Santa Barbara City College in the early 1990s, struck a balance between the universal and the particular in his brand of Chicano politics. Alvarado cited the band's local border roots in El Paso and Ciudad Juárez as central to their musical and political identity. "We are a Chicano band because we possess a certain identity in terms of what is going to separate Border Roots from any other international reggae band." At the same time, he continued, "we wanted to create something that stands out, something that represents issues that affect everyone such as [the] cultural, political, social, and philosophical."[34] "Even though we're on the Mexican border," he elaborated, "we know our music reach[es] out and touch[es] people all over the world and that's a great feeling."[35]

An interracial and transnational Chicanx sensibility was also apparent in the music itself, which often integrated the sounds, instruments, and rhythms of Mexican *corridos* and folk, salsa and cumbia, rhythm and blues and jazz, ska and punk with the reggae vibe to create a Chicanx-Afro-Latinx border soundscape. The Quinto Sol bassist Martin Perez and Mizraim Leal noted that being from Mexicano families in Los Angeles, they "listened to puro cumbias and salsa and all this good stuff, you know in the fiestas growing up as little kids." They added, "That's why we have that blend because that's what came natural. . . . The reggae was the hard part! We were really just a bunch of Chicanos trying to play reggae. So people say, 'Hey, you guys blend in all this bad Afro-Cuban, salsa, cumbia, mixed with reggae . . .' That was already in the blood. We didn't have to learn none of that stuff. . . . Most of what we know was just from listening growing up." Their sound and politics were also shaped by several band members' affinity for ska, punk, skateboard culture, and anarchism in their younger years.[36] Quino McWhinney's musical project Quinazo, which released its album, *La Ofrenda*, in 2009, explored the contours of Chicanismo more directly than Big Mountain had in its recorded music. Quinazo's Chicano awakening was in part a result of Quino's developing engagement with Chicano folk music and Mexican *corridos*, an influence that stemmed partially from his friendship and collaboration with longtime San Diego Chicano musicians Ramon

"Chunky" and Rick Sanchez, who were active in the city's Chicano music scene and grassroots politics for more than forty years as part of their band Los Alacranes and the city's Chicano Park Steering Committee.[37] Like many other Chicanx reggae bands, Radio La Chusma cited Bob Marley as a formative musical and political influence. They also noted Santana, Los Lobos, the Beatles, James Brown, Toots and the Maytals, Manu Chau, Ozomatli, and "all Mexican music: mariachi, cumbia, corridos, boleros" as inspiration for their amalgamation of reggae, rock, and cumbia.[38] The guitarist Raul "Scoop" Valdez appropriately described La Chusma's sound as "Bob Marley meets Carlos Santana."[39] In their own diversified portfolio, a number of members of Border Roots got their start in Tejano and rock, and the band's own website described their sound as "Chicanos influenced by roots reggae, Rasta, the farm worker movement, civil rights, Bob Marley, Malcolm X, MLK, Cesar Chavez, Benny Moore, Motown, oppressed workers all over the world, Chicano youth and our mothers and fathers."[40] Border cities from San Diego to Los Angeles to El Paso were thus sites for ethnic Mexican, Indigenous, Black American, and Afro-Caribbean cultural fusion by Chicanx reggae artists.

While Chicanx reggae was drawn from Black American and Black Caribbean historical influences, among the most important influences shaping the music and identity of the artists was everyday life in the borderlands. Border life was evident in the themes and bilingual lyrics of much border reggae, which was often sung in Spanish, English, and, in the case of Quinto Sol, Nahuatl. Most followed conventional reggae recipes of struggle against oppression, colonialism, and imperialism in many of their jams, but often with a local Chicanx twist that stressed border living, immigration, Indigeneity, and Latinidad. El Paso's Border Roots affirmed the importance of their physical location on the US-Mexican border in El Paso–Ciudad Juárez in more than their name. When the band emerged, Chicanx reggae was a top draw in the city's nightclubs and across the border in Juárez in part because the music, lyrics, and politics were rooted in border life. Speaking of his pursuit of degrees in Chicanx and Border Studies at the University of Texas, El Paso (UTEP), Border Roots' Mark Alvarado asserted that "living on the border has taught me to look at things in a different perspective, one of the biggest things that blew me away was when you go to the state-of-the-art library at UTEP and you look out the window you see complete and utter poverty."[41] Alvarado's observations were reminiscent of Gloria Anzaldúa's observation that "the US-Mexican border es una herida abierta (is an open wound) where the Third World grates against the first and bleeds. And before a scab forms it hemorrhages again, the lifeblood of two worlds merging to form a third country—a border culture."[42] This border sensibility informed both the cover art of Border Roots' first CD, *Barrio Reggae*, which depicted a conquering Rasta lion with a red, gold, and green flag amid a telephone wire- and shanty-filled *colonia* that might be on either side of the El Paso–Juárez divide, and the music and lyrics that illuminated their views on border living and Chicanx identity.[43] Radio La Chusma similarly anchored their approach in the El Paso–Juárez area. "Our main goal," argued Ernie Tinajero, "was to expose everybody to the border region," a charge that manifested itself in their full-length albums, *Sonidos de la Gente* and *91.5 MexM*, which explored everything from cruising El Paso to *La llorona* to Afro-Mexica politics and spirituality.[44]

Farther west and closer to the Southern California border with Mexico, Big Mountain, Quinazo, and Quinto Sol also simultaneously rooted their reggae in their most immediate surroundings and in a broadly imagined landscape of Chicanx politics. Among Big Mountain's more political tunes was "Border Town," a heavy roots track about life in San Diego that was an incisive critique of immigration policy, the militarization of the border, and "silly fools in their big green vans" (border patrol agents); at the same time, it was a passionate plea to see the connections between US Chicanxs and Mexican immigrants, since "if it weren't for fate we might be each other."[45] On *New Day*, Quino explained that the entire album told "the story of the United States—about the different people coming here and their stories and exactly how we're gonna deal with the fact that we're all very unique. We're not blending into this melting pot that everyone talked about since its inception." Quino viewed the album as a critique of global capitalism and the ways it determined the life conditions of many immigrants.[46] McWhinney's more recent *La Ofrenda* with Quinazo included odes to the mixing of Mexica-Rasta traditions, life "up north," and a call for "huelga en general" (general strike) for human rights and dignity in a peaceful manner.[47] Up the coast in Los Angeles, Quinto Sol's solo and joint-venture albums paid homage to their Mixteca, Afro-Caribbean, and Chicano roots in East Los Angeles.[48] As Victor Viesca, Josh Kun, and Yvette Doss have shown, the broader context in which the Quinto Sol sound evolved from their 1993 beginnings was shaped by shared performances, social space, and organizing with East LA bands Quetzal, Ozomatli, Aztlan Underground, Ollin, Slowrider, and others who were involved in unionization and early

Zapatista activism, as well as efforts to create and sustain, for at least a year, the Eastside Peace and Justice Center.[49]

Quinto Sol is not alone as Chicanx reggae artists who have integrated their multiracial and translocal musical sensibilities with their networks of political organizing and activism. Others have also demonstrated that border reggae's hybrid musicality correlated with participation in social movements that prioritized the betterment of Chicanx, Mexican, and border communities. Indeed, it is sometimes difficult to gauge where the music ends and politics begin, as they are often one and the same. Virtually all of the Chicanx reggae artists under scrutiny here were long active in local barrio politics, struggles for immigrant rights, Zapatista solidarity work, border issues, labor organizing, independent art and cultural work, and the global justice movement. Back in El Paso, Border Roots and Radio La Chusma had long track records of appearing at progressive Chicanx and border fundraisers, rallies, and protests in support of maquiladora and farmworkers, immigrant rights, and *colonia* and barrio organizations, including regular gigs at Cinco de Mayo, Mexican Independence Day, and Cesar Chavez Day celebrations. Radio La Chusma, for example, was the featured entertainment at the February 2009 "A Day in the Sun: Adios ASARCO, Hello Future" event that celebrated grassroots efforts to oppose the reopening of the ASARCO smelter company near El Paso, a century-long corporate presence in the area that, as Monica Perales illustrated, was responsible for devastating lead contamination in the company town where its largely Mexican workforce lived.[50] Border Roots' Alvarado also complemented his musical career with work for El Paso Community College and the city of El Paso geared toward aiding workers displaced by NAFTA; neighborhood revitalization; community development in rural *colonias* along the border; and urban programs in health, education, and social services.

Less than twenty miles north of Tijuana, Quino McWhinney's reggae-influenced Chicanx activism dates back to at least the 1990s when he enlisted the aid of Mark Alvarado of Border Roots to develop a border coalition for immigrant rights.[51] McWhinney's community organizing crystallized in his more recent work with Quinazo and Rebel Ink, his independent music and art media group devoted to "conscious artistic expression for conscious people." Following La Gran Marcha, the massive immigrant rights marches across the country on May Day 2006, when McWhinney mused that "on May 1 we're gonna shut this country down," Quinazo became a fixture at San Diego–area pro-immigrant, anti-deportation events and helped organize student protests.[52] Staying true to the band's interracial, transnational, and fluid Chicanx sensibility, Quino elaborated the community-based and collaborative logic behind the group's public activism and his own efforts for independently supported Chicanx cultural production. Rebel Ink was about "bridges of understanding between communities, conduits or parallels that will allow us to recognize areas of solidarity that will allow us to work together."[53] He further underscored his belief that "the more we concentrate on our own labels, our own newspapers, our magazines, this is where the real progress goes . . . the real concrete change that's happening in the community, that's what we're really all fighting for."[54] In the same vein, like their San Diego and El Paso counterparts, Quinto Sol's Martin Perez and Mizraim Leal continued to steadfastly perform at LA-area Chicanx and Latinx festivals, fundraisers for community institutions like author/poet Luis Rodriguez's Tía Chucha Café Cultural, and their own barrio music and art store, and they provided free music lessons for youth.[55] These grassroots efforts were more than community engagement. They manifested a border(lands) where militarization and anti-immigrant hysteria did not go unchallenged and where the dreams in Chicanx reggae came to life, recalling John Storey's claim that the "entanglement of hope and desire can take many forms, both written and practiced, but, at its core, it is seeking somewhere better, seeking to make the news from nowhere manifest somewhere."[56]

As much as such political activity was oriented around Chicanx, Indigenous, and border issues, however, most Chicanx reggae musicians ascribed Bob Marley and Jamaican Rastafarianism as among their most formative *political*, not just musical, influences. Quinto Sol duo Perez and Leal say as much when they recalled that when they came across Marley, "we wanted to do what they were doing for the black people, we wanted to for the brown people . . . uplifting music, speaking conscious stuff, stuff for a better tomorrow."[57] As much as the music itself, the politics of Chicanx reggae was interracial and inclusive, local and transnational, and constitutive of a kind of contemporary border Chicanx movement fueled by reggae music. This new *movimiento*, however, was more a movement of movements, one in which a range of local struggles, from LA to San Diego to El Paso to Juárez, were loosely affiliated through shared ideology and personal relationships, and one that was less concerned with sparking a capital "R" "Revolution" than cultivating lots of small "r" revolutions. In this, Chicanx reggae artists demonstrated a sophisticated understanding of the Zapatismo that inspired many of them after 1994 while also revealing their analysis of the first Chicano Movement's nationalist limitations and internationalist possibilities.[58]

Chicanx reggae exhibited a multiplicity, perhaps an infinite number, of musical aesthetics, cultural identities, and political struggles that were uniquely situated in border(land) locales while recognizing common links, experiences, and histories with one another. The music and activism of these artists was at once transnational, even postnational, in its aesthetics and politics. Border reggae conveyed that it was possible to live beyond paradigms of nationalism that informed earlier Chicano politics, documented a world where intensified patterns of globalization often resulted in political and economic crises for the nation-state, and encouraged cultural and political alliances across borders.[59] Yet border reggae also reminded listeners that border dwellers dealt with the imposing structural, economic, and social conditions of the nation-state every day by claiming dignity and envisioning a better world in the wake of neoliberalism's dehumanization and militarization.

AFRO-MEXICA REGGAE

Border reggae boasted a similarly burgeoning scene in urban areas just south of the geopolitical boundary. Mainly in Tijuana, but also in Mexicali, the early 2000s saw the rise of what observers labeled "Afro-Mexica" reggae. Played mostly by young Mexican men, with lyrics in both Spanish and English, it was inspired by the Chicanx reggae of San Diego, Marley, and touring Jamaican artists who frequented beach and bar venues in Tijuana and Rosarito, as well as *rock en español*, ska, punk, and Mexican cumbia. It was similar to its Chicanx cousin north of the border and pointed to the hidden history of Black cultural and political presence in Tijuana and patterns of Mexican-Black interaction in the area. Afro-Mexica reggae recalled African American musicians' fascination with the border city, including, as I noted in chapter 2, Gerald Wilson's "Viva Tirado" during World War II (later of El Chicano cover fame in the 1960s), Charles Mingus's 1957 *Tijuana Moods*, and earlier twentieth-century Black forays across the border by Jack Johnson, Jelly Roll Morton, Sonny Clay, and others, such as those involved in efforts to establish autonomous African American agricultural colonies to the south and east of Tijuana in the 1920s and '30s.[60] Afro-Mexica reggae grew from this often hidden interracial past, but it was also deeply rooted in the contemporary Mexican border experience. As Pablo Vila argued about border dwellers more generally, these artists displayed the ability and willingness to cross multiple borders while reinforcing others to ensure their ethnic and cultural uniqueness.[61] Everyday border living was saturated with experiences, relationships, and opportunities that opened up the "possibility of enacting and performing the tissue of daily life differently."[62] Afro-Mexica artists articulated a Mexican identity and sensibility that was interracial and transnational and, as the poet Bobby Byrd might say, "*puro* border," filled with "cross-contamination of our language and culture. It is like a biological weapon, an organism that grows into the shape of who we are and where we live. It feeds on words and sentences spoken in the streets and alleys of our cities and towns and pueblos on both sides of the line."[63]

Not surprisingly, the Tijuana scene and its interracial, cross-border sensibilities were dramatically influenced by Southern California reggae. Not only did California bands like Quinto Sol have histories of performing in Tijuana, but international tours that frequented San Diego and LA periodically swung through Tijuana beginning in the early 1990s, especially for big beach festivals held in nearby Rosarito that drew thousands of partiers from south and north of the border. Those Jamaican artists with exceptional followings in San Diego—it's still not uncommon, for example, to hear Eek-a-Mouse's "Skidip" or Barrington Levy's "Broader Than Broadway" booming from cars at red light intersections—consistently played Tijuana over the years, with visits to the city inspiring songs like Eek's "Border Patrol," about difficulties navigating US border control and customs.[64]

The local San Diego scene, in particular, had a big impact on the rise of Afro-Mexica reggae in Tijuana. As the Astrorumberos member and native Tijuanense Carlos Garcia noted, "the radio doesn't play reggae down here," so many turned to airwaves carrying reggae shows from San Diego.[65] San Diego's own Makeda "Dread" Cheatom was at the forefront of helping grow the Afro-Mexica scene from Tijuana's sister city to the north. As the longtime hostess of the weekly "Reggae Makossa" program on San Diego's 91X FM, who also served as director of the World Beat Center, located near downtown San Diego in Balboa Park and long home to touring reggae shows and related culture in the city, Cheatom took a keen interest in developing reggae south of the border. She was instrumental in organizing, advertising, and emceeing annual Bob Marley Day festivities and other concerts in Tijuana. For Cheatom, the Afro-Mexica scene "is a good opportunity for Mexicans to recognize that Africa is part of their history.... This is the perfect time to recognize the diversity that exists in Mexico." If Afro-Mexicans, perhaps most widely associated with the Veracruz and Oaxacan coast regions, "are Mexico's forgotten roots," Cheatom saw Afro-Mexica reggae as a potentially important connective tissue in coalitions and support among African American and Chicanx communities in Southern California.[66] Cheatom's claims that many Mexican youth in Tijuana learned more about Mexico's Black history and the African Diaspora through reggae than any other source may not be far off the mark. Chris Fregoso, the keyboardist for Tijuana reggae bands Esencia and De Raíz, said as much. In addition to the bootleg videos and tapes of Marley that circulated around Tijuana, Fregoso recalled that he and many other Tijuana youth grew up listening to "Reggae Makossa" every Sunday night and that "we'd hear in the music, the similarities between Jamaican and Mexican cultures—the struggle for poor people to survive."[67]

Just as the impetus for growth in the music came from transnational cultural encounters, so, too, did it stem from the rootedness of Afro-Mexica artists' experience in Tijuana. Esencia's Fregoso helped cultivate the local scene, particularly since he saved money from his non-music-related job as a driving instructor to build Comunidad Rubydreads, a recording studio in the barrio of Colonia Valle del Rubí. The studio became something of a nerve center for the Afro-Mexica scene in Tijuana, in part because, as Fregoso explained, reggae's message of struggle and resistance struck a chord in the neighborhood. "Rubí is working-class. A lot of people here work in the *maquiladoras*. Some are teachers; some are carpenters and construction workers.... Today if you are living here in La Colonia, it's the same as in ... other parts of Latin America. There are the same problems and troubles—lack of jobs, high crime and overcoming poverty and drug addiction."[68] As much as Afro-Mexica was a product of the transnational flow of reggae vibes via the African Diaspora and south across the border from San Diego, it was also very much a uniquely *Tijuas* scene.

Reggae and the urban border context combined to create a vibrant and growing Afro-Mexica scene that articulated an interracial, Afro-inspired, and transnational Mexicanidad that was rooted in local Tijuana experiences and history. Particularly visible since the turn of the new millennium, Tijuana bands like Esencia, Cáñamo, Los Astrorumberos, Cartel de Zion, and Yumanos helped build a diverse reggae and Rasta scene in the city. With regular gigs at venues like El Foro, Bar Berlin, Tilly's, and the Voodoo House and Tijuana Roots and Culture, their own reggae specialty shop on Avenida Revolución in the heart of the city started by Ras Alfonso, an original member of the band Natural, Afro-Mexica artists constructed a cultural infrastructure in support of their music.

The hybrid musical aesthetic of Afro-Mexica reggae mirrored and reinvented claims to Indigeneity, pan-Latinidad, Afro-Caribbean links, and, in some cases, radical politics seen in Chicanx reggae. As with their musical kin to the north, utopian impulses could be gleaned from Afro-Mexica in ways described by Peter Thompson's musing that "little abstracted sparks of utopia exist all around us in everyday life, but they cannot yet add up to a utopian process until and unless they become radicalized, grasped at their roots."[69] Border reggae artists didn't always make the leap between "sparks" and "process," but many tried to or at least shifted in that direction. Maíz, led by the singer and trumpeter Karlos Páez, who was also the front man for the more well-known San Diego and Tijuana favorite B-Side Players, popularized tunes like "La Raza" and "Tierra Maya," which emphasized cultural and ethnic pride. In a brand of body politics and Rasta-inspired Indigeneity, Páez's dreadlocks and tattoos of the Aztec calendar and Zapotec corn god visually captured the seemingly disparate cultural streams of Afro-Mexica.[70] Los Astrorumberos' style was labeled "Latin dub Afro-beat" for their combination of English-language covers of Bob Marley classics and Spanish-language originals. And though their own material may have lacked the political edge of Marley—in that they are not alone—their bassist, Carlos Garcia, made it clear that among the band's motivations was that "we are kind of angry about racism and problems at the border."[71] In their two demos, "Botas" and "La Quedijimos," Cáñamo combined reggae, jazz, rock, blues, bosa nova, and cumbia with lyrics ranging from general calls for peace and unity to shout-outs to border crossers. The band conveyed their sense of the local and global by claiming they played for those "who walk through the streets and corners of Tijuana and the entire planet."[72]

Another example of Afro-Mexica's diversity and progressive cultural politics was the popularity of San Diego–based Elijah Emanuel and the Revelations in Tijuana. Demonstrating the cross-border and interracial ethos of the scene, Emanuel's band has been as popular in Tijuana as in San Diego since its inception in the 1990s. Emanuel was born a military brat in Panama, where he was introduced to reggae and Rastafarian culture by Jamaicans who worked on the Panama Canal. He was among the first *reggae en español* artists, with most of his recordings and live performances fairly evenly split between English and Spanish lyrics.

Musically, he dropped African polyrhythms, Native American chants, Cuban tres, jazz horns, and cello into his reggae groove. Emanuel's unique sound drew a devoted following among Tijuana youth in the late 1990s and early 2000s and helped spawn the Afro-Mexica scene. His attention to border politics and immigration rights resulted in songs and lyrics that supported undocumented immigrants in the United States, questioned the dehumanizing discourse of "illegal aliens," voiced solidarity with the Zapatistas and contemporary Indigenous struggles in Mexico, and highlighted the presence of African Diasporic cultural productions in the borderlands.[73] Although his music was rooted in the San Diego–Tijuana border region, Emanuel claimed a universalism not uncommon to the reggae form. "Where I want to take it [reggae]?" he avowed, "Where it's not localized to one geography and not limited to one culture."[74]

Lest one think Afro-Mexica's politics were not entrenched in the particularities of Tijuana, one need only look at how artists addressed popular discourse on both sides of the border in the 2000s, characterizing the city as overrun with drug trafficking, gang violence, kidnappings, and danger. This was especially the case in debates over US "homeland security" following 9/11 and amid revivals of the century-old "Mexican problem" that expressed fear of the perceived immoral, socially deviant, and economically draining impact of Mexican immigration. Rather than ignore or accept their city and people being labeled as dangerous or threatening, Afro-Mexica artists created, sustained, and circulated a different Tijuas narrative in their music. Alluding to both the social and political turmoil in the city and the cultural response by Afro-Mexica artists, Cáñamo bandleader Osvaldo Julián urged that "Tijuana is super-inspiring. In Tijuana, you see things that don't happen in the rest of Mexico." Julián put his finger on the city's cultural pulse that led one area literary agent to state that "people are continuing to work and showing that here there's more than shootouts and kidnappings. Violence is not going to stop Tijuana's rhythm, and it's not going to stop the creativity of its artists."[75]

Afro-Mexica reggae in Tijuana generated an infusive Mexicanidad, one open to interracial histories, the African Diaspora, transnational cultural and political projects, and local inflections of living in Mexico's largest *frontera* city. As Alejandro L. Madrid showed in his study of Nortec music in Tijuana, both Mexican and US residents long viewed the city in contradictory ways. People in the United States often viewed Tijuana as both a symbol of immorality and perversion and a site of emancipation where red zones and party culture made it a place of desire and excess. People in Mexico might have seen the city as inhabiting the geographical and cultural periphery of Mexicanidad and an entry point to American modernity.[76] As part of this cultural terrain, Afro-Mexica reggae was one site to map the political possibilities of a Black/brown, Mexican/American, cross-border cultural scene that inspired its practitioners to imagine a different Tijuana, one where dignity might be rescued from the clenches of neoliberalism's inhumanity along the border.

IS ANOTHER BORDER(LANDS) POSSIBLE?

Is another border(lands) possible? As much as border reggae suggested that Chicanxs and Mexicans crafted identities and politics with an interracial and transnational timbre, they were not without imposing limits. If border reggae was part of a new type of geographically and demographically diverse cultural politics, its greatest strength and weakness might have been its lack of formal organization or singular sense of purpose. The music, moreover, came with pitfalls and contradictions related to commercialization, gender, and race that risked short-circuiting the reach and impact of its utopian impulses.

Border reggae artists exploited the same networks of global capital to open new political possibilities that restructured borderlands communities. George Lipsitz noted that popular music embodies the contradictions of commercialized culture and serves as a "dangerous crossroads," "an intersection between the undesirable saturation of commercial culture in every area of human endeavor and the emergence of a new public sphere that uses circuits of commodity production and circulation to envision and activate new social relations."[77] To be sure, border reggae revealed more than an oppression/resistance or colonialist/colonized binary. The very presence of border reggae was a testament to transnational cultural streams that illuminated a spectrum of border identities and experiences that ranged from destabilizing and challenging local forces of globalization to feeding the neoliberal machine. Just as border reggae served as a vehicle to critique militarization or helped spark and support new social movements, for example, it was just as easily used to sell border tourism in the form of weekend getaways to Rosarito for a big reggae beach festival or even to pick up red-, gold-, and green-colored ponchos bought by Americans crossing back north. At the same time, border reggae and border tourism more generally, as Alejandro L. Madrid proposed, offered a forum for borderlanders themselves to recast their identity in unconventional ways to take advantage of and create room to maneuver in the globalization unfolding around them.[78]

The case of Joaquín "Quino" McWhinney and Big Mountain is helpful here. Despite commercial success in the 1990s, in part because of their reggae remake of Peter Frampton's "Baby, I Love Your Way" for the soundtrack to the movie *Reality Bites*, McWhinney and the band struggled to maintain control over their artistic product after they were signed to Warner Brothers and in subsequent dealings with a Japanese-owned record label. More than a decade later, McWhinney was juggling his independently owned and community-based Rebel Ink label with his full-time job as a multimedia vocational schoolteacher in Chula Vista, California, while his new band, Quinazo, found fresh outlets.[79] Fast-forward to 2017 and "Baby, I Love Your Way" found new success on the big screen when it was featured in the blockbuster *Jumanji* franchise, two films that starred Dwayne "The Rock" Johnson. Though McWhinney's journey through and entanglement with pop music's commercialism may not be unique, it underscored that just as border reggae was commodified, bought, and sold, the risk remained that its social identities and political movements might suffer the same fate. For McWhinney and other border reggae artists, however, such struggles were less about banal debates over authenticity, selling out, or "keeping it real" and more about what the performance studies scholar Ramón Rivera-Servera labeled "sincerity." As they navigated the pitfalls of the global music industry, border reggae artists believed the intent was as important as the content of their music, their sense of self as important as the CDs, mp3s, and concert tickets they sold, and whether fueling social movements, commercialism, or both, sincerity was often contested and contradictory.[80]

It is also apparent that border reggae, at least among those who produced the music, was a largely masculine affair. All of the bands discussed above were fronted by men, with few women musicians and backup singers involved. In some ways, this inequity reflected the gender hierarchy of the larger music industry and reggae, specifically, but in other ways it replicated much of the male-dominated, patriarchal, macho, and hypermasculine character of Mexican and Chicanx communities along the border. While there was a conscious effort by many border artists to address such concerns in their music and lyrics, one overriding propensity was to equate resistance and rebel-like activity with manhood, a tendency that resulted, at least in the context of certain live performances, from male reggae artists entertaining largely male audiences. Another common feature was the construction of a typology of Chicana, Mexicana, or Indigenous women as either objects of male sexual desire or feminine protectors of the old ways and traditional culture. As Michael Bucknor argued about the reggae aesthetic more broadly, these tendencies not only risked reinforcing long-standing patterns of patriarchy but also obscured and silenced a wider range of gender and sexual identities and voices.[81] Border reggae thus often privileged dominant or heroic masculinities, couched in terms of sexual prowess or political power, against the subordination of alternative masculine, feminine, or sexual identities.

The conflicting gender politics of border reggae mirrored developments evident in reggae's digital dancehall genre since the late 1980s, where male performers often assumed the ability to understand women and know what they wanted in ways that uncritically accepted troubling assumptions about patriarchal power. Such trends not only blunted the empowering possibility of border reggae, because they limited the agency of Chicanas, Mexicanas, and others, but also suggested that the social movements and broader struggles for social transformation of which border reggae was an active part needed to more critically interrogate their gender and sexual politics. There was no easy answer, but the political possibilities of border reggae necessarily hinged on the engagement with and recognition of such disruptive and counterproductive patterns. Whether border reggae's unequal gender relations stemmed from male artists' presumption about understanding women, their local borderlands communities, the popular music industry, or all of the above, it was forced to reckon with issues that, as Bucknor asserted, demonstrated that border reggae often "elides the politics of gender and sexuality in the favor of artistic revolt."[82]

It is also worth noting that the encounter between border reggae artists and the African Diaspora was not uniformly smooth and without conflict. It was sometimes shrouded in competition over the racial and cultural ownership and authenticity of reggae. Despite cross-border gigs and demographics that suggested a stable market for border reggae, it was not a sure thing. Border Roots' Mark Alvarado remembered, for example, that it "was difficult to get a following in Chihuahua, Mexico. Every time we played there, they always wanted us to play songs by Carlos Santana, in fact one time they booed us off the stage."[83] As comments from Maíz's Karlos Páez and Elijah Emanuel demonstrated, such conflict took different shapes, too. Páez recalled that when Maíz first opened for the legendary Jamaican reggae group Black Uhuru, they were "dissed" and "perceived as posers."[84] Emanuel admitted that "sometimes I question when Latin Americans embrace reggae music. Its ideologies and beliefs come from a black, African consciousness. If you don't put a lot of thought into those beliefs, you're mimicking the culture."[85] Despite its racial and geographic crossings, Chicanx and Afro-Mexica reggae still struggled to find meaning in its cultural and political fusion.

Although this chapter focuses largely on the emergence of border reggae in the interval between the lead-up to NAFTA in the early 1990s and the first decade of the 2000s, it is worth noting that border reggae continued to flourish. One illustrative example of border reggae's more recent political charge was Big Mountain's return with their 2018 single "Deportation Nation." It was released amid outcries over the Trump administration's vicious practice of family separation at the border, which stripped children, including infants and toddlers, from parents and guardians with whom they had crossed the border. With parents incarcerated, children were placed under the control of Health and Human Services, and both were subjected to prison-like quarters, poor diets, and a lack of basic services. Although the exact number of children affected is not clear, thousands were moved without their parents to remote locations in the interior of the United States without any plan for reunification with their families. During the same period, thousands more immigrants and refugees from around the world seeking political asylum in the United States were imprisoned in detention centers with little legal recourse and similarly disturbing conditions. "Deportation Nation" was one border reggae response to the latest chapters in a longer history of violent attempts to stem immigration, deport undocumented migrants, and persecute refugees.[86]

"Deportation Nation" exposed the history of anti-immigrant policy and the hostile discourse about immigrants and refugees rampant in 2018. As they'd done back in 1994 with their song "Bordertown," the band deployed music as a political weapon. With a pulsating drum and bass rhythm behind it, the lyrics flowed, in part:

> I and I live in a deportation nation
> I don't want to hear about no civilization
> So they can round up the population with no explanation
> Right in front of our face

With direct reference to family separation, the song continued:

> First they came for the weakest among us
> Those without a voice that belong in a school bus
> We let down the children
> And history is watching

In addition to spitfire vocals by Quino McWhinney and his brother James, the track included a spoken-word interlude by John Márquez, professor of Latinx Studies at Northwestern University, who met Quino in immigrant rights and anti-police brutality activist circles in San Diego in the 1990s.[87] His haunting delivery on the track went as follows:

> Lock our children in cages and they will reinvent our world. Redefine what it means to be a nation. You know not what you do. The steel is making us stronger. Our radical traditions are rooted in how we live and love otherwise. Despite you, we bond with one another. Lock us up, deport or separate us, and we still find ways to connect and love radically and insurgently with a love that burns with the power of the sun.

The song was played and discussed on mainstream media outlets like CNN, Telemundo, and Univisión. One outlet described it as a "fierce roots reggae rebuke to [the] Trump administration's immigration and border enforcement policy and broader history of border militarization."[88]

Quino described the inspiration to write the song: "We wanted to demonstrate to our undocumented immigrant sisters and brothers that the band Big Mountain stands in solidarity with their plight. We believe that all people have a right to travel far and wide to fulfill their dreams, especially when it comes to bettering their lives and the lives of their families."[89] He also made clear it was a censure of the Trump administration: "The United States cannot survive without labor from undocumented people. That is the reality. What is the alternative? What are we gonna do? Because we can't just keep on deporting people every 20, 30 years. And we decide, some populist whacko becomes President and decides to take advantage of people's emotions. That's not a world I want to live in. That's not a world I'm gonna stand for."[90]

Like the longer history of reggae in the region, "Deportation Nation" showed how border folk regenerated identities and politics with an eye to a better future. Though their musical and political activity didn't always lead to substantive change in border communities, it was part of people's ongoing attempts to imagine a better border(lands). It recalled Shana Redmond's declaration that "beyond its many pleasures, music allows us to do and imagine things that may otherwise be unimaginable or seem impossible."[91] Their creativity yielded utopian impulses in as much as "virtually all utopian thought is the conviction in an ideal society that diminishes suffering, fully realizes human potential, and pushes the boundaries of what seems possible."[92] Border reggae's interracial and transnational qualities were ingrained in the fibers of *frontera* life and efforts to make it better. Its utopian impulses salvaged dignity and hope from the hostile conditions of the nation-state and neoliberalism. Summing up the song "Deportation Nation," Quino said as much. "That's why we make the art that we make. If we want a better world, first it has to be imagined. And that's the responsibility of singers, painters, poets. We're the ones that imagine a better world. And then we hand it off to the people that are supposed to do the hard work."[93] If we are wise, we will listen to border reggae and consider how it might help us consider the possibilities of a *frontera* soundscape.

Coda
NGĀTAHI

In 2004, the Maori hip-hop artist, activist, and filmmaker Dean Hapeta visited Los Angeles while making his "rapumentary"/documentary film, *Ngātahi: Know the Links*. During his stay, he met Joseph "Nuke" Montalvo, the renowned Chicano muralist and graffiti artist, who introduced Hapeta to LA street art and several Chicanx- and Indigenous-themed murals in the city. Among the works he shared was the massive *Undiscovered America* mural near the corner of Fourth Place and Hewitt Street. Created in 1992 by the Earth Crew, which included Montalvo, Erick "Duke" Montenegro, Benjamin James Frank Jr., and Rojelio "Angst" Cabral, it was one of the first murals painted in what was then "skid row" but would become the revamped LA Art District. As Nuke explained, it was made "in honor of the native cultures . . . all the way from Alaska to the tip of South America," as an "anti–Christopher Columbus mural" in the quincentennial year of his arrival in the Americas. The mural featured "a medicine wheel in the center in celebration of the healing of relations among all peoples of the world."[1] It was also completed just a few short months after rebellion and violence swept Los Angeles following the acquittal of four LAPD officers for the beating of Rodney King. "Globally and locally there was a lot of turmoil," Nuke recalled, and the mural was intended to acknowledge the Indigenous presence in the Americas and represent a "front line" in struggles for racial justice in LA and beyond.[2]

Scenes of Nuke and Hapeta discussing *Undiscovered America*, common ground between Chicanxs and Maori, and doing the "hongi," the traditional Maori greeting in which two people press noses together, manifested the "links" in *Ngātahi*. Dozens more examples between Hapeta and others he met around the world were included in the six-part series produced between 2003 and 2012. For nearly a decade, Hapeta, armed with only a handheld video camera and a few contacts in destination cities, left Aotearoa (New Zealand) to experience hip-hop, spoken word, and social movements in aggrieved communities. His journey took him to more than twenty countries, where he accumulated spectacular footage of concerts, protests, and informal interviews from Los Angeles to London to Wounded Knee to the West Bank and points in between. Hapeta, who was cameraman, director, and editor all-in-one, stayed afloat with personal funds and support from the Screen Innovation Production Fund, several Maori tribal councils, and calling in favors to cut costs.[3] Back home in between trips, Hapeta put his backyard film studio to use, producing films that, in his words, invite the viewer to "step into a zone where hip-hop and activism are one" to experience "an elated dose of urban vitality immersed in conscious awareness."[4] The result was a rich cultural history of what some have labeled the Fourth World War, or the contemporary struggle for global justice and against neoliberalism, a shining example of pop culture fomenting grassroots movements for change across racial and geographic boundaries.[5] Chicanx and Latinx folk are featured in only a few segments, accounting for just a sliver of Ngātahi's airtime, but, nonetheless, their stories, performances, and activism enriched Hapeta's chronicle of how people's local struggles linked to others in faraway places.[6] Ngātahi, after all, means "togetherness" in Maori.

What does a lone globetrotting Maori have to teach us about Chicanx utopias? Quite a bit, if we listen to what Hapeta and his Chicanx friends along the Ngātahi trail said about why they see themselves in one another. Utopia in the films, to borrow from Jean Pfaelzer, "is not a set of blueprints or political recipes for class, gender, and racial equality. Rather, utopia is a view, indeed, a vision, that the ingredients for a just, respectful, and even playful future are imminent in our capitalist, racist, and sexist society."[7] Hapeta's films drew connections between seemingly variant experiences of poverty, racism, and police brutality and shared histories of resistance to colonialism. They showed that while Indigenous and aggrieved communities have long shouldered the destructive consequences of imperialism and development, their cultural practices fought such conditions by fostering solidarity with distant people and places. Hapeta, Chicanxs, and others in Ngātahi were part of a diaspora, one based on interlinked struggles for dignity rather than any place or ethnic-based affiliation. Against the indignity and dehumanization wrought by neoliberal globalization, they rendered dominant race or power relations unworkable on the ground, if only for a moment at a festival, protest, or spontaneous performance. The art and activism in *Ngātahi* enabled people to speak out against their own erasure by making a record of injustice and calls for change that might otherwise go unrecorded. Chicanxs were part of *Ngātahi*, and *Ngātahi* was part of their popular culture because they actively cultivated alliances and exchange with Hapeta and many others in his films. Despite being the brainchildren of a Maori from well beyond the borders of Aztlán, the films embodied the interracial, transnational, and politically engaged currents that bubbled in the history of Chicanx pop culture.

In the rest of this coda, I ponder first the Chicanx segments in *Ngātahi* and then whether the films offer any contemplation of Chicanx utopias, pop culture, and social movements. Far from a full treatment of *Ngātahi*, it is more of a closing riff meant to provocatively urge consideration of Chicanx utopias from wide-ranging and disorienting points of view.[8] Without completely decentering Chicanx figures and history, my aim is to complement and complicate preceding chapters by probing anew how Chicanx utopias encompass and are encompassed by a range of pop cultural and political movements.

CHICANX LOS ANGELES IN *NGĀTAHI*

Hapeta's travels took him to six continents, from Europe to the Pacific and up and down the Americas, all in search of grassroots art and activism fighting the effects of neoliberalism and colonialism.[9] Out of nearly one hundred segments in *Ngātahi*'s five parts, Chicanxs appear in only a handful. Predictably, these were based on Hapeta's visits to San Francisco and Los Angeles in 2001 and 2004 when he met Chicanx rappers, poets, and artists. The parts on LA, in particular, brimmed with a Chicanx presence and were interspersed with clips of ordinary street life in the city, which led one reviewer to comment that "everyday movement from walking to surfing is displayed as if it was break dancing."[10] Hapeta's encounters with the pioneering Chicanx rap group Aztlan Underground, the poet Marisol, and the muralist Nuke were interwoven with appearances by Filipinx and Indigenous poets and rappers and members of the local All-African People's Revolutionary Party, presenting LA as a fusion of Black and brown. Like others in *Ngātahi*, the LA scenes discussed art and music as weapons in fights against police brutality, settler colonialism, and global capital—all backed by a soundtrack featuring local artists or Hapeta's own band, Upper Hutt Posse (UHP), which was at the forefront of a rebirth in cultural nationalism among Maori youth in the mid-1980s. The resulting portrait is a Chicanx LA in which artists and activists were knit together as part of a global network of aggrieved communities battling to make life better for everyone.

Hapeta's visit with Aztlan Underground opens *Ngātahi #3*. He first met the band at an Indigenous rights conference in Adelaide, Australia, where he was screening a festival cut of *Ngātahi #1* and they were on the bill.[11] A few years later, while filming in Los Angeles, Hapeta attended an Aztlan Underground rehearsal and interviewed members Joe Galarza, Yaotl, and Bulldog. Their conversation stressed Aztlan Underground's commitment to making socially conscious music and their identification with Indigenous rights, anti-police brutality, and global justice efforts around the world. Galarza described their music as "a vibrational prayer that we send out to the world . . . , for the betterment of humanity, to take away these mental borders that we're so colonized with." Yaotl added, "Our music . . . embodies not only a cultural awakening but also a social-political analysis of our surroundings in the world . . . and our connection to all the native people throughout the world, all the world's indigenous human beings of the earth, because we share the experience of being colonized." Hapeta's segment with Aztlan Underground featured their rock/rap tune "Blood on Your Hands," repeating its lyrics "stains the glory for which you stand" and splicing clips of their interview, shots of LA freeways and beaches, and contrasting images of Beverly Hills and East Los Angeles. Evoking the thorny association between Chicanx and Indigenous politics discussed in chapter 5, Hapeta and Aztlan Underground found common ground in their different relationships with and shared critique of the legacy of European colonization. The segment also included extended clips with the poet Marisol waxing lyrically on the historical significance of Aztlán and border crossing for Chicanx and native history and her own spoken word. She noted, "Aztlán is a place where the Mexica or the Aztecas originated from, which is north of the Mexican border. So, we're up here again, you know, it's like an ongoing cycle you cannot stop. It's like natural force, it's like the wind, the water, you can't impose control on it, it's gonna happen, we're gonna cross back and forth, this is our natural heritage."[12]

From Aztlan Underground and Marisol, Hapeta transitioned in *Ngātahi #3* to Black and Filipinx Los Angeles. The next segment, "No More Prisons," featured Dedon Kamathi, a Pan-African activist, former Black Panther, president of the Black Surfer's Association, and host of

KPFK's *Freedom Now* radio program, and Faith Santilla, a Pinay spoken-word and hip-hop artist and international women's rights activist. It begins with Kamathi and Macheo Shabaka of the All-African People's Revolutionary Party in a living room in South Central LA. With books scattered at their feet and Bob Marley, "Free Palestine," African Liberation, George Jackson, and "Smash the FBI-CIA" posters on the walls, Kamathi and Shabaka shared thoughts on racism as a global phenomenon and the need for "the fight back" to cultivate links between Pan-African and Maori, Aborigine, Khoi Khoi, Korean, and Irish struggles against colonialism. The scene then flips to Faith Santilla in the middle of an unnamed LA city street at dusk. As a helicopter hovered in the sky above her, Santilla delivered her poem "No More Prisons" on neoliberal, for-profit exploitation of prison labor in the United States; the hyperfunding of prisons compared to the underfunding of state-sponsored education; and shout-outs to the Filipinos on death row. The scene shifts back and forth between Kamathi/Shabaka and Santilla: different political discussions linked by a shared desire for a future where disparate struggles unite and work together. Hapeta's own UHP provided musical backdrop.[13]

Hapeta's tour of Los Angeles continued with the segment "By All Means Bring Unity." It introduced Native Guns, the Filipino/Chinese American rap group featuring Jonah Deocampo, also known as Bambu (which stands for "By All Means Bring Unity"). In clips that mixed their live performance with a casual curbside interview, Bambu vigorously condemned police brutality and urged interracial togetherness. "They put us in a police state and we live in fear of them, so I'm saying fuck them!" He continued, "'We' is my community. The brown, the black, red man, all of us who live in the inner city, people who have been shitted on, the oppressed people of the world. . . . In the big scheme of things, our struggles are all the same. We need to overcome the same shit that they need to overcome and Latino people need to overcome. And that's oppression."[14] Deocampo was Filipino American, raised in Watts, and he joined the Marine Corps when he was eighteen. After his stint in the military, he took his music career solo, blending his politics and emcee skills in songs about worker and immigrant rights, the prison industrial complex, gentrification, and police brutality. He was consistently involved in Asian American youth leadership programs and community reform efforts, explaining, "Ultimately, my music is trying to get folks to organize. It's not to create fans but to create organizers to actually go out there and get the change they hear me reflecting in songs."[15]

The Chicanx murals and graffiti of Joseph "Nuke" Montalvo were the next stop on Hapeta's LA expedition. Together they explored murals across East Los Angeles with images of Cesar Chavez, Emiliano Zapata, and Frida Kahlo, with Montalvo providing a history of LA street art and its debt to Chicano Movement–era muralists along the way. He emphasized the power of art to help bring communities together. "We all have roots with each other," he said. "And through art, slowly but surely, we'll start to break the code and tap into our hidden genetic code and genetic information we all carry. I think that's where art helps. . . . You're not going to be able to control it, when one mural goes up and another mural goes up and another mural goes up. You know? It's like consciousness spreading from mind to mind and heart to heart."[16]

Like many others in *Ngātahi*, Montalvo practiced what he preached. He was commissioned for multiple public art projects across LA, has worked consistently with Zapatista communities in Chiapas since 1994, and, in addition to providing tours of LA's street art scene, has supported a myriad of grassroots cultural efforts in his native Boyle Heights and beyond.[17]

Hapeta closed his Los Angeles circuit by chatting with the Indigenous-inspired hip-hop outfit Culture of Rage. The segment fused interviews with the rappers Urban Native Son and Phoenix 51/50 with their song "Godless America." The soundtrack urged "Refuse, resist!" to a rap/rock rhythm and referenced Wounded Knee, East Timor, Tlatelolco, Acteal, and Palestine, among other historical sites of Indigenous resistance and slaughter. In the interviews, the two rappers touched on their music as critique of the blurred lines between California's K-12 education system and the prison industrial complex, talked about how learning about the worldwide history of genocide against Indigenous communities inspired the launch of their band, and noted the influence of Malcolm X on their political development. Hapeta responded, "This is so much of us, our story, this same story. Reading *The Autobiography of Malcolm X*, everything."[18]

The Los Angeles scenes made up the first half hour of *Ngātahi #3*. Not everyone in them classified themselves or their visions as utopian, but their art, music, film, and politics expressed the desire for a better way of living, conjuring José Esteban Muñoz's contention that the "not-yet-conscious is knowable, to some extent, as a utopian feeling."[19] Hapeta and the Chicanxs in *Ngātahi* reminded us that music, film, and art were often home to utopian utterances that were not articulated, at least in the same ways, in other arenas of life. It was as if they innately made sense of utopia in a similar way to Ruth Levitas, who rejected any "classificatory definition that says this is utopian, that is not. Rather, it is an analytic definition that allows that many cultural forms may have a utopian element. This approach allows us to look at the variety of forms, contents, functions, and locations of utopian expressions; to make connections between different forms; and to marry detailed historical specificity with theoretical questions."[20]

From LA, Hapeta moved on to Mexico City and Chiapas before returning north to Whitehorse, Wounded Knee, and Rapid City, South Dakota. The Chicanxs and others he met back in Southern California do not reappear in the films, but they were linked to the rappers, poets, and activists Hapeta encountered elsewhere. Their belief in the possibility of a better world, one in which pop culture served as an incubator for global justice, brought them together.

NGĀTAHI AND CONCENTRIC UTOPIAS

Ngātahi illuminated shared visions of utopia among Chicanxs, Hapeta, and others in the films. Despite coming from different places and backgrounds, they found common ground against legacies of colonialism and global capitalism. Their art and activism claimed dignity by rejecting humiliation and dehumanization and establishing channels of cultural and political exchange.[21] *Ngātahi* recalled James Scott's observation that struggles for dignity are often considered less important than material exploitation, but, nonetheless, can illumine a diagnostics of political power, its limits, and possibilities.[22] *Ngātahi* laid bare what we might call concentric utopias, visions of a better world that shared similar axes of struggle. The Chicanxs in *Ngātahi* were in dialogue and aware of how their plight and dreams of the future grew from conditions shared with Hapeta and others. Their connections were a kind of globalization from below, a diaspora of dignity that was as much forward looking to possible links as it was backward looking to any common place of origin, kinship, or race. Much as Vivek Bald described overlapping diasporas in early twentieth-century United States, *Ngātahi* comprised "movements and relations between multiple locations," moved "away from an overdetermining focus on 'homeland,'" and departed from "a singular emphasis on particular racial, ethnic or national groups."[23] For Bald and Hapeta, diaspora operated more as "a process of encounter, intermixture, and the negotiation of difference across all these lines."[24]

As did other Chicanx utopias, *Ngātahi* sprouted from seemingly dystopian circumstances, including the prevalence of police brutality, land loss, tourism, and corporate greed, and the ongoing racism, poverty, and poor life chances of so many. While such conditions could be said to breed a diaspora of misery or exploitation, *Ngātahi* revealed a world of interconnected activists and artists working toward new and powerful alternatives. Assessing the utopian/dystopian balance in *Ngātahi*, Hapeta declared, "I feel happy about it. I feel inspired by the films. Yeah, I'm an optimist. Although, you know, I'm always talking about the bad shit." He added, "Shit, man, if there wasn't optimism there'd be no use in doing this. I wouldn't do it."[25]

Hapeta's easygoing, if slightly unorthodox methods underscored the idea that utopia was always a job unfinished, never a finished product or a final destination. His free-flowing ethnography, described by one critic as "guerilla filmmaking," consisted of grabbing his camera and walking the streets of whichever city he found himself in.[26] *Ngātahi* relied on Hapeta's mobility and travel, supporting James Clifford's contention that travel enabled "reflections on conditions for human connection, alliances cutting across class, race, gender, and national locations." Like Clifford, Hapeta intuitively understood ethnography as an encounter in which movement created contacts while sustaining ideas of home, dwelling, and discrete regions. These "roots" with a double *o* and "routes" with an *ou* were very much alive in *Ngātahi*.[27] Contacts and travel opportunities popped up unexpectedly—there was not necessarily a set plan—and the experience mattered as much as, if not more than, the end result. In Los Angeles, for instance, Urban Native Son from Culture of Rage introduced Hapeta to several additional contacts on the fly, leading Hapeta to declare that Urban Native Son "made this LA part tick and work properly."[28] In another instance, Hapeta even received help from the New Zealand ambassador to the Philippines, who, despite knowing of Hapeta's leftist politics, aided him in meeting locals and avoiding travel problems.[29] Hapeta viewed his network as the result of shared openness and reciprocity among artists and activists, so much so that he felt "like I can go and see any of these people in ten years' time" and the links will remain strong.[30] "Activists are the best people on the planet," he continued. They "give up contacts no problem, not like the music business! . . . With activism it's about something greater than your career, greater than the music industry. It's about people's lives for real. People living and dying. So people are all too willing to share their links."[31] Utopia in *Ngātahi* was more than an on-screen representation; rather, as Herman

Gray elaborated, it was its own politics of articulation that asked "how and where different and sometimes unsettling alternative visions, practices, and forms of organization operate, and with what cultural and political effect."[32]

Ngātahi was also a reminder that global justice—some might say the utopia of global justice—depended on hard work and small acts.[33] Neither Hapeta nor the Chicanxs in *Ngātahi* generated a world-changing event or anything close to it, but they did seek to create multiple transcendent moments. Their rapping, dancing, poetry, organizing, and freestyle philosophizing bore witness to how cultural labor fostered global justice, recalling Ernst Bloch's claim that everyday life was filled with hopes waiting to be transformed into social and political activity.[34] A contentious and slippery idea, global justice often serves as shorthand for diverse struggles around the planet seeking full and universally realized socioeconomic and civil-political rights.[35] The "full" and "universal" aspects of such a notion are tricky, for they substitute difference and diversity for homogeneity and cohesion. Rather than an abstract set of morals or ethics, institutional or legislative fiat, or even solidarity between distinct social movements or NGOs, *Ngātahi* offered an alternative sense of global justice. Hapeta and the folks in his movies practiced what Fuyuki Kurasawa called "the work of global justice." More than a long-term war of position that rarely entailed victory over the "powers that be,"[36] global justice in *Ngātahi* encompassed organizing a political rally; writing or performing a poem, song, or speech; or painting a mural. If, as Immanuel Wallerstein argued, sustained effort for radical democracy must take place over the middle run and long term, Hapeta, the Chicanxs, and others in *Ngātahi* reminded us that short-term politicization often plants seeds that might take time to bloom.[37] Sketching the links between an abundance of seemingly small feats, *Ngātahi* showed that global justice as an "inter-struggle struggle" was alive and well. It projected global justice as splintered and local, unique to Chicanxs in Los Angeles, but also dialogic and sweeping, powered by connections that extended well beyond Chicanx LA. Rather than assume global justice was an unreachable utopian goal, *Ngātahi* showed that it was routinely attained in the aid, forgiving, redress, and solidarity evident in the cultural creativity of artists and activists.[38]

Like other pop cultural moments of Chicanx utopia before it, *Ngātahi* was not without pitfalls. It hearkened back to the perils and promise of commercialization, begging the question of who actually viewed the films. Though it was screened at many festivals, including Sundance in 2004, Hapeta never actively sought venues or television opportunities. While *Ngātahi #1–2* were screened on Maori television in Aotearoa, *#3* and *#4* were not accepted for television, leading Hapeta to declaim, "Ah, fuck TV in New Zealand! I don't even care to do that. But people have always said to me, 'Man, it should be on TV! People should be seeing it!' And I says, 'Well, I didn't make it for those clowns!'"[39] He preferred to "just put it into stories and let it find its audience," largely through cyberspace and word of mouth in international hip-hop, Indigenous, and activist circles.[40] Like many of the artists he featured in the films, Hapeta rejected the conventional movie, music, and entertainment industry in lieu of working toward the decommodification of hip-hop, film, and politics. Even if it meant fewer viewers, the process of making *Ngātahi* was valuable for what it produced *off-screen*. Hapeta noted, "This is what *Ngātahi: Know the Links* is all about. It's not necessarily about waking up all of those idiots out there. It's necessarily about making links amongst us who fight and resist and have knowledge about how we should go about taking out the beast and that we need to be strong in who we are so that humanity can continue to survive on this planet."[41] *Ngātahi*'s utopia was for those who appeared in the films as much as anyone, suggesting that pop culture isn't always just a reflection of existing politics but can trigger and strengthen social movements and even function as its own movement for change.

At the same time, *Ngātahi* raised questions about who crafted its utopian visions. The Chicanx scenes in LA, as well as those from other cities, for example, were determined by the different ways Hapeta met and engaged men and women. Footage of concerts, rehearsals, and lengthier interviews were mostly with men, perhaps because they were scheduled in advance. Women were more often featured in spontaneous, individual performance pieces, with fewer monologues or long interviews. Hapeta admitted that he had "to work a bit harder" to find women for the films. "I really do go out and look for women as well," he said, "but as a guy, it's easy for me to find guys."[42] As a result, parts of *Ngātahi* mirrored the hypermasculinity of larger hip-hop and entertainment industries and contained traces of the Maori and South Pacific rap and reggae scenes that equated warriors and resistance with manliness.[43] There are uneasy moments when hypermasculine or essentialist politics—not to mention the fetishization of anything or anyone deemed critical of globalization—threatened *Ngātahi*'s inclusive diaspora of dignity. If people experienced assaults against race and class identities in gendered ways, it stood to reason they made links with others on gendered ground.

Nonetheless, as in the case of other Chicanx utopias, gender dynamics in *Ngātahi* raised important questions about how the promise of togetherness, dignity, and everyday utopia was curtailed or even undermined.

Ngātahi's brilliance lay in its links between people and its warnings about how efforts for social change might be derailed or left unrealized. Nor is it always clear how we move from *knowing the links* to addressing the structural and material conditions left in the wake of neoliberalism, differential colonialisms, and uninterrogated nationalisms. If the films provide an answer, it is to constantly regenerate links and utopia anew through everyday culture and politics.

FROM *SALT OF THE EARTH* TO *NGĀTAHI*

It may seem odd to close with *Ngātahi*. Although Chicanx history in Los Angeles may seem incongruent with that of a Maori from Aotearoa, *Ngātahi* put them (and many others) in the same story of pop-cultural utopia. If previous chapters covered the likes of Frances Williams, Shin Miyata, Freddie Prinze, and Favianna Rodriguez, among others, all non-Chicanx figures laboring alongside Chicanxs in pop culture and related social movements, Hapeta was not dissimilar. Earlier figures worked with or in opposition to Mexican American unionists, brown-eyed soul and border reggae artists, sitcom writers and media activists, and poster artists in ways that reimagined Chicanx identity. They practiced a Chicanx identity, culture, and politics infused with interracial relationships and transnational experiences. Their production, consumption, and circulation of popular culture stretched the territorial and racial logics of what it meant to be Chicanx. Aztlán, *mestizaje*, Mexicans, even the US-Mexico border were not always sufficient points of reference for making sense of Chicanx pop culture and history. In light of this longer trajectory, it may not be far-fetched to include *Ngātahi* here.

Albeit from an outside-in sight line, *Ngātahi* showcased how Chicanx utopias in pop culture came to be. Chicanx visions of the future were the product of hard work, cultural exchange and collaboration, deep connections to local places, and an understanding that building a new world depended on acute recognition of the past and present. Chicanx utopias were less objects of study than historically grounded analytic categories that help us understand how Chicanxs made sense of the world around them.[44] Pop culture helps us see Chicanx utopias more clearly because it is one place where they can be glimpsed and where they were given license to be imagined. Chicanx pop culture also reminds us that utopia is not a privilege afforded only to those with great amounts of monetary wealth and power. In fact, its history demonstrates that folks with the least money and political pull might have the most to teach us about how to imagine a better world. From *Salt of the Earth* to *Ngātahi*, the utopian imagination was an everyday struggle that rested on cultural labor. Rather than think of utopia as an ever-elusive ideal society or a massive transformation that solved everyone's problems, Chicanx pop culture shows us it is an ongoing process that, if we're lucky, consists of many small moments when a better world is within reach. Such moments may be fleeting and elusive, but they are worth fighting for.

Acknowledgments

Many folks made this book possible. Kerry Webb was a joy to work with at the University of Texas Press. Her steady hand as editor and deep engagement with ideas in the book made it better. Andrew Hnatow was a whiz with the logistics, and Robert Devens expressed support and enthusiasm at every opportunity. Carlos Blanton and Lorrin Thomas are fabulous series editors, and I'm thankful to call them colleagues.

Fellowship support from the Institute for Humanities Research (IHR) at Arizona State University and the Charles Warren Center for Studies in American History at Harvard University were crucial during formative stages of writing. At the IHR in 2009–2010, Director Sally Kitch, Rachel Bowditch, Megha Budruck, Anne Feldhaus, Tracey Fessenden, Ann Kaplan, and Pegge Vissicaro were a fabulous cohort of Fellows to learn from during our weekly seminars on the topics of "Utopias, Dystopias, and Social Transformation." Their feedback on the big ideas that frame the book and early versions of what would become the coda were invaluable. At the Warren Center in 2012–2013, Robin Bernstein and Samuel Zipp convened an extraordinary group of scholars for their seminar "Everyday Life: The Textures and Politics of the Ordinary, Persistent, and Repeated." Jayna Brown, Bruce Dorsey, Karen Hansen, Martha Hodes, David Jaffee, Ann Pellegrini, Kyla Wazana Tompkins, Sara Warner, and Harvey Young provided friendship and generative collegiality. Their response to an early version of chapter 1—along with the extensive notes by the Warren Center administrative director Arthur Patton-Hock—was outstanding. Additionally, a Manuscript Forum grant from the Institute of Arts and Humanities (IAH) at UC San Diego was crucial in securing images and copyright permissions.

Huge thanks to Sandra Garcia-Meyers and staff at the Cinematic Arts Library and David L. Wolper Center at the University of Southern California; Christine Marine and staff in Chicano/a Research Collection and Special Collections at Arizona State University; Carol Wells and staff from the Center for the Study of Political Graphics in Los Angeles; and staff from the Department of Special Collections at UC Santa Barbara. Their mastery of the archives and willingness to always dig up additional material or provide new leads was invaluable. My extra special appreciation goes to Carol Wells for her incredibly close and thoughtful reading of chapter 4. Thanks, too, to the staff at Getty Images in Los Angeles for their assistance with images for chapters 2 and 3.

My heartfelt thank-you and admiration to all of the artists, musicians, actors, and activists who appear in this book. Their tireless labor and extraordinary creativity made me want to write this book and remind me that a better world is possible. I am especially grateful to Lalo Alcaraz, Melanie Cervantes, Raoul Deal, Favianna Rodriguez, and Mark Vallen for agreeing to have their beautiful images appear in the book. Melanie Cervantes and Raoul Deal also offered instrumental comments on chapter 4.

Chapter 2 is a revised version of a chapter that previously appeared in Brian Behnken's excellent anthology *The Struggle in Black and Brown: African American and Mexican American Relations during the Civil Rights Era*. It was coauthored with Daniel Widener, and his intellectual stamp remains on the version in this book. Our original chapter was made better by Brian Behnken's feedback.

I first toyed with the ideas in chapter 3 as a contributor to Carlos Blanton's exciting anthology *A Promising Problem: The New Chicana/o History*. His generative feedback, along with that of fellow contributors during our seminar hosted by the History Department and Glasscock Center for Humanities Research at Texas A&M University, helped shape my thinking as my early thoughts grew into the chapter in this book. Many thanks to Carlos Blanton, Michael Olivas, Lilia Fernandez, Perla Guerrero, Felipe Hinojosa, and Sonia Hernandez for their comradery and brilliant discussions.

An earlier version of chapter 5 previously appeared in Alejandro L. Madrid's exceptional volume *Transnational Encounters: Music and Performance at the U.S.-Mexico Border*. It benefited greatly from our contributors seminar at the University of Illinois, Chicago, in 2010, which included Alejandro L. Madrid, Sydney Hutchinson, Mark C. Edberg, Donald Henriques, José Limón, Helena Simonett, Joan Titus, Jesús

Ramos-Kittrell, Margaret Dorsey, Miguel Díaz-Barriga, Josh Kun, Ignacio Corona, Estevan Azcona, Brenda Romero, Lillian Gorman, Cathy Ragland, and Ramón Rivera-Servera.

I am grateful for many wonderful friends and colleagues at UC San Diego and beyond who helped shape this book in ways big and small. Extra special thanks go to Dave Gutiérrez and Danny Widener for always having my back and blazing a trail for me to follow. Many more thanks are due to friends and colleagues who read chapter drafts, helped me make sense of what I wanted to say, or invited me to participate in lectures or conferences over the years where the pieces of this book came together, including Carlos Blanton, Mary Pat Brady, Rachel Buff, Juan Flores, Alan Gómez, Nicole Guidotti-Hernández, Frank Guridy, Dave Gutiérrez, Felipe Hinojosa, George Lipsitz, John Márquez, Anthony Macías, Verónica Martínez, Natalia Molina, Alicia Schmidt Camacho, Nayan Shah, Victor Viesca, Helena María Viramontes, Danny Widener, Howie Winant, and Emilio Zamora.

I finished writing this book while on sabbatical with my family in Barcelona, Catalunya, in 2019–2020. Despite the COVID-19 pandemic, it was a magical year because of the amazing group of friends we made. A massive shout-out to the entire Friyays crew, especially Thomas Kunambi, Arnold Lee, Mark Liu, David Lynch, and Akida Mashaka. Their friendship, adventurous spirit, and late-night chats about music, politics, and everything else under the sun fueled my writing. See you all back on the plaza soon!

Marilyn Espitia gave me the love, time, and space necessary to write this book. Our two amazing daughters—Hesley and Indira—remind me every day of life's extraordinary possibilities. Without them, this book would not be.

Notes

INTRODUCTION

1. As discussed at the end of this introduction, I embrace the terms "Chicanx" and "Latinx" as a gender-inclusive way of referring to people of Mexican and Latin American descent in the United States. Since many of the figures and moments discussed in this book populated time periods before the terms entered common usage, however, I also make use of the terms Mexican American, Chicana/o, or Latina/o as applicable.
2. Gray, *Watching Race*, 2.
3. Benjamin, *The Arcades Project*.
4. Ransby and Matthews, "Black Popular Culture," 535.
5. Levitas, *Utopia as Method*, xiii.
6. Hall, "Notes on Deconstructing 'The Popular,'" 227–240.
7. Buck-Morss, *Dreamworld and Catastrophe*.
8. Harvey, *A Brief History of Neoliberalism*, 2.
9. Dávila, *Barrio Dreams*, 9. See also Comaroff and Comaroff, "Millennial Capitalism," 291–343.
10. Dávila, *Barrio Dreams*, 8.
11. Gutiérrez, "The Politics of the Interstices," 89–120; Chambers, *Room for Maneuver*.
12. Berlant, *Cruel Optimism*, 2.
13. Following well-established understandings of race as a social construct with historical and material consequences, I use the term "interracial" to refer to ways in which processes of racial formation and experiences of racialization occurred between and within different racial groups, often in the context of cultural or political expression and exchange.
14. Guterl, *Seeing Race in Modern America*, 10–11.
15. Fischlin, Heble, and Lipsitz, *The Fierce Urgency of Now*, xix.
16. Reed, *The Art of Protest*, xiii.
17. Lipsitz, *Time Passages*.

18. Levitas, *Utopia as Method*, xii.
19. Merriam-Webster, s.v. "impulse," https://www.merriam-webster.com/dictionary/impulse.
20. Kelley, *Race Rebels*, 8.
21. Dolan, *Utopia and Performance*, 5, 6, 13.
22. Goldfarb, *The Politics of Small Things*.
23. Ernst Bloch, quoted in Korstvedt, *Listening for Utopia*, 3.
24. Grossberg, *Cultural Studies in the Future Tense*, 278.
25. Berlant, *Cruel Optimism*, 8.
26. Stuart Hall, oral presentation, Minneapolis, Minnesota, April 3, 1987, quoted in Lipsitz, *Time Passages*, 260.
27. Alicia Schmidt Camacho notes that imaginaries function as a "symbolic field in which people come to understand and describe their social being." Camacho, *Migrant Imaginaries*, 5.
28. Grewal, *Transnational America*, 23. Grewal notes the complex and multiple characters of transnational "connectivities" (as opposed to outright "connections") where there are a "variety of connections that exist," "strong and weak connectivities," and that we need to examine "how some get translated and transcoded, how some are unevenly connected, others strongly connected, and still others [are] incommensurable and untranslatable." Ibid.
29. Cooper, *Everyday Utopias*, 3.
30. Ibid., 2, 3; Levitas, *Utopia as Method*.
31. Stewart, *Ordinary Affects*, 1–2.
32. Bloch, *Utopian Function of Art and Literature*, 12.
33. Bloch, *Principle of Hope*. For trenchant discussion of Bloch's writing on utopia, especially relative to music, see Levitas, "Singing Summons the Existence of the Fountain," 219–245; Korstvedt, *Listening for Utopia in Ernst Bloch's Musical Philosophy*.
34. Jacoby, *Picture Imperfect*, xiv; Levitas, *Utopia as Method*, xvi.
35. Abensour, *Utopia*; Williams, "Utopia and Science Fiction," 208. Elaborating on Abensour's observation, Raymond Williams noted the strengths and weaknesses of "heuristic" and "systematic" utopias. "Heuristic" utopias, he observed, functioned as a "vision against the grain" that "can settle into isolated and in the end sentimental desire." "Systematic" utopias expressed a "strength of conviction that the world really can be different," but "in its insistent organization, it seems to offer little room for any recognizable life." Ibid.
36. Storey, *Radical Utopianism and Cultural Studies*, 11, 2.
37. Bowditch and Vissicaro, *Performing Utopia*, 6.
38. Levitas, *Utopia as Method*, xiii.
39. Molina, "Examining Chicana/o History," 522.
40. See, for instance, Molina, *How Race Is Made in America*; Rosas, *South Central Is Home*; Márquez, *Black-Brown Solidarity*; Behnken, *Fighting Their Own Battles*; Araiza, *To March for Others*; Mantler, *Power to the Poor*; Guerrero, *Nuevo*

South; Ortiz, *An African American and Latinx History of the United States*; Widener, *Black Arts West*; Johnson, *Spaces of Conflict, Sounds of Solidarity*.

41. Molina, *How Race Was Made in America*.
42. Hong and Ferguson, *Strange Affinities*, 18.
43. Widener, *Black Arts West*, 14–15.
44. Johnson, *Spaces of Conflict, Sounds of Solidarity*, x.
45. Marquez, *Black-Brown Solidarity*, 14.
46. See, for instance, Habell-Pallán, *Loca Motion*; Gómez, *The Revolutionary Imaginations of Greater Mexico*; Rosas, *Abrazando El Espíritu*; Rueda, *Students of Revolution*.
47. Seminal studies that inspire this approach include Lipsitz, *Time Passages*; Kelley, *Race Rebels*; Reed, *The Art of Protest*.
48. Gordin, Tilley, and Prakash, *Utopia/Dystopia*, 4.
49. Sánchez, *Becoming Mexican American*; Macías, *Mexican American Mojo*; Ramírez, *The Woman in the Zoot Suit*; Ruiz, *From Out of the Shadows*; Johnson, *Spaces of Conflict, Sounds of Solidarity*.
50. Featherstone and Miles, "Utopias: An Introduction," 129.
51. See, for example, Hébert, "Worlds Not Yet in Being," https://journals.openedition.org/am/604; Holloway and Peláez, *Zapatista! Reinventing Revolution in Mexico*; Khasnabish, *Zapatismo Beyond Borders*; Esteva and Prakash, *Grassroots Postmodernism*; Callahan, "Why Not Share a Dream?," 6–37; Graeber, "The New Anarchists," 61–73.
52. Hidalgo, *Revelation in Aztlán*; López-Lozano, *Utopian Dreams, Apocalyptic Nightmares*.
53. See, for example, Zamalin, *Black Utopia*; Johnson and Lubin, *Futures of Black Radicalism*. For a provocative discussion of the intersections between Afrofuturism and Chicanafuturism in science fiction, see Ramírez, "Afrofuturism/Chicanafuturism: Fictive Kin," 185–194.
54. Vincent, "Black Hopes in Baja California," 204–213; McBroome, "Harvests of Gold," 149–180; McBroome, "All Men Up and No Man Down," 59–84.
55. Chan and Ventura, "Introduction: Articulating Race and Utopia," 2.
56. Zamalin, *Black Utopia*, 11.
57. Flores, "Reclaiming Left Baggage," 187–206.
58. Guidotti-Hernández, *Unspeakable Violence*, 14.
59. Reed, *The Art of Protest*, xvii.
60. Levitas, *Utopia as Method*, xi.
61. Gordin, Tilley, and Prakash, *Utopia/Dystopia*, 3, 4.

CHAPTER 1: SALT OF THE EARTH

1. "New Mexicans Parade Against Leftist Film," *Los Angeles Times*, March 5, 1953.

2. *Congressional Record*, 83rd Congress, 1st Session, February 24, 1953, vol. 99, Part 1, 1371–1372.

3. Elizabeth Kerby, "Violence in Silver City: Who Caused the Trouble?," *Frontier: The Voice of the New West*, May 1953, pages 5–10, Clinton Jencks Papers, Department of Archives and Special Collections, University Libraries, Arizona State University (hereafter CJP), Mss. 137, Box 1, Folder 13.

4. *Variety*, March 17, 1954; and *New York Times*, March 15, 1954, both in CJP, Mss. 137, Box 1, Folder 14.

5. Pfaelzer, "*Salt of the Earth*," 121.

6. Lorence, *The Suppression of* Salt of the Earth; Baker, *On Strike and on Film*; Balthaser, "Cold War Re-Visions," 347–371; Camacho, *Migrant Imaginaries*, especially chapter three, "No Constitution for Us: Class Racism and Cold War Unionism."

7. Camacho, *Migrant Imaginaries*; Baker, *On Strike and on Film*.

8. Cooper, *Everyday Utopias*, 7.

9. Pfaelzer, "*Salt of the Earth*," 121.

10. Holloway, "Dignity's Revolt," 159–198.

11. Gutiérrez, *Walls and Mirrors*, 161.

12. Camacho, *Migrant Imaginaries*, 115–119. Camacho considers the deportation of Revueltas in the same vein as the targeted arrests and persecution of several other Latina radical activists in the 1950s, including Luisa Moreno, Josefina Fierro, and Emma Tenayuca.

13. Scott, *Domination and the Arts of Resistance*, xii.

14. Efforts to curtail the power of labor unions during the Cold War were enhanced by the 1947 Taft-Hartley Act that severely limited the ability of unions to organize for worker rights in the name of national security and states' rights. Taft-Hartley is widely considered to be at least a partial repeal of the 1935 Wagner Act, or National Labor Relations Act. It paved the way for the National Labor Relations Board (NLRB) oversight of union elections, cracked down on cross-union solidarity by banning secondary boycotts and sympathy strikes, and required union leaders to disavow the Communist Party in writing. For a detailed description of Taft-Hartley, see Lipsitz, *Rainbow at Midnight*, 171–179.

15. Cargill, "Empire and Opposition," 189; Weinberg, "*Salt of the Earth*," 41; Lorence, *The Suppression of* Salt of the Earth, 25–26; Baker, *On Strike and on Film*; Camacho, *Migrant Imaginaries*, 121–122.

16. Baker, *On Strike and on Film*, 102–103.

17. García, "Mexican American Labor and the Left," 65–86; Gutiérrez, *Walls and Mirrors*, 173; Camacho, *Migrant Imaginaries*, 125–127; Baker, *On Strike and on Film*, 102–107; Lorence, *The Suppression of* Salt of the Earth, 8–11.

18. Gómez-Quiñones, *Mexican American Labor, 1790–1990*; Vargas, *Labor Rights Are Civil Rights*.

19. Baker, *On Strike and on Film*, 203–204.

20. Lorence, *The Suppression of* Salt of the Earth, 58.

21. Ceplair, *The Marxist and the Movies*, 137–145; Baker, *On Strike and on Film*, 202–205; Lipsitz, *Rainbow at Midnight*, 292; Lorence, *The Suppression of* Salt of the Earth, 56–62.

22. "Mexicans Demand Release of 'Race' Film Actress," *Atlanta Daily World*, March 3, 1953.

23. The making of *Salt* thus functioned as what Mary Louise Pratt calls a "contact zone." Pratt explains contact zones as "the spatial and temporal copresence of subjects previously separated by geographical and historical disjunctures, whose trajectories now intersect." Pratt, *Imperial Eyes*, 7.

24. Chacón, "Union Made," 180.

25. Biberman, *Salt of the Earth*, 81–82. Biberman's book was initially published in 1965 to little fanfare. Like the film, it garnered more attention in later years and was republished.

26. Ibid., 83–84.

27. Chacón, "Union Made," 182.

28. Michael Wilson, quoted in Deborah Silverton Rosenfelt, "Commentary," in Wilson, *Salt of the Earth*, 127–128.

29. Jarrico and Biberman, "Breaking Ground," 170.

30. Lipsitz, *Rainbow at Midnight*, 292.

31. Clinton Jencks, quoted in Baker, *On Strike and on Film*, 217.

32. *Congressional Record*, 83rd Congress, 1st Session, February 24, 1953, vol. 99, Part 1, 1371–1372.

33. Chacón, "Union Made," 180.

34. Clinton Jencks, quoted in Rosenfelt, "Commentary," 117.

35. Rosenfelt, "Commentary," 118.

36. Unnamed document, CJP, Mss. 137, Box 1, Folder 13.

37. Paul Jarrico, quoted in Ceplair, *The Marxist and the Movies*, 141.

38. Biberman, *Salt of the Earth*, 55.

39. Christian, *Meet It, Greet It, and Defeat It*, 161.

40. "Biography," Frances E. Williams Papers, 1965–1995 (Mss. 086); "Frances E. Williams, Actress, 89, Is Dead," *New York Times*, January 12, 1995, p. B11; Christian, "Frances E. Williams."

41. Williams, "To Hell with Bandannas," interview.

42. Christian, *Meet It, Greet It, and Defeat It*, 157–166.

43. Williams, "To Hell with Bandannas," interview.

44. Ibid.

45. Chacón, "Union Made."

46. "What's New in Labor," August 1954, CJP, Mss. 137, Box 1, Folder 14.

47. Christian, *Meet It, Greet It, and Defeat It*, 161.

48. Ibid.; Williams, "To Hell with Bandannas," interview.

49. Lorence, *The Suppression of* Salt of the Earth, 59.

50. Christian, *Meet It, Greet It, Defeat It*, 162–163.

51. Wilson, *Salt of the Earth*, 130.

52. Ibid., 166.
53. Bernstein, *Bridges of Reform*.
54. Rosenfelt, "Commentary," 94, 153.
55. Baker, *On Strike and on Film*, 11.
56. May, *Homeward Bound*.
57. Camacho, *Migrant Imaginaries*, 120.
58. Baker, *On Strike and on Film*, 213–214.
59. Ibid., 170–171.
60. Weinberg, *Salt of the Earth*, 43.
61. Rosenfelt, "Commentary," 141.
62. José Fuentes, quoted in Rosenfelt, "Commentary," 142.
63. Camacho, *Migrant Imaginaries*, 134.
64. Baker, *On Strike and on Film*, 246.
65. Rosenfelt, "Commentary," 142.
66. Ibid., 95.
67. Ibid., 107.
68. *La Prensa*, San Antonio, Texas, February-March, 1953.
69. Camacho, *Migrant Imaginaries*, 119–121.
70. *Congressional Record*, 83rd Congress, 1st Session, February 24, 1953, vol. 99, Part 1, 1371–1372.
71. Balthaser, "Cold War Revisions," 347–371.
72. Gómez-Quiñones, *Mexican American Labor, 1790–1990*, 186.
73. On the transborder organizing of Mine-Mill, see Vargas, *Labor Rights Are Civil Rights*, 168–170.
74. Von Eschen, *Race Against Empire*; Dudziak, *Cold War Civil Rights*; Borstelman, *The Cold War and the Color Line*.
75. Hobsbawm, *The Age of Extremes*.

CHAPTER 2: BROWN-EYED SOUL

This chapter was originally coauthored with Daniel Widener and appeared in *The Struggle in Black and Brown: African American and Mexican American Relations during the Civil Rights Era*, edited by Brian D. Behnken (Lincoln: University of Nebraska Press, 2011), 211–236.

1. Don Snowden, "Latino Bands—High-Riders of the Future?" *Los Angeles Times*, January 8, 1984, p. 60.

2. Ibid.; Macías, "California's Composer Laureate," 34–51; Loza, *Barrio Rhythm*, 102–104; McCarthy, *Voices of Latin Rock*, 16–17; El Chicano, accessed July 18, 2019, http://www.elchicanomusic.com/.

3. Rodriguez, *Guide to the Eddie Davis West Coast East Side Sound Archive*, n.p.

4. Buddy Seigal, "Chicano Rock Will Add Spice to Holiday Fiesta," *Los Angeles Times*, July 4, 1994, p. OCF3.
5. Ibid.
6. Levitas and Moylan, "Introduction: The Once and Future Orpheus," 205–206. Levitas and Moylan ask "whether there is something distinctly utopian in the objects related to music (be it the music itself, the lyrics, the performance, and/or the social constellations clustered around the production and reception of music)" (ibid., 206).
7. Chávez, *Sounds of Crossing*, 7.
8. Johnson, *Spaces of Conflict, Sounds of Solidarity*, 193.
9. Molina, "The Importance of Place-Makers," 71.
10. Hidalgo, *Revelation in Aztlan*, 4.
11. Zamalin, *Black Utopia*, 6.
12. Muñoz, *Cruising Utopia*, 4.
13. Macías, "California's Composer Laureate."
14. For a discussion of multiracial patterns in wartime Los Angeles, see, for example, Alvarez, *The Power of the Zoot*; Macías, *Mexican American Mojo*; Leonard, *The Battle for Los Angeles*; Varzally, *Making a Non-White America*.
15. Grendysa, "The Making of Rhythm and Blues," n.p.
16. Widener, "Perhaps the Japanese Are to Be Thanked?," 135–181; Macías, "Rock con Raza, Raza con Jazz."
17. Robinson, *After Camps*; Greg Robinson, "The Great Unknown and the Unknown Great: African American Attorney Was Defender of Japanese Americans during World War II," *Nichi Bei Times Weekly* (Los Angeles), June 7, 2007, 1, 5; Kurashige, *The Shifting Grounds of Race*; Leonard, "'In the Interest of All Races,'" 309–340.
18. Alvarez, *The Power of the Zoot*; Leonard, *The Battle for Los Angeles*; Pagán, *Murder at the Sleepy Lagoon*; Escobar, *Race, Police, and the Making of a Political Identity*.
19. Johnson, "Constellations of Struggle," 156–157; Johnson, *Spaces of Conflict, Sounds of Solidarity*.
20. Horne, *Fire This Time*; McGirr, *Suburban Warriors*; Matthew Dallek, *The Right Moment*.
21. Bernstein, *Bridges of Reform*.
22. "2009 Persons Attend Cultural Programs at Soto, Michigan," *California Eagle*, November 23, 1952.
23. Sánchez, "What's Good for Boyle Heights Is Good for the Jews," 633–661.
24. Reyes and Waldman, *Land of a Thousand Dances*, 13.
25. Ibid.
26. Ibid., 33.
27. Millar, "Chicano Rock: Down Mexico Way," 16–17; Lipsitz, *Time Passages*, 140–143.

28. Garcia, *A World of Its Own*.
29. Macías, *Mexican American Mojo*, 4–5.
30. Bryant et al., *Central Avenue Sounds*.
31. Macías, *Mexican American Mojo*, 159–160.
32. Kun, "The Tijuana Sound," 246.
33. Ruiz, *On the Rim of Mexico*, 51.
34. Balkan, "Way Out West on Central," 43–45.
35. Lipsitz, *How Racism Takes Place*.
36. Allan and Bruce Phillips, interview by Josh Kun, August 18, 2011, http://phillipsmusiccompany.tumblr.com.
37. Reed Johnson, "Celebrating a Piece of Boyle Heights History," *Los Angeles Times*, August 27, 2011; Jessica Perez, "The Democracy of Music in Boyle Heights," *Boyle Heights Beat*, August 4, 2011.
38. Sánchez, "What's Good for Boyle Heights Is Good for the Jews," 644–645.
39. Johnson, "Celebrating a Piece of Boyle Heights History."
40. Narváez, "Influences of Hispanic Cultures," 175–196.
41. Johnson, "'Sobre Las Olas,'" 225–237.
42. Narváez, "Influences of Hispanic Cultures," 211.
43. For detailed accounts of the musical history of the Eastside sound in the 1960s, see Molina, *Chicano Soul Music*; Reyes and Waldman, *Land of a Thousand Dances*; *Chicano Rock! The Sounds of East Los Angeles* (Latino Public Broadcasting, 2008), directed by Jon Wilkman; *Brown Eyed Soul: The Sound from East LA Vol. 1–3* (Rhino Records, 1997).
44. Ernst Bloch famously contended that music was the most socially conditioned of the arts, a crucial observation to which I might add only that society is also musically conditioned.
45. Rando, *Hope and Wish Image in Music Technology*, 23.
46. Dolan, *Utopia in Performance*, 7.
47. Muñoz, *Cruising Utopia*, 3.
48. Molina, *Chicano Soul Music*; Del Barco, "The Story of 'Whittier Blvd.'"
49. Ibid.
50. Rando, *Hope and Wish Image in Music Technology*, 7.
51. Don Snowden, "The Sound of East LA, 1964," *Los Angeles Times*, October 28, 1984, p. T6.
52. Mark Guerrero, "The Premieres," personal website and archive, https://markguerrero.net/11.php. Son of the legendary Chicano musician Lalo Guerrero and former front man for his band Mark and the Escorts, Guerrero hosts a website and archive of original articles on Chicano music history, many based on oral histories with artists active since the 1960s.
53. Mark Guerrero, "The Blendells," personal website and archive, https://markguerrero.net/12.php.
54. "Photo Standalone 16—No Title," *Los Angeles Sentinel*, January 25, 1968, p. B8.

55. Richard Cromelin, "Latinos Send a Big Sign to R&B Singer Brenton Wood," *Los Angeles Times*, August 21, 1992.
56. Ibid.
57. Rando, *Hope and Wish Image in Music Technology*, 35.
58. Fischlin, Heble, and Lipsitz, *The Fierce Urgency of Now*, xv.
59. Cromelin, "Latinos Send a Big Sign to R&B Singer Brenton Wood."
60. Ersi Arvizu, interview by Mark Guerrero, August 31, 2019. Aired on *Mark Guerrero's Chicano Music Chronicles* podcast.
61. Vargas, *Dissonant Divas in Chicana Music*, ix.
62. Ibid., xiv.
63. *West Coast Eastside Sound Documentary*, chapter one, "The Eddie Davis Story," http://cemaweb.library.ucsb.edu/musicWCESS.html. Eddie Davis West Coast East Side Sound Archives, CEMA.
64. Ibid.
65. Ibid.; Ben Quiñones, "Naa Na Na Na Naa," *LA Weekly*, December 29, 2005; Billy Cardenas, interview by Mark Guerrero, June 2, 2019, aired on *Mark Guerrero's Chicano Music Chronicles* podcast.
66. For an extensive archive of posters and flyers, see Mark Guerrero, "'60s Eastside Flyers," https://markguerrero.net/flyers.php.
67. Macías, "Bringing Music to the People," 693–717; Garcia, *A World of Its Own*.
68. Cooper, *Everyday Utopias*, 2.
69. Snowden, "The Sound of East LA, 1964."
70. Chávez, *Sounds of Crossing*, 7.
71. Martin Hawkins, "Tex Mex Makes Your Feet Smile," *Melody Maker*, March 22, 1980; Peña, *Música Tejana*, 155–158.
72. Young, *Soul Power*; Pulido, *Black, Brown, Yellow, and Left*.
73. Oropeza, *¡Raza Si! ¡Guerra No!*; Ernesto Chavez, *¡Mi Raza Primero! (My People First)*.
74. Mariscal, *Brown-eyed Children of the Sun*.
75. Araiza, *To March for Others*.
76. Rosas, *South Central Is Home*.
77. Lipsitz, *American Studies in a Moment of Danger*; Young, *Soul Power*.
78. West Coast Eastside Sound Documentary, chapter three, "The Vietnam Draft," http://cemaweb.library.ucsb.edu/Davis3.html.
79. Snowden, "The Sound of East LA, 1964."
80. Robert Hilburn, "Chicano Rock on Bill at Cal State LA," *Los Angeles Times*, September 16, 1972, p. 6; Snowden, "Latino Bands."
81. Hilburn, "Chicano Rock on Bill at Cal State LA."
82. Dennis Hunt, "War: Warriors in Recording Industry Combat," *Los Angeles Times*, August 19, 1973, p. 50; Sharon Lawrence, "Burdon Tries New Musical Direction with War Group," *Los Angeles Times*, July 17, 1970, p. 15; Mike Jahn, "Eric Burdon Bows with New Group," *New York Times*, September 27, 1970, p. 84.

83. Ann Powers, "Broken Barriers and Disk Generosity," *New York Times*, November 13, 1992, p. 7.
84. Keith Altham, "War: The Battle Against Unlove," *New Musical Express*, July 21, 1973.
85. Storey, *Radical Utopianism and Cultural Studies*, 1.
86. Davis, "Uprising and Repression in LA," 142.
87. MIWON is a coalition of five immigrant rights organizations: the Coalition for Humane Immigrant Rights (CHIRLA), Koreatown Immigrant Workers Alliance (KIWA), Instituto de Educación Popular del Sur de California (IDEPSCA), the Garment Worker Center (GWC), and the Pilipino Workers Center (PWC). MIWON has been active since 1999.
88. Widener, "Another City Is Possible," 188–219.
89. Doss, "Choosing Chicano in the 1990s," 191–202; Kun, *Audiotopia*; Viesca, "The Battle of Los Angeles," 719–739.
90. Kun, *Audiotopia*, 219.
91. Viesca, "The Battle of Los Angeles," 731.
92. Gonzalez, *Chican@ Artivistas*.
93. Widener, "Radical Rhythms," 25.
94. Fogelson, *The Fragmented Metropolis*.
95. Baraka, "The Changing Same."
96. Hector Becerra, "Eastside Record Label Still Spinning Out the Music," *Los Angeles Times*, January 8, 2013.
97. Ibid.
98. Mark Guerrero, "Shin Miyata: Chicano Music's Bridge to Japan," http://www.markguerrero.com/misc_63.php, based on Guerrero's interview of Miyata on December 9, 2007; interview with Shin Miyata on "Discos Immigrantes," April 24, 2012, aired on Radio Sombra, a community-based internet radio station in Boyle Heights, East Los Angeles.
99. Benjamin, *The Author as Producer*, 220–238.
100. Levitas, *"In eine bess're Welt entrückt,"* 220–221.

CHAPTER 3: *CHICO AND KOTTER*

1. Alicia Sandoval and Paul Macías, "Chico and the Man: Some Chicanos Are Not Amused," *Los Angeles Times*, October 27, 1974. Sandoval was a USC PhD candidate in education and a local talk show host. Macías was an actor at Universal Studios and a member of the Teatro Nacional de Aztlán (TENAZ), a national network of Chicana/o theater groups.
2. Formisano, *Boston Against Busing*; Delmont, *Why Busing Failed*.
3. Gregg Kilday, "Kotter Unwelcome: Boston Bans ABC Comedy," *Los Angeles Times*, August 28, 1975, p. E31.
4. Gray, *Watching Race*, xiv.

5. Cooper, *Everyday Utopias*, 3. Cooper draws this assessment from the scholarship of Ruth Levitas, who, in turn, built on the seminal, three-volume work on utopian studies by Ernst Bloch, *The Principle of Hope*.

6. Levitas, "In eine bess're Welt entrückt," 324.

7. Chan and Ventura, "Introduction: Articulating Race and Utopia."

8. Brooks and Marshe, *The Complete Directory*.

9. Berger, *The Hidden 1970s*.

10. Dávila, *Barrio Dreams*, 10–11.

11. Ibid., 10–11.

12. Rando, *Hope and Wish Image in Music Technology*, 22.

13. It is worth noting that Freddie Prinze's portrayal of Chico occasionally disrupted the "macho" masculine trope.

14. Spigel, *Make Room for TV*; Gray, *Watching Race*.

15. Flach, "Tell It Like It Is"; Lear, *Even This I Get to Experience*.

16. Deeny Kaplan, "An Interview with Norman Lear and James Komack," *Millimeter*, September 1977, David L. Wolper Collection, USC Warner Bros. Archive (hereafter DWC), Box 266; "Producer Is Caught in Race Controversy," *Journal Herald*, Dayton, Ohio, October 6, 1975, DWC, Box 265, Folder 027, Press Clippings 1975 (originals).

17. Gray, *Watching Race*, xvii.

18. Acham, *Revolution Televised*.

19. For a rich case study of Latina/o viewership of a 1970s TV sitcom, see Chávez-García, "Coming Home to *The Brady Bunch*," 430–460.

20. Dávila, *Barrio Dreams*; Davis, *Magical Urbanism*; Villa, *Barrio-Logos*; De Genova and Ramos-Zayas, *Latino Crossings*.

21. Brooks and Marshe, *The Complete Directory*.

22. Ibid.

23. "Freddie Prinze: Too Much, Too Soon," *Time*, February 7, 1977, p. 37. Following Prinze's death, the network considered canceling the series. Instead, it continued with Chico having left Ed's garage to go into business with his father. In his stead, a twelve-year-old runaway from Mexico named Raul became the new "chico" and sidekick to Ed.

24. Justicia press release, January 30, 1974, DWC, Box 262, Folder 007, "Chicano and the Man, Publicity (Chicano Community)."

25. Zamalin, *Black Utopia*, 11–12.

26. Cecil Smith, "Why Shouldn't a Hunga-Rican Play a Chicano?" *Tulsa World*, December 15, 1974, DWC, Box 262, Folder 16, "Chico Press Clippings, '74 copies."

27. "NBC Insults the Chicano Community," undated press release, Cal State, Los Angeles, DWC, Box 22, Folder 21, "T.V. Series-Correspondence."

28. Sandoval and Macías, "Chico and the Man: Some Chicanos Are Not Amused."

29. Mark Littman, "Chicano Group Raps 'Chico,'" October 25, 1974, DWC, Box 22, Folder 21, "T.V. Series-Correspondence."

30. "What It Is, Que Onda or Lowriders vs. Chico and the Man," *Lowrider Magazine*, January, 1977, 3.

31. Littman, "Chicano Group Raps 'Chico.'"

32. Letter from the Los Angeles Hispanic Urban Center to NBC president Robert Howard, reprinted in "Under Fire: Chico and the Man," *Los Angeles Times*, September 30, 1974.

33. John H. Brinsley, Letter to the Editor, "Chico and the Man," *Los Angeles Times*, November 18, 1974.

34. "NBC Insults the Chicano Community," undated press release, Cal State, Los Angeles, DWC, Box 22, Folder 21, "T.V. Series-Correspondence."

35. Noriega, *Shot in America*, 71.

36. Charles Witbeck, "Komack Knows Comedy," *Baltimore Sun*, December 1, 1974, DWC, Box 262, Folder 16, "Chico Press Clippings, '74 copies."

37. Al Antezak, "Chico and the Man Program Protested," *Texas Catholic*, October 11, 1974, DWC, Box 262, Folder 16, "Chico Press Clippings, '74 copies."

38. "'Chico' Had a Rocky Beginning," Associated Press, *Lakeland Ledger*, April 28, 1975.

39. "NBC Insults the Chicano Community," undated press release, Cal State, Los Angeles.

40. Mark Littman, "Chicano Group Raps 'Chico.'"

41. Letter to Mr. Arthur L. Ginsburg, Chief Complaints Board, Complaints and Compliance Department Broadcast Bureau, Federal Communications Commission, Washington, DC, from Migdia Varela, Los Angeles, CA, undated, DWC, Box 22, Folder 21, "T.V. Series-Correspondence."

42. Penny Anderson, "'Chico' Associate Producer Is the Real Chicano," *Toledo Times*, December 19, 1974, DWC, Box 262, Folder 16, "Chico Press Clippings, '74 copies."

43. Ibid.

44. "Chico's Associate Producer Andrade Unhappy over Show's Chicano Image," *Daily Variety*, September 19, 1974; Oguss, "Whose Barrio Is It?," 3–21.

45. "NBC Insults the Chicano Community," undated press release, Cal State, Los Angeles.

46. Ibid.

47. "Chicanos Picket NBC to Protest 'Chico' Content," *Daily Variety*, September 13, 1974, DWC, Box 262, Folder 16, "Chico Press Clippings, '74 copies"; Gary Deeb, "Freddie Prinze Under Attack: Popular Program Draws Some Fire," *The Blade*, Toledo, Ohio, October 1974, DWC, Box 262, Folder 16, "Chico Press Clippings, '74 copies"; Colin Dangaard, "Ban 'Racist' Show, Say Chicanos," *National Star*, October 5, 1974, DWC, Box 262, Folder 16, "Chico Press Clippings, '74 copies."

48. Mark Littman, "Chicano Group Raps 'Chico,'" October 25, 1974.

49. "KNBC-TV License Challenged by Chicanos," *Montebello Comet*, November 21, 1974, DWC, Box 262, Folder 16, "Chico Press Clippings, '74 copies."

50. Ibid.

51. "Chicanos Grouchy about 'Chico'; See Ethnic Putdown by 'The Man,'" *Variety*, October 9, 1974, DWC, Box 262, Folder 16, "Chico Press Clippings, '74 copies."

52. Jim O'Brien, "'Chico' Only Part Chicano," *Philadelphia Daily News*, November 18, 1974, DWC, Box 262, Folder 16, "Chico Press Clippings, '74 copies."

53. Letter to Jimmie Komack from David Wolper, June 26, 1974, DWC, Box 22, Folder 021, "T.V. series—Correspondence."

54. David Wolper, Alan Sacks, memo, December 3, 1974, DWC, Box 22, Folder 021, "T.V. series—Correspondence."

55. "Producer Caught in Race Controversy," *Journal Herald*, Dayton, Ohio, October 6, 1975, DWC, Box 265, Folder 027, "Press Clippings 1975 (originals)."

56. Jim O'Brien, "'Chico' Only Part Chicano," *Philadelphia Daily News*, November 18, 1974, DWC, Box 262, Folder 16, "Chico Press Clippings, '74 copies."

57. Bill Davidson, "Get Out of Here and Take Your Flies with You," *TV Guide*, November 23, 1974, DWC, Box 262, Folder 16, "Chico Press Clippings, '74 copies."

58. Bob Thomas, "How Chico Stayed on Air," *The Baltimore Evening Sun*, April 18, 1975, DWC, Box 263, Folder 16, "Chico Press Clippings, '75 copies."

59. Witbeck, "Komack Knows Comedy."

60. "Streetwise Road to Stardom," *Dallas Morning News*, December 22, 1974, DWC, Box 262, Folder 16, "Chico Press Clippings, '74 copies."

61. Vernon Scott, UPI, *Houston Chronicle*, October 26, 1974, DWC, Box 262, Folder 16, "Chico Press Clippings, '74 copies."

62. "Hot Hungarican," *Newsweek*, November 11, 1974, DWC, Box 262, Folder 16, "Chico Press Clippings, '74 copies."

63. Cecil Smith, "Why Shouldn't a Hunga-Rican Play a Chicano?" *Tulsa World*, December 15, 1974, DWC, Box 262, Folder 16, "Chico Press Clippings, '74 copies."

64. Cecil Smith, "Chico's Casting Loco?," *New Orleans Times-Picayune* (*Los Angeles Times* syndicated), November 10, 1974, DWC, Box 262, Folder 16, "Chico Press Clippings, '74 copies."

65. Betelou Peterson, "Chico's Rolling with the Critical Punches," *St. Louis Globe-Democrat*, November 23, 1974, DWC, Box 262, Folder 16, "Chico Press Clippings, '74 copies."

66. Vernon Scott, "Chicanos Get TV Turn," *Omaha World Herald*, November 3, 1974, DWC, Box 262, Folder 16, "Chico Press Clippings, '74 copies."

67. "Streetwise Road to Stardom," *The Dallas Morning News*, December 22, 1974, DWC, Box 262, Folder 16, "Chico Press Clippings, '74 copies."

68. Davidson, "Get Out of Here and Take Your Flies with You."

69. Lipsitz, *American Studies in a Moment of Danger*, 176.

70. Cooper, *Everyday Utopias*, 3.

71. "Pilot Script," DWC, Box 136, Folder 006; "'Kotter' Survives Ban by Boston," *Seattle Post-Intelligencer*, January 11, 1976, DWC, Box 131, Folder 21.

72. Brooks and Marshe, *The Complete Directory*.

73. "Gabe Says Sweathogs Are Universal," August 30, 1976, *The Capital Times*, Madison, Wisconsin, DWC, Box 265.

74. Kaplan, "An Interview with Norman Lear and James Komack."

75. Memorandum to "welcome back, kotter gang" from Irwin Russell, June 18, 1976, DWC, Box 265.

76. "P.S. 166-Outline (n.d.)," DWC, Box 136, Folder 005.
77. "Gabe Says Sweathogs Are Universal," *Capital Times* (Madison, Wisconsin).
78. David Wiegand, "RIP Arnold Horshack: Was He TV's Gay 'Sweathog'?" *SFGate*, August 14, 2012, https://blog.sfgate.com/dwiegand/2012/08/14/rip-arnold-horshack-was-he-tvs-gay-sweathog/.
79. *Screen Stars*, "Sweathogs' Yearbook," New York, October 1976, DWC, Box 265.
80. Negro Ensemble Company Records, 1967–1993, Schomburg Center for Research in Black Culture, Manuscripts, Archives, and Rare Books Division, The New York Public Library, "Overview" and "Detailed Description."
81. "P.S. 166-Outline (n.d.)," DWC, Box 136, Folder 005.
82. Vernon Scott, "He Sought a Light Touch and Got the Heat Instead," *San Diego Union* (UPI), September 24, 1975, DWC, Box 265, Folder 027, "Press Clippings 1975 (originals); "Welcome Back Kotter's Horshack, 63," *Jewish Press*, August 15, 2012, https://www.jewishpress.com/news/breaking-news/welcome-back-kotters-horshack-63/2012/08/15/.
83. Meredith Blake, "As Arnold Horshack, Ron Palillo was an Iconic TV Nerd—and More," *Los Angeles Times*, August 14, 2012, https://www.latimes.com/entertainment/tv/la-xpm-2012-aug-14-la-et-st-arnold-horshack-welcome-back-kotter-iconic-tv-nerd-20120814-story.html.
84. Wiegand, "RIP Arnold Horshack."
85. "P.S. 166-Outline (n.d.)," DWC, Box 136, Folder 005.
86. Tanny, "A Bad, Bold, Big-Nosed Biblical Brother," 106.
87. "The Return of Hotsy Totsy," *Welcome Back, Kotter*, season 3, episode 26, May 11, 1978.
88. "Angie," *Welcome Back, Kotter*, season 3, episode 18, January 12, 1978.
89. "The Election," *Welcome Back, Kotter*, season 1, episode 5, October 7, 1975.
90. Tanny, "A Bad, Bold, Big-Nosed Biblical Brother," 106.
91. *TV News*, October 23, 1976, DWC, Box 131, Folder 20.
92. Tanny, "A Bad, Bold, Big-Nosed Biblical Brother," 106.
93. Zurawik, *Jews of Prime Time*, 102.
94. Harry Harris, "There Are Lots of Jews on TV, but No One Is Emphasizing It," *Philadelphia Inquirer*, October 29, 1975, DWC, Box 265, Folder 027, "Press Clippings 1975 (originals)"; ibid.
95. "Follow the Leader (Part 1)," *Welcome Back, Kotter*, season 1, episode 16, January 20, 1976.
96. "Teachers and TV: Friends or Foes," *TV Guide*, October 22, 1977, in DWC, Box 266.
97. Rana Arons, "Kotter Could Have Been Me!," unnamed publication, DWC, Box 131, Folder 21.
98. *Chicago Defender*, January 31, 1976, DWC, Box 131, Folder 21.
99. Bill Kaufman, "Kotter Based on Real Life," *Syracuse Post-Standard*, January 25, 1976, DWC, Box 265.

100. Sherry Woods, no title, *Miami News*, August 8, 1975, DWC, Box 265.

101. "Gabe Says Sweathogs Are Universal," *Capital Times* (Madison, Wisconsin).

102. Featherstone and Miles, "Utopias: An Introduction," 125–131.

103. "*Welcome Back, Kotter* Review," *TV Guide*, December 6, 1975, DWC, Box 265.

104. "TV Program Research, ABC memorandum," February 15, 1978, DWC, Box 265, Folder "Kotter Marketing Research (Group Discussions)."

105. Formisano, *Boston Against Busing*; Delmont, *Why Busing Failed*.

106. "Race Riots Erupt!," *Screen Stars*, New York, August 1976, DWC, Box 265.

107. Article by Ken Emerson, *Boston Phoenix*, November 11, 1975, DWC, Box 265, Folder 027, "Press Clippings 1975 (originals)."

108. Ibid.

109. "TV as It Is Today," unnamed periodical, DWC, Box 265, Folder 027, "Press Clippings 1975 (originals)."

110. "James Komack in Hot Water," *Wichita Sunday Eagle and Beacon*, February 22, 1976, DWC, Box 131, Folder 21; "Jim Komack in Trouble," *Indianapolis Star*, October 5, 1975, DWC, Box 265; Jack Allen, "Fans Find 'Kotter' a Regular Guy," *Courier Express Buffalo*, November 2, 1975, DWC, Box 265, Folder 027, "Press Clippings 1975 (originals)"; Dean Schott, "Sweathogs behind Violence?" *Columbus Citizen-Journal*, December 7, 1977, DWC, Box 266.

111. Arthur Unger, "How Series TV Distorts American Life," *Christian Science Monitor*, November 28, 1977, DWC, Box 266.

112. Article by Ken Emerson, *Boston Phoenix*, November 11, 1975.

113. Ibid.

114. "'Kotter' Survives Ban by Boston," *Seattle Post-Intelligencer*, January 11, 1976, DWC, Box 131, Folder 21.

115. Ibid.

116. "Race Riots Erupt!," *Screen Stars*, New York, August 1976.

117. "Komack, TV's New Prolific Producer," *Sacramento Bee*, August 8, 1976, DWC, Box 132, Folder 005, "Press Clippings."

118. "James Komack in Hot Water," *Wichita Sunday Eagle and Beacon*, February 22, 1976, DWC, Box 131, Folder 21.

119. Bill Carter, "Mr. T and Tina Is No Longer Offensive and Stupid; now It's just Stupid," *Baltimore Sun*, September 24, 1976, DWC, Box 265.

120. Ibid.

121. "On All Channels: James Komack Is One Indie Producer Who Isn't Crying about Deficit Financing," *Daily Variety*, May 17, 1976, DWC, Box 265.

CHAPTER 4: *NO HUMAN BEING IS ILLEGAL*

1. In this chapter, I follow the use of the term "immigrant" adopted by the CSPG and most artists in *NHBI*, in part because the activist and policy focus of the

exhibition is largely on experiences referring specifically to the United States. This acknowledges, as Nick De Genova argued, that the term "migrant" can "do a certain epistemological work, to serve as a category of analysis that disrupts the implicit teleology of the more conventional term 'immigrant,'" which can "imply a one-directional and predetermined movement of outsiders coming in and thus are conceptual categories that necessarily can be posited only from the standpoint of the (migrant-receiving) U.S. nation-state." De Genova, *Working the Boundaries*, 2–3.

2. *No Human Being Is Illegal! Posters on the Myths and Realities of the Immigrant Experience*, Center for the Study of Political Graphics, Exhibition Guide, http://www.politicalgraphics.org/no-human-being-is-illegal.

3. Gonzalez-Barrera and Lopez, "A Demographic Portrait of Mexican-Origin Hispanics in the United States," May 1, 2013, Pew Research: Hispanic Trends Project, http://www.pewhispanic.org/2013/05/01/a-demographic-portrait-of-mexican-origin-hispanics-in-the-united-states.

4. Fernández-Kelley and Massey, "Borders for Whom?"; Gutiérrez, "An Historic Overview of Latino Immigration."

5. Chavez, *Covering Immigration*; Chavez, *The Latino Threat*; Santa Ana, *Brown Tide Rising*.

6. Chávez, *Sounds of Crossing*, 4.

7. Byrd, *The Sounds of Latinidad*, 2.

8. Dávila, *Barrio Dreams*, 11.

9. Storey, *Radical Utopianism and Cultural Studies*, 1–2.

10. Lipsitz, *American Studies in a Moment of Danger*, 181.

11. Cooper, *Everyday Utopias*, 11.

12. Storey, *Radical Utopianism and Cultural Studies*, 1.

13. Rogger, Voegeli, Widmer, Zurich University of the Arts, and Museum für Gestaltung Zürich, *Protest: The Aesthetics of Resistance*, 39–40.

14. Mendoza, *raúlsalinas and the Jail Machine*, 296.

15. Zamalin, *Black Utopia*, 16.

16. Mehan, "The Discourse of the Illegal Immigration Debate," 249–270; The Editorial Board, "Time to Retire the Term 'Alien,'" *New York Times*, October 20, 2015; Hong, "The Ten Parts of 'Illegal.'"

17. See, for example, CARECEN Washington, DC's, website, www.carecendc.org.

18. Hong, "The Ten Parts of 'Illegal,'" 55; Rosove, "No Human Being Is Illegal! Elie Wiesel"; immigration attorney Shahid Haque website, Border Crossing Law Firm, http://nohumanbeingisillegal.com/Home.html.

19. Featherstone and Miles, "Utopias: An Introduction," 129.

20. "Mark Vallen: A Short Biography," Mark Vallen website, https://www.art-for-a-change.com/content/bio.htm.

21. American Friends Service Committee website, www.afsc.org.

22. Lipsitz, *American Studies in a Moment of Danger*, 170.

23. CultureStrike, "How We Work," http://archive.culturestrike.org/about/ and https://www.culturalpower.org/origin-story; emphasis in original.

24. Rodriguez, "Being Grounded in Oakland Feeds My Artist Power," January 15, 2020, https://www.artpractical.com/feature/being-grounded-in-oakland-feeds-my-artist-power/.

25. Ibid.

26. Cooper, *Everyday Utopias*, 9.

27. Lipsitz, *American Studies in a Moment of Danger*, 169.

28. Interview with Jesús Barraza by Ilan Stavans, "Posters Are for the People: An Interview with Jesús Barraza," February 16, 2014, https://dignidadrebelde.com/?p=2233.

29. Ibid.

30. Hector Tobar, "Father Luis Olivares, Voice for the Poor, Dies of AIDS," *Los Angeles Times*, March 20, 1993.

31. Notes on the history of the *No Human Being Is Illegal* exhibition provided by Carol Wells, director, Center for the Study of Political Graphics, Los Angeles.

32. Ibid.

33. Massey and Pren, "Unintended Consequences of US Immigration Policy," 1–29, https://www.ncbi.nlm.nih.gov/pmc/articles/PMC3407978/?report=classic.

34. Lesser and Batalova, "Central American Immigrants in the United States."

35. Valerie J. Nelson, "Octavio Gomez, 71; Cameraman Helped Cover Latino Civil Rights Movement," *Los Angeles Times*, January 27, 2006.

36. Gordin, Tilley, and Prakash, *Utopia/Dystopia*, 2.

37. Devan Cole and Caroline Kelly, "Cuccinelli Rewrites Statue of Liberty Poem to Make Case for Limiting Immigration," CNN.com, August 13, 2019, https://www.cnn.com/2019/08/13/politics/ken-cuccinelli-statue-of-liberty/index.html.

38. Fairchild, "Urban Farm Workers."

39. Klein, *No Is Not Enough*, 141.

40. American Civil Liberties Union, "Chronology of Proposition 187," press release, July 29, 1999, https://www.aclu.org/press-releases/cas-anti-immigrant-proposition-187-voided-ending-states-five-year-battle-aclu-rights?redirect=immigrants-rights/cas-anti-immigrant-proposition-187-voided-ending-states-five-year-battle-aclu-righ.

41. Ibid.

42. Fernández L'Hoeste, *Lalo Alcaraz*.

43. López-Lozano, *Utopian Dreams, Apocalyptic Nightmares*, 37.

44. Fernández-Kelley and Massey, "Borders for Whom?"

45. López-Lozano, *Utopian Dreams, Apocalyptic Nightmares*, 37, 38.

46. Alcaraz, *Migra Mouse*, 71.

47. Fernández L'Hoeste, *Lalo Alcaraz*, 169.

48. Ibid., 173.

49. Lalo Alcaraz interview, www.laloalcaraz.com.

50. Cooper, *Everyday Utopias*, 6–7; Levitas, *Utopia as Method*.

51. Alcaraz also cofounded the political comedy troupe Chicano Secret Service, cohosted the infamous "Pocho Hour of Power" on KPFK in Los Angeles (90.7 FM), and served as coproducer of the Fox television show *Bordertown*. His collaborators have included Esteban Zul of the rap group Aztlan Nation, the academic Ilan Stavans, and the writer Gustavo Arellano of the *Orange County Weekly* "Ask a Mexican" column.

52. Poblete, "The Archeology of the Post-social in the Comics of Lalo Alcaraz."

53. Ibid.

54. Lalo Alcaraz, www.laloalcaraz.com.

55. Bachman, "Think Again, 1997–2012," https://www.sabachman.com/think-again.

56. Attyah and Bachman, *A Brief History of Outrage*, introduction.

57. Lazos Vargas, "The Immigrant Rights Marches (Las Marchas)," 781; Bada, Fox, and Selee, *Invisible No More*, v, https://www.wilsoncenter.org/sites/default/files/Invisible%20No%20More_0.pdf.

58. Bada, Fox, and Selee, *Invisible No More*, 36.

59. Featherstone and Miles, "Utopias: An Introduction," 126–127; Rando, *Hope and Wish Image in Music Technology*, 33; Jameson, *Archaeologies of the Future*, 231–232.

60. Martínez, "'Flowers from the Same Soil,'" 557–579; Cisneros, "(Re)Bordering the Civic Imaginary," 26–49; Lazos Vargas, "Immigrant Rights Marches (Las Marchas)."

61. Cindy Carcamo, "With Only One Left, Iconic Yellow Road Sign Showing Running Immigrants Now Borders on the Extinct," *Los Angeles Times*, July 7, 2017.

62. Favianna Rodriguez, "Biography," https://favianna.com/about/biography. The "first-generation" quote appeared in an earlier version of her website but is no longer included on the revised website.

63. CultureStrike, "How We Work," http://archive.culturestrike.org/about/ and https://www.culturalpower.org/origin-story.

64. The Center for Cultural Power, "Keep Powering the Culture Wave," https://www.culturalpower.org/about.

65. In 1996, California voters passed Proposition 209, banning affirmative action by prohibiting state institutions from considering race, sex, color, ethnicity, or national origin in the operation of public employment, education, or contracting. In 2000, California voters passed Proposition 21, which increased penalties for youth and gang-related crimes. Like Proposition 187, both of these propositions were deemed by many to target racialized and immigrant communities.

66. Jesús Barraza, interview by Matthew Harrison Tedford, "Visiting Artist Profiles: Taller Tupac Amaru," May 4, 2013, https://www.artpractical.com/column/taller_tupac_amaru/.

67. Ibid.

68. Dignidad Rebelde, "Melanie Cervantes: Artist and Cultural Worker," https://dignidadrebelde.com/?page_id=740.

69. Dignidad Rebelde, "Jesús Barraza: Artist and Master Printer," https://dignidadrebelde.com/?page_id=748.

70. Barraza and Cervantes, "Empujando Tinta," 209.

71. Dignidad Rebelde, "Dignidad Rebelde," https://dignidadrebelde.com/?page_id=8.

72. Barraza and Cervantes, "Empujando Tinta," 209.

73. Dignidad Rebelde website, "Dignidad Rebelde," https://dignidadrebelde.com/?page_id=8.

74. Ibid.

75. Barraza and Cervantes, "Empujando Tinta," 213.

76. Dignidad Rebelde, "Dignidad Rebelde," https://dignidadrebelde.com/?page_id=8; DeMirjyn, "Dignidad Rebelde's Art Activism," 213–215.

77. Justseeds Artists' Cooperative, https://justseeds.org/about/.

78. Mohl, "The Politics of Expulsion," 42–67.

79. Barraza and Cervantes, "Empujando Tinta," 214.

80. Melanie Cervantes, email exchange with author, November 2020.

81. Smithsonian American Art Museum,¡*Printing the Revolution*¡ *The Rise and Impact of Chicano Graphics, 1965 to Now*, Washington, DC, https://americanart.si.edu/exhibitions/chicano-graphics.

82. Truax, *Dreamers*.

83. Ibid., 24.

84. Raoul Deal, email exchange with author, November 2020.

85. *Migration Now!*, portfolio organized by Favianna Rodriguez and Roger Peet, coproduced by CultureStrike and Justseeds, https://justseeds.org/portfolio/migration-now/.

86. Dreamers Adrift, "About Us," http://dreamersadrift.com/about.

87. *No Human Being Is Illegal! Posters on the Myths and Realities of the Immigrant Experience*, Center for the Study of Political Graphics, Exhibition Guide, http://www.politicalgraphics.org/no-human-being-is-illegal.

88. Cucher, "Concrete Utopias from the Central Valley to Southern California," 28.

CHAPTER 5: BORDER REGGAE

1. I occasionally use the term "border(lands)" to encompass both the territory within proximate distances to the US-Mexico border and those areas that Mike Davis refers to as the "third border" (in addition to the geopolitical boundary between nation-states and the extended border checkpoints) that "polices daily intercourse between two citizen communities: its outrageousness [is] redoubled by the hypoc-

risy and can't be used to justify its existence. Invisible to most Anglos, it slaps Latinos across the face." Davis, *Magical Urbanism*, 61.

2. Rando, *Hope and Wish Image in Music Technology*, 35.

3. Ibid., 4.

4. Levitas, "Singing Summons the Existence of the Fountain," 222, 223, quoting Ernst Bloch, *The Principle of Hope*, 1063, 1088.

5. For discussion of the wide-ranging appeal of reggae's political aesthetics, see Redmond, *Anthem*.

6. Hall, "Cultural Identity and Diaspora," 222.

7. Byrd, *The Sounds of Latinidad*, 7.

8. Johnson, *Spaces of Conflict, Sounds of Solidarity*, 172.

9. Redmond, *Anthem*, 1.

10. Yúdice, "Afro Reggae," 53.

11. Flynn, "We Are the Border," 311–330.

12. López-Lozano, *Utopian Dreams, Apocalyptic Nightmares*, 17.

13. Ortiz, *An African American and Latinx History of the United States*, 5.

14. Solnit, *A Paradise Built in Hell*.

15. Lipsitz, *Footsteps in the Dark*, 70.

16. Gordin, Tilley, and Prakash, *Utopia/Dystopia*, 2.

17. Andreas, "Borderless Economy, Barricaded Border," 14–21.

18. Ibid.; Eschbach et al., "Death at the Border."

19. Andreas, *Border Games*; Nevins, *Operation Gatekeeper*; Dunn, *Militarization of the US-Mexico Border*.

20. Huntington, "The Hispanic Challenge," 30–45.

21. See chapter 4 for discussion of Proposition 187, HR 4437, and SB 1070.

22. Viesca, "The Battle of Los Angeles."

23. Alvarez, *Mangoes, Chiles, and Truckers*, 3.

24. Rando, *Hope and Wish in Music Technology*, 5.

25. Savishinsky, "Transnational Popular Culture," 259–281; Spencer, "Chanting Change around the World," 253–265.

26. More commonly known as Azteca or the Aztecs, "Mexica" refers to the Indigenous group that migrated from what is now the US Southwest to the central valley of Mexico in the twelfth century.

27. Mizraim Leal and Martin Perez (of Quinto Sol), interview by Panquetzani, http://www.youtube.com/watch?v=AlEpl97d6EM.

28. "Night After Night," *San Antonio Express-News*, April 17, 2009.

29. Radio La Chusma, interview by convictedartist.com, February 2009, http://www.convictedartist.com/radiolachusma.html.

30. Joaquín McWhinney, interview by Steve Serpiente, February 2003, http://www.jahworks.org/music/interview/big_mtn1.html.

31. Saldaña-Portillo, "Who's the Indian in Aztlán?," 403.

32. Liner notes from Big Mountain, *Unity*, Giant Records, 1994.

33. Ibid. "Incidents at Oglala" refers to the pillaging of land and labor in West Papua, Indonesia, by multinational mining interests.

34. Davi Kallman, "12 Questions for Mark Alvarado, Border Roots," *Newspaper Tree—El Paso's Original News Source*.

35. Press release from the city of El Paso's Museums and Cultural Affairs office for "Border Roots: El Paso's Own Reggae Band to open the Alfresco! Friday's Season," June 20, 2008.

36. Mizraim Leal and Martin Perez (of Quinto Sol), interview; Zachary Stahl, "Rasta-Meets-Aztec: Crew Quinto Sol Performs in King City," *Monterey County Weekly*, November 20, 2008.

37. Joaquín McWhinney video blog, April 25, 2009, http://www.rebelink.com; this video blog is no longer available, but other McWhinney and Big Mountain videos are available on their YouTube channel, https://www.youtube.com/channel/UCHrLFGDPL1yS3xpSrsN6Trg; liner notes from Quinazo, *La Ofrenda*, Rebel Ink, 2009.

38. Radio La Chusma, interview by convictedartist.com.

39. Doug Pullen, "Radio La Chusma Takes Wing," *El Paso Times*, August 4, 2009.

40. Border Roots, http://www.myspace.com/borderroots; this URL is no longer active.

41. Davi Kallman, "12 Questions for Mark Alvarado, Border Roots."

42. Anzaldúa, *Borderlands/La Frontera*, 25.

43. Border Roots, *Barrio Reggae*, Hard Man Fe Dead/Shade Records, 2009.

44. Doug Pullen, "Radio La Chusma Takes Wing"; Radio La Chusma, *Sonidos de la Gente*, 2003; Radio La Chusma, *91.5 MexM*, 2007.

45. Big Mountain, "Border Town," *Unity*, Giant Records, 1994.

46. Joaquín McWhinney, interview by Steve Serpiente.

47. Quinazo, *La Ofrenda*, Rebel Ink, 2009; Pablo Jaime Sainz, "Best Bet: 'This record is an offering to my people,'" *San Diego Union Tribune*, June 18, 2009.

48. Quinto Sol, *Cuicacalli*, Xicano Records and Film, 1999; Quinto Sol, *Barrio Roots*, Xicano Records and Film, 2003.

49. Doss, "Choosing Chicano in the 1990s," 191–202; Viesca, "Straight Out the Barrio," 445–473; Kun, *Audiotopia*, 219–225; Widener, "Another City Is Possible," 189–219.

50. Perales, "Fighting to Stay in Smeltertown," 41–64.

51. Ortega, "Chicano Reggae: The Story of Mark Moses Alvarado," http://www.texasreggae.org/docs/borderroots.pdf; this URL is no longer active.

52. Ken Leighton, "Guevara with a Guitar," *San Diego Reader*, June 10, 2009; Ken Leighton, "Have Guitar, Will Revolt," *San Diego Reader*, April 20, 2006.

53. Joaquín McWhinney video blog, April 25, 2009.

54. Van Pelt, "Big Mountain: Waking Up to Unity," http://incolor.inebraska.com/cvanpelt/bigmountain.html.

55. Stahl, "Rasta-Meets-Aztec: Crew Quinto Sol Performs in King City."
56. Storey, *Radical Utopianism and Cultural Studies*, 12.
57. Mizraim Leal and Martin Perez (of Quinto Sol), interview.
58. Alvarez, "From Zoot Suits to Hip Hop," 53–75.
59. Corona and Madrid, "Introduction," 3–5.
60. Balkan, "Way Out West on Central," 43–45; Vincent, "Black Hopes in Baja California"; McBroome, "Harvests of Gold"; McBroome, "All Men Up and No Man Down."
61. Vila, "Identity and Empowerment on the Border," 40–45.
62. Cooper, *Everyday Utopias*, 9.
63. Byrd, "Introduction," 13.
64. Eek-a-Mouse, "Border Patrol," *Uneek*, Island Records, 1991.
65. "The Astrorumberos," http://www.sandiegoreader.com/bands/astrorumberos.
66. Pablo Jaime Sainz, "Afro-Mexicans: Mexico's Forgotten Roots: Bob Marley Day Festival in Tijuana Will Celebrate Mexico's Black History," *La Prensa San Diego*, February 18, 2005.
67. Gil Griffin, "Kingston in Tijuana: Afro-Mexica-Style Reggae Is More Than Just Music—It's also a Call for Social Reform," *San Diego Union Tribune*, August 6, 2004.
68. Ibid.
69. Thompson, "Introduction," 13.
70. Griffin, "Kingston in Tijuana."
71. "The Astrorumberos."
72. Cáñamo, https://www.myspace.com/canamotjreggae.
73. Elijah Emanuel, *La Lucha Continua*, self-released, 2001; Elijah Emanuel, *Persistence of Vision*, self-released, 2004; Elijah Emanuel, *Tres sangres*, self-released, 2008.
74. "Elijah Emanuel and the Revelations," http://www.jambase.com/Artists/9379/Elijah-Emanuel-and-The-Revelations-Bio.
75. Sandra Dibble, "Amid Tijuana's Violence, Cultural Pulse Is Vibrant," *San Diego Union Tribune*, June 2, 2008.
76. Madrid, *Nor-Tec Rifa!*, 14–16.
77. Lipsitz, *Dangerous Crossroads*, 12.
78. Madrid, *Nor-Tec-Rifa!*, 16.
79. Ken Leighton, "Guevara with a Guitar."
80. Rivera-Servera, "Musical Trans(actions)."
81. Bucknor, "Staging Seduction," 67–81.
82. Ibid., 72.
83. Davi Kallman, "12 Questions for Mark Alvarado, Border Roots."
84. Griffin, "Kingston in Tijuana."
85. Ibid.
86. Buff, *Against the Deportation Terror*.

87. Not coincidentally, Márquez's academic work includes the study of Mexican American–African American cultural and political struggles in Houston and along the Gulf Coast. See Márquez, *Black-Brown Solidarity*.

88. "Short Documentary: Big Mountain-Deportation Nation," Reggaeville .com, December 23, 2018, https://www.reggaeville.com/artist-details/big-mountain /news/view/short-documentary-big-mountain-deportation-nation/.

89. Ibid.

90. "Deportation Nation," short documentary, 2018, directed by Juan Zapata, https://www.reggaeville.com/artist-details/big-mountain/news/view/short-docu mentary-big-mountain-deportation-nation/.

91. Redmond, *Anthem*, 1.

92. Zamalin, *Black Utopia*, 5.

93. Joaquín McWhinney and John Márquez, interview on CNN, November 18, 2018, https://www.youtube.com/watch?v=j3nO_Ag7fzg.

CODA: NGĀTAHI

1. *Ngātahi: Know the Links #3*, Kia Kaha Productions, 2007; Earth Crew 2000, "*Undiscovered America*: A Mural of Resistance," https://www.laweekly.com/undis covered-america-a-mural-of-resistance/.

2. *Ngātahi: Know the Links #3*; Joseph Montalvo, interview with Art Share LA, "An Interview with Muralist and Artist, Nuke," 2018, https://artsharela.org/nuke interview/.

3. For each of the five completed parts of the *Ngātahi* series between 2001 and 2008, Hapeta was awarded NZ$10,000 from the Screen Innovation Production Fund, a partnership between Creative New Zealand and the New Zealand Film Commission, at least half of which went toward airfare.

4. *Ngātahi: Know the Links*, Kia Kaha Productions, 2003.

5. Subcomandante Marcos, "'The Fourth World War,'" November 20, 1999, reprinted in *La Jornada*, October 21, 2001; see also the documentary film *The Fourth World War*, Big Noise Films, 2004.

6. Chicanas/os and Latinas/os are included in *Ngātahi* #1 (San Francisco and New York) and #3 (Los Angeles).

7. Pfaelzer, "*Salt of the Earth*," 121.

8. For further discussion of *Ngātahi*, see Alvarez, "Building Dignity's Diaspora through Rapumentary Film," 233–254.

9. *Ngātahi #1–2*, released in 2003, included Paris, France; Ottawa and Toronto, Canada; London, GB; Detroit, Honolulu, New York, San Francisco, and Washington, DC, USA; Medellín and Bogotá, Colombia; Kingston, Jamaica; Havana, Cuba; Sydney, Australia; and Aotearoa, New Zealand. *Ngātahi #3* (2007) included Mexico City and Chiapas, Mexico; Los Angeles; Whitehorse, Wounded Knee, and Rapid City, South Dakota. *Ngātahi #4* (2007) included Cape Town, South Africa; Arusha,

Tanzania; and Tahiti. *Ngātahi #5* (2008) included the West Bank, Palestine; Belfast and Derry, Northern Ireland; and Manila and Baguio, Philippines. *Ngātahi #6* (2012) included Budapest, Hungary; Belgrade, Serbia; Beijing, China; Rio de Janeiro and São Paulo, Brazil.

10. Collins, "Culture and Identity in the Asia-Pacific," 95–96.
11. *Ngātahi: Know the Links #3*, commentary track.
12. *Ngātahi: Know the Links #3*.
13. Ibid.
14. Ibid.
15. Burlison, "From Gangs to Glory," *KQED*, March 9, 2015, https://www.kqed.org/arts/10445851/from-gangs-to-glory-bambus-political-hip-hop-for-the-people.
16. *Ngātahi: Know the Links #3*.
17. NukeOne, https://nuke.one.
18. *Ngātahi: Know the Links #3*, commentary track.
19. Muñoz, *Cruising Utopia*, 3.
20. Levitas, "*In eine bess're Welt entrückt*," 217.
21. Holloway, "Dignity's Revolt"; Callahan, "Why Not Share a Dream?"
22. Scott, *Domination and the Arts of Resistance*, xi–xii.
23. Bald, "Overlapping Diasporas, Multiracial Lives," 7.
24. Ibid.
25. *Ngātahi: Know the Links #5*, Kia Kaha Productions, 2008, commentary track.
26. Simon Sweetman, *The Dominion Post*, October 24, 2003, accessed October 27, 2010, www.tekupu.com/Ngātahi-review.1.html; URL no longer active.
27. Clifford, *Routes*, 18.
28. *Ngātahi: Know the Links #3*, commentary track.
29. Simon Sweetman, *The Dominion Post*; no current URL available.
30. *Ngātahi: Know the Links #5*, commentary track.
31. Ibid.
32. Gray, *Cultural Moves*, 3.
33. Gilroy, *Small Acts*; Goldfarb, *The Politics of Small Things*.
34. Bloch, *The Principle of Hope*; Rando, *Hope and Wish Image in Music Technology*, 12.
35. Kurasawa, *The Work of Global Justice*, 1.
36. Ibid.
37. Wallerstein, "Remembering Andre Gunder Frank."
38. Kurasawa, *The Work of Global Justice*, 17.
39. *Ngātahi: Know the Links #5*, commentary track.
40. Graham Reid, *New Zealand Herald*, September 16, 2003, accessed October 27, 2010, http://www.tekupu.com/Ngātahi-review.3.html; URL no longer active.
41. *Ngātahi: Know the Links #3*, commentary track.
42. *Ngātahi: Know the Links #5*, commentary track.
43. Alvarez, "Reggae Rhythms in Dignity's Diaspora."
44. Gordin, Tilley, and Prakash, *Utopia/Dystopia*, 3.

Bibliography

PRIMARY SOURCES: ARCHIVAL COLLECTIONS,
INTERVIEWS, AND CULTURAL MEDIA

Alcaraz, Lalo. www.laloalcaraz.com.
American Civil Liberties Union. "Chronology of Proposition 187." Press release, July 29, 1999. https://www.aclu.org/press-releases/cas-anti-immigrant-proposition-187-voided-ending-states-five-year-battle-aclu-rights?redirect=immigrants-rights/cas-anti-immigrant-proposition-187-voided-ending-states-five-year-battle-aclu-righ.
American Friends Service Committee. www.afsc.org.
Arvizu, Ersi. Interview by Mark Guerrero, August 31, 2019. Aired on *Mark Guerrero's Chicano Music Chronicles* podcast, https://markguerrero.net/chronicles.php.
Attyah, David John, and S. A. Bachman. *A Brief History of Outrage*. Venice, CA: Politicizing Pictures Press, 2004.
Bachman, S. A. "Think Again, 1997–2012." https://www.sabachman.com/think-again.
Barraza, Jesús. Interview by Ilan Stavans. "Posters Are for the People: An Interview with Jesús Barraza," February 16, 2014. https://dignidadrebelde.com/?p=2233.
———. Interview by Matthew Harrison Tedford. "Visiting Artist Profiles: Taller Tupac Amaru," May 4, 2013. https://www.artpractical.com/column/taller_tupac_amaru/.
Big Mountain. *Unity*. Giant Records, 1994.
Border Roots. *Barrio Reggae*. Hard Man Fe Dead/Shade Records, 2009.
———. http://www.myspace.com/borderroots. URL no longer active.
Brown Eyed Soul: The Sound from East LA Vol. 1–3. Rhino Records, 1997.
Cáñamo Tijuana Reggae. https://www.facebook.com/CanamoTjreggae/; or https://myspace.com/canamotjreggae.
Cardenas, Billy. Interview by Mark Guerrero, June 2, 2019. Aired on *Mark Guerrero's Chicano Music Chronicles* podcast, https://markguerrero.net/chronicles.php.

Chicano Rock! The Sounds of East Los Angeles. Documentary. Directed by Jon Wilkman. Latino Public Broadcasting, 2008.

Chico and the Man. Television series aired on NBC from 1974 to 1978. Directed by Peter Baldwin, Jack Donohue, and James Komack. The Komack Company and Wolper Productions.

Clinton Jencks Papers. Department of Archives and Special Collections, University Libraries, Arizona State University, Tempe, Arizona.

Cole, Devan, and Caroline Kelly. "Cuccinelli Rewrites Statue of Liberty Poem to Make Case for Limiting Immigration." CNN.com, August 13, 2019. https://www.cnn.com/2019/08/13/politics/ken-cuccinelli-statue-of-liberty/index.html.

Congressional Record. 83rd Congress, 1st Session, February 24, 1953, vol. 99, Part 1.

CultureStrike. http://archive.culturestrike.org/about/.

David L. Wolper Collection. David L. Wolper Center, The Cinematic Arts Library, University of Southern California, Los Angeles.

Del Barco, Mandalit. "The Story of 'Whittier Blvd.,' a Song and Place Where Latino Youth Found Each Other." *All Things Considered; American Anthem: Music That Challenges, Unites and Celebrates,* National Public Radio, November 29, 2018. https://www.npr.org/2018/11/29/671688096/the-story-of-whittier-blvd-a-song-and-place-where-latino-youth-found-each-other.

Dignidad Rebelde. https://dignidadrebelde.com/?page_id=740.

Dreamers Adrift. http://dreamersadrift.com.

Earth Crew 2000. "*Undiscovered America*: A Mural of Resistance." By Daniel Ortega, *LA Weekly*, December 12, 2018. https://www.laweekly.com/undiscovered-america-a-mural-of-resistance/.

Eddie Davis West Coast East Side Sound Archives. California Ethnic and Multicultural Archives (CEMA), Department of Special Research Collections, University of California, Santa Barbara. https://www.library.ucsb.edu/special-collections/cema/WCESS.

Eek-a-Mouse. *Uneek*, Island Records, 1991.

El Chicano. http://www.elchicanomusic.com/. Accessed July 18, 2019.

Emanuel, Elijah. *La Lucha Continua*. Self-released, 2001.

———. *Persistence of Vision*. Self-released, 2004.

———. *Tres Sangres*. Self-released, 2008.

The Fourth World War. Directed by Rick Rowley. Big Noise Films, 2004.

Frances E. Williams Papers, 1965–1995 (Mss. 086). Southern California Library for Social Studies and Research, Los Angeles, California. https://oac.cdlib.org/institutions/Southern+California+Library+for+Social+Studies+and+Research.

Guerrero, Mark. https://markguerrero.net.

Justseeds Artists' Cooperative. https://justseeds.org/about/.

McWhinney, Joaquín. "A 'New Day' for Big Mountain." Interview by Steve Serpiente, November 2002, https://jahworks.org/steve_serpiente/a-new-day-for-big-mountain/#.YJsxyS2ZMQ8.

---. Video blog, April 25, 2009. http://www.rebelink.com. URL no longer active; other Big Mountain videos available at https://www.youtube.com/channel/UCHrLFGDPL1yS3xpSrsN6Trg.

McWhinney, Joaquín, and John Márquez. Interview on CNN by John Vause, November 18, 2018. https://www.youtube.com/watch?v=j3nO_Ag7fzg.

Migration Now! Portfolio organized by Favianna Rodriguez and Roger Peet, coproduced by CultureStrike and Justseeds. https://justseeds.org/portfolio/migration-now/.

Miyata, Shin. Interview on "Discos Inmigrantes," April 24, 2012; aired on Radio Sombra, a community-based internet radio station in Boyle Heights, East Los Angeles, California.

Montalvo, Joseph. Interview with Art Share LA, "An Interview with Muralist and Artist, Nuke," 2018. https://artsharela.org/nukeinterview/.

Negro Ensemble Company Records, 1967–1993. Schomburg Center for Research in Black Culture, Manuscripts, Archives, and Rare Books Division, The New York Public Library.

Ngātahi: Know the Links #1–2. Film. Kia Kaha Productions, 2003.

Ngātahi: Know the Links #3. Film. Kia Kaha Productions, 2007.

Ngātahi: Know the Links #4. Film. Kia Kaha Productions, 2007.

Ngātahi: Know the Links #5. Film. Kia Kaha Productions, 2008.

Ngātahi: Know the Links #6. Film. Kia Kaha Productions, 2012.

No Human Being Is Illegal! Posters on the Myths and Realities of the Immigrant Experience. Exhibition Guide, Center for the Study of Political Graphics, Los Angeles, California. http://www.politicalgraphics.org/no-human-being-is-illegal.

NukeOne. https://nuke.one.

Phillips, Allan, and Bruce Phillips. Interview by Josh Kun, August 18, 2011. http://phillipsmusiccompany.tumblr.com.

Quinazo. *La Ofrenda.* CD. Rebel Ink, 2009.

Quinto Sol. *Barrio Roots.* CD. Xicano Records and Film, 2003.

———. *Cuicacalli.* CD. Xicano Records and Film, 1999.

Radio La Chusma. Interview by convictedartist.com, February 2009. http://www.convictedartist.com/radiolachusma.html.

———. *91.5 MexM.* CD. 2007.

———. *Sonidos de la Gente.* CD. 2003.

Rodriguez, Favianna. "Being Grounded in Oakland Feeds My Artist Power," January 15, 2020. https://www.artpractical.com/feature/being-grounded-in-oakland-feeds-my-artist-power/.

———. https://favianna.com.

Rodriguez, Luis. *Guide to the Eddie Davis West Coast East Side Sound Archive,* California Ethnic and Multicultural Archive (CEMA), Department of Special Research Collections, University of California, Santa Barbara, 2010. https://www.library.ucsb.edu/special-collections/cema/WCESS.

Short Documentary: Big Mountain-Deportation Nation. Reggaeville.com, December 23, 2018. https://www.reggaeville.com/artist-details/big-mountain/news/view/short-documentary-big-mountain-deportation-nation/.

Smithsonian American Art Museum. *¡Printing the Revolution¡ The Rise and Impact of Chicano Graphics, 1965 to Now.* https://americanart.si.edu/exhibitions/chicano-graphics.

Vallen, Mark. "Mark Vallen's Art for a Change." https://www.art-for-a-change.com/content/bio.htm.

Welcome Back, Kotter. Television series aired on ABC from 1975 to 1979. Created by Gabe Kaplan and Alan Sacks. The Komack Company and Wolper Productions.

Williams, Frances. Interview by Karen Anne Mason and Richard Cándida Smith. "To Hell with Bandannas: Oral History Transcript, 1992–1993." Oral History Program, University of California, Los Angeles. https://archive.org/details/tohellwithbandanoowill.

SECONDARY SOURCES

Abensour, Miguel. *Utopia: From Thomas More to Walter Benjamin.* Minneapolis: Univocal, 2017.

Acham, Christine. *Revolution Televised: Prime Time and the Struggle for Black Power.* Minneapolis: University of Minnesota Press, 2005.

Alcaraz, Lalo. *Migra Mouse: Political Cartoons on Immigration.* Brooklyn, NY: Akashik Books, 2004.

Alvarez, Luis. "Building Dignity's Diaspora through Rapumentary Film: Learning from *Ngātahi*." *KALFOU: A Journal of Comparative and Relational Ethnic Studies* 2, no. 2 (2015): 233–254.

———. "From Zoot Suits to Hip Hop: Towards a Relational Chicana/o History." *Latino Studies* 5, no. 1 (2007): 53–75.

———. *The Power of the Zoot: Youth Culture and Resistance during World War II.* Berkeley: University of California Press, 2008.

———. "Reggae Rhythms in Dignity's Diaspora: Globalization, Indigenous Identity, and the Circulation of Cultural Struggle." *Popular Music and Society* 31, no. 5 (2008): 575–597.

Alvarez, Robert R., Jr. *Mangoes, Chiles, and Truckers: The Business of Transnationalism.* Minneapolis: University of Minnesota Press, 2005.

Andreas, Peter. *Border Games: Policing the US-Mexican Divide.* Ithaca, NY: Cornell University Press, 2000.

———. "Borderless Economy, Barricaded Border." *NACLA Report on the Americas* 33, no. 3 (1999): 14–21.

Anzaldúa, Gloria. *Borderlands/La Frontera: The New Mestiza.* San Francisco: Aunt Lute Books, 1994.

Araiza, Lauren. *To March for Others: The Black Freedom Struggle and the United Farm Workers*. Philadelphia: University of Pennsylvania Press, 2014.

Bada, Xóchitl, Jonathan Fox, and Andrew Selee, eds. *Invisible No More: Mexican Migrant Civic Participation in the United States*. Washington, DC: Woodrow Wilson Center, 2011. https://www.wilsoncenter.org/sites/default/files/media/uploads/documents/Invisible_No_More.pdf.

Baker, Ellen R. *On Strike and on Film: Mexican American Families and Blacklisted Filmmakers in Cold War America*. Chapel Hill: University of North Carolina Press, 2007.

Bald, Vivek. "Overlapping Diasporas, Multiracial Lives: South Asian Muslims in U.S. Communities of Color, 1880–1950." *Souls: A Critical Journal of Black Politics, Culture, and Society* 8, no. 4 (2006): 3–18.

Balkan, Michael. "Way Out West on Central: Jazz in the African-American Community of Los Angeles before 1930." In *California Soul: Music of African Americans in the West*, edited by Jacqueline Cogdell DjeDje and Eddie S. Meadows, 23–78. Berkeley: University of California Press, 1998.

Balthaser, Benjamin. "Cold War Re-Visions: Representation and Resistance in the Unseen Salt of the Earth." *American Quarterly* 60, no. 2 (June 2008): 347–371.

Baraka, Amiri. "The Changing Same (R&B and New Black Music)." *Black Music*, 180–211. New York: Morrow, 1968.

Barraza, Jesús, and Melanie Cervantes. "Empujando Tinta: The Work and Politics of Dignidad Rebelde." *Aztlán: A Journal of Chicano Studies* 41, no. 2 (Fall 2016): 209–220.

Behnken, Brian D. *Fighting Their Own Battles: Mexican Americans, African Americans, and the Struggle for Civil Rights in Texas*. Chapel Hill: University of North Carolina Press, 2011.

———, ed. *The Struggle in Black and Brown: African American and Mexican American Relations during the Civil Rights Era*. Lincoln: University of Nebraska Press, 2011.

Benjamin, Walter. *The Arcades Project*. Translated by Howard Eiland. Cambridge, MA: Harvard University Press, 1999.

———. "The Author as Producer." In Walter Benjamin, *Reflections: Essays, Aphorisms, Autobiographical Writings*, edited by Peter Demetz, 220–238. New York: Schocken, 1986.

Berger, Dan, ed. *The Hidden 1970s: Histories of Radicalism*. New Brunswick, NJ: Rutgers University Press, 2010.

Berlant, Lauren. *Cruel Optimism*. Durham, NC: Duke University Press, 2011.

Bernstein, Shana. *Bridges of Reform: Interracial Civil Rights Activism in Twentieth-Century Los Angeles*. Oxford: Oxford University Press, 2011.

Biberman, Herbert. *Salt of the Earth: The Story of a Film*. New York: Sag Harbor, 2002.

Bloch, Ernst. *The Principle of Hope*. Oxford: Blackwell Press, 1986.

———. *The Utopian Function of Art and Literature*. Translated by Jack Zipes and Frank Mecklenberg. Cambridge, MA: MIT Press, 1993.

Borstelman, Thomas. *The Cold War and the Color Line: American Race Relations in the Global Arena*. Cambridge, MA: Harvard University Press, 2001.

Bowditch, Rachel, and Pegge Vissicaro, eds. *Performing Utopia*. New York: Seagull, 2017.

Brooks, Tim, and Earle Marshe. *The Complete Directory to Prime Time Network and Cable TV Shows, 1946-Present*. New York: Ballantine, 2009.

Bryant, Clora, Buddy Collette, William Green, Steven Isoardi, Jack Kelson, Horace Tapscott, Gerald Wilson, and Marl Young, eds. *Central Avenue Sounds: Jazz in Los Angeles*. Berkeley: University of California Press, 1998.

Buck-Morss, Susan. *Dreamworld and Catastrophe: The Passing of Mass Utopia in East and West*. Cambridge, MA: MIT Press, 2002.

Bucknor, Michael. "Staging Seduction: Masculine Performance or the Art of Sex in Colin Channer's Reggae Romance *Waiting in Vain?*" *Interventions* 6, no. 1 (2004): 67–81.

Buff, Rachel Ida. *Against the Deportation Terror: Organizing for Immigrant Rights in the Twentieth Century*. Philadelphia: Temple University Press, 2017.

Burlison, Dani. "From Gangs to Glory: Bambu's Political Hip-Hop for the People." *KQED*, March 9, 2015. https://www.kqed.org/arts/10445851/from-gangs-to-glory-bambus-political-hip-hop-for-the-people.

Byrd, Bobby. "Introduction." In *Puro Border: Dispatches, Snapshots and Graffiti from La Frontera*, edited by Luis Humberto Crosthwaite, John William Byrd, and Bobby Byrd, 9–20. El Paso, TX: Cinco Puntos, 2003.

Byrd, Samuel K. *The Sounds of Latinidad: Immigrants Making Music and Creating Culture in a Southern City*. New York: New York University Press, 2015.

Callahan, Manuel. "Why Not Share a Dream? Zapatismo as Political and Cultural Practice." *Humboldt Journal of Social Relations* 29, no. 1 (2005): 6–37.

Camacho, Alicia Schmidt. *Migrant Imaginaries: Latino Cultural Politics in the US-Mexico Borderlands*. New York: New York University Press, 2008.

Cargill, Jack. "Empire and Opposition: The 'Salt of the Earth' Strike." In *Labor in New Mexico: Unions, Strikes, and Social History since 1881*, edited by Robert Kern, 183–267. Albuquerque: University of New Mexico Press, 1983.

Ceplair, Larry. *The Marxist and the Movies: A Biography of Paul Jarrico*. Lexington: University Press of Kentucky, 2007.

Chacón, Juan. "Union Made." *California Quarterly* 2, no. 4 (Summer 1953), reprinted in Wilson, *Salt of the Earth: Screenplay*, 180–182. New York: Feminist Press, 1978.

Chambers, Ross. *Room for Maneuver: Reading (the) Oppositional (in) Narrative*. Chicago: University of Chicago Press, 1991.

Chan, Edward K., and Patricia Ventura. "Introduction: Articulating Race and Utopia." *Utopian Studies* 30, no. 1 (2019): 1–7.

Chávez, Alex E. *Sounds of Crossing: Music, Migration, and the Aural Poetics of Huapango Arribeño*. Durham, NC: Duke University Press, 2017.

Chávez, Ernesto. *"¡Mi Raza Primero!" (My People First): Nationalism, Identity, and Insurgency in the Chicano Movement in Los Angeles, 1966–1978*. Berkeley: University of California Press, 2002.

Chavez, Leo R. *Covering Immigration: Popular Images and the Politics of the Nation*. Berkeley: University of California Press, 2001.

———. *The Latino Threat: Constructing Immigrants, Citizens, and the Nation*. Stanford: Stanford University Press, 2008.

Chávez-García, Miroslava. "Coming Home to *The Brady Bunch*: In Search of Latina/o Identity." *Southern California Quarterly* 101, no. 4 (2019): 430–460.

Christian, Anna. "Frances E. Williams." In *Oxford African American Studies Center*, edited by Henry Louis Gates Jr. Oxford: Oxford University Press, 2013. https://oxfordaasc.com/view/10.1093/acref/9780195301731.001.0001/acref-9780195301731-e-38205?rskey=Kdg2Mi&result=1.

———. *Meet It, Greet It, and Defeat It: The Biography of Frances Williams, Actress/Activist*. Los Angeles: Milligan Books, 1999.

Cisneros, Josué David. "(Re)Bordering the Civic Imaginary: Rhetoric, Hybridity, and Citizenship in La Gran Marcha." *Quarterly Journal of Speech* 97, no. 1 (Feb. 2011): 26–49.

Clifford, James. *Routes: Travel and Translation in the Late Twentieth Century*. Cambridge, MA: Harvard University Press, 1997.

Collins, Francis Leo. "Culture and Identity in the Asia-Pacific." *Graduate Journal of Asia-Pacific Studies* 2, no. 1 (2004): 95–96.

Comaroff, Jean, and John L. Comaroff. "Millennial Capitalism: First Thoughts on a Second Coming." *Public Culture* 12, no. 2 (2000): 291–343.

Cooper, Davina. *Everyday Utopias: The Conceptual Life of Promising Spaces*. Durham, NC: Duke University Press, 2013.

Corona, Ignacio, and Alejandro L. Madrid. "Introduction: The Postnational Turn in Music Scholarship and Music Marketing." In *Postnational Musical Identities: Cultural Production, Distribution, and Consumption in a Globalized Scenario*, edited by Ignacio Corona and Alejandro L. Madrid, 3–5. Lanham, MD: Lexington, 2007.

———, eds. *Postnational Musical Identities: Cultural Production, Distribution, and Consumption in a Globalized Scenario*. Lanham, MD: Lexington Books, 2007.

Crosthwaite, Luis Humberto, John William Byrd, and Bobby Byrd, eds. *Puro Border: Dispatches, Snapshots and Graffiti from La Frontera*. El Paso, TX: Cinco Puntos, 2003.

Cucher, Michael. "Concrete Utopias from the Central Valley to Southern California: Repurposing Images of Emiliano Zapata in Chicana/o Murals." *Aztlan: A Journal of Chicano Studies* 43, no. 1 (Spring 2018): 25–59.

Dallek, Matthew. *The Right Moment: Ronald Reagan's First Victory and the Decisive Turning Point in American Politics*. Oxford: Oxford University Press, 2000.

Dávila, Arlene. *Barrio Dreams: Puerto Ricans, Latinos, and the Neoliberal City*. Berkeley: University of California Press, 2004.

Davis, Mike. *Magical Urbanism: Latinos Reinvent the U.S. Big City*. London: Verso, 2000.

———. "Uprising and Repression in LA." *Covert Action Information Quarterly* (Summer 1993). Reprinted in *Reading Rodney King/Reading Urban Uprising*, edited by Robert Gooding-Williams. New York: Routledge, 1993.

De Genova, Nicholas. *Working the Boundaries: Race, Space, and "Illegality" in Mexican Chicago*. Durham, NC: Duke University Press, 2005.

De Genova, Nicholas, and Ana Ramos-Zayas. *Latino Crossings: Mexicans, Puerto Ricans, and the Politics of Citizenship*. London: Routledge, 2003.

Delmont, Matthew F. *Why Busing Failed: Race, Media, and the National Resistance to School Segregation*. Berkeley: University of California Press, 2016.

DeMirjyn, Maricela. "Dignidad Rebelde's Art Activism: Looking Back, Seeing Forward." *Revista de Estudios Globales y Arte Contemporáneo* 7, no. 1 (2020): 211–235.

Dolan, Jill. *Utopia and Performance: Finding Hope at the Theater*. Ann Arbor: University of Michigan Press, 2005.

Doss, Yvette. "Choosing Chicano in the 1990s: The Underground Music Scene of Los(t) Angeles." *Aztlan: A Journal of Chicano Studies* 23, no. 2 (1998): 191–202.

Dudziak, Mary. *Cold War Civil Rights: Race and the Image of American Democracy*. Princeton, NJ: Princeton University Press, 2000.

Dunn, Timothy. *The Militarization of the U.S.-Mexico Border, 1978–1992*. Austin: University of Texas Press, 1995.

Eschbach, Karl, Jacqueline Hagan, Nestor Rodriguez, Rubén Hernández-León, and Stanley Bailey. "Death at the Border." *International Migration Review* 33, no. 3 (1999): 430–454.

Escobar, Edward. *Race, Police, and the Making of a Political Identity: Mexican Americans and the Los Angeles Police Department, 1900–1945*. Berkeley: University of California Press, 1999.

Esteva, Gustavo, and Madhu Suri Prakash. *Grassroots Postmodernism: Remaking the Soil of Cultures*. London: Zed Books, 1998.

Fairchild, Stephanie. "Urban Farm Workers: A History of the Justice for Janitors Campaign as a Response to Neoliberal Restructuring and Union Decline." PhD diss., University of California, San Diego, 2018.

Featherstone, Mark, and Malcolm Miles. "Utopias: An Introduction." *Cultural Politics* 10, no. 2 (July 2014): 125–131.

Fernández-Kelley, Patricia, and Douglas S. Massey. "Borders for Whom? The Role of NAFTA in Mexico-U.S. Migration." *Annals of the American Academy of Political and Social Science* 610, no. 1 (2007): 98–118.

Fernández L'Hoeste, Héctor D. *Lalo Alcaraz: Political Cartooning in the Latino Community*. Oxford: University Press of Mississippi, 2017.

Fischlin, Daniel, Ajay Heble, and George Lipsitz. *The Fierce Urgency of Now: Improvisation, Rights, and the Ethics of Cocreation*. Durham, NC: Duke University Press, 2013.

Flach, Kathryn L. "Tell It Like It Is: Television and Social Change, 1960–1980." PhD diss., University of California, San Diego, 2018.
Flores, Juan. "Reclaiming Left Baggage: Some Early Sources for Minority Studies." *Cultural Critique* 59 (Winter 2005): 187–206.
Flynn, Donna K. "We Are the Border: Identity, Exchange, and the State along the Bénin-Nigeria Border." *American Ethnologist* 24, no. 2 (1997): 311–330.
Fogelson, Robert. *The Fragmented Metropolis: Los Angeles, 1850–1930*. Berkeley: University of California Press, 1993.
Formisano, Ronald P. *Boston Against Busing: Race, Class, and Ethnicity in the 1960s and 1970s*. Chapel Hill: University of North Carolina Press, 1991.
García, Mario. "Mexican American Labor and the Left: The Asociación Nacional México-Americana, 1949–1954." In *The Chicano Struggle: Analyses of Past and Present Efforts*, edited by John A. García, Teresa Córdova, and Juan A. García, 65–86. Binghamton, NY: Bilingual Press/Editorial Bilingüe, 1984.
Garcia, Matt. *A World of Its Own: Race, Labor, and Citrus in the Making of Greater Los Angeles, 1900–1970*. Chapel Hill: University of North Carolina Press, 2001.
Gilroy, Paul. *Small Acts: Thoughts on the Politics of Black Cultures*. London: Serpent's Tail, 1994.
Goldfarb, Jeffrey C. *The Politics of Small Things: The Power of the Powerless in Dark Times*. Chicago: University of Chicago Press, 2006.
Gómez, Alan Eladio. *The Revolutionary Imaginations of Greater Mexico: Chicana/o Radicalism, Solidarity Politics, and Latin American Social Movements*. Austin: University of Texas Press, 2016.
Gómez-Quiñones, Juan. *Mexican American Labor, 1790–1990*. Albuquerque: University of New Mexico Press, 1994.
Gonzalez, Martha. *Chican@ Artivistas: Music, Community, and Transborder Tactics in East Los Angeles*. Austin: University of Texas Press, 2020.
Gonzalez-Barrera, Ana, and Mark Hugo Lopez. "A Demographic Portrait of Mexican-Origin Hispanics in the United States." *Pew Research: Hispanic Trends Project*, May 1, 2013. http://www.pewhispanic.org/2013/05/01/a-demographic-portrait-of-mexican-origin-hispanics-in-the-united-states.
Gordin, Michael D., Helen Tilley, and Gyan Prakash, eds. *Utopia/Dystopia: Conditions of Historical Possibility*. Princeton, NJ: Princeton University Press, 2010.
Graeber, David. "The New Anarchists." *New Left Review* 13 (January/February 2002): 61–73.
Gray, Herman. *Cultural Moves: African Americans and the Politics of Representation*. Berkeley: University of California Press, 2005.
———. *Watching Race: Television and the Struggle for Blackness*. Minneapolis: University of Minnesota Press, 2004.
Grendysa, Pete. "The Making of Rhythm and Blues." *Collecting Magazine* (1985): N.p.
Grewal, Inderpal. *Transnational America: Feminisms, Diasporas, Neoliberalisms*. Durham, NC: Duke University Press, 2005.

Grossberg, Lawrence. *Cultural Studies in the Future Tense.* Durham, NC: Duke University Press, 2010.
Guerrero, Perla M. *Nuevo South: Latinas/os, Asians, and the Remaking of Place.* Austin: University of Texas Press, 2017.
Guidotti-Hernández, Nicole. *Unspeakable Violence: Remapping U.S. and Mexican National Imaginaries.* Durham, NC: Duke University Press, 2011.
Guterl, Matthew Pratt. *Seeing Race in Modern America.* Chapel Hill: University of North Carolina Press, 2013.
Gutiérrez, David G. "An Historic Overview of Latino Immigration and the Demographic Transformation of the United States." *American Latinos and the Making of the United States: A Theme Study.* Washington, DC: National Park System Advisory Board, 2015.
———. "The Politics of the Interstices: Reflections on Citizenship and Non-Citizenship at the Turn of the Twentieth Century." *Race/Ethnicity* 1, no. 1 (Autumn 2007): 89–120.
———. *Walls and Mirrors: Mexican Americans, Mexican Immigrants, and the Politics of Ethnicity.* Berkeley: University of California Press, 1995.
Habell-Pallán, Michelle. *Loca Motion: The Travels of Chicana and Latina Popular Culture.* New York: New York University Press, 2005.
Hall, Stuart. "Cultural Identity and Diaspora." In *Identity: Community, Culture, Difference*, edited by Jonathan Rutherford, 222–237. London: Lawrence and Wishart, 1990.
———. "Notes on Deconstructing 'The Popular.'" In *People's History and Socialist Theory*, edited by Raphael Samuel, 227–240. London: Routledge, 1981.
Harvey, David. *A Brief History of Neoliberalism.* Oxford: Oxford University Press, 2007.
Hébert, Martin. "Worlds Not Yet in Being: Reconciling Anthropology and Utopianism." *Anthropology and Materialism: A Journal of Social Research* 3 (2016). https://journals.openedition.org/am/604.
Hidalgo, Jacqueline M. *Revelation in Aztlán: Scriptures, Utopias, and the Chicano Movement.* New York: Palgrave Macmillan, 2016.
Hobsbawm, Eric. *The Age of Extremes: A History of the World, 1914–1991.* New York: Vintage, 1994.
Holloway, John. "Dignity's Revolt." In *Zapatista!: Reinventing Revolution in Mexico*, edited by John Holloway and Eloína Peláez, 159–198. London: Pluto, 1998.
Holloway, John, and Eloína Peláez, eds. *Zapatista! Reinventing Revolution in Mexico.* London: Pluto Press, 1998.
Hong, Grace Kyungwon, and Roderick A. Ferguson, eds. *Strange Affinities: The Gender and Sexual Politics of Comparative Racialization.* Durham, NC: Duke University Press, 2011.
Hong, Kari E. "The Ten Parts of 'Illegal' in 'Illegal Immigration' That I Do Not Understand." *UC Davis Law Review Online* 50, no. 43 (2017). https://ssrn.com/abstract=2942303.

Horne, Gerald. *Fire This Time: The Watts Uprising and the 1960s*. New York: Da Capo, 1997.
Huntington, Samuel P. "The Hispanic Challenge." *Foreign Policy* 141 (2004): 30–45.
Jacoby, Russell. *Picture Imperfect: Utopian Thought for an Anti-Utopian Age*. New York: Columbia University Press, 2005.
Jameson, Fredric. *Archaeologies of the Future: The Desire Called Utopia and Other Science Fictions*. London: Verso, 2005.
Jarrico, Paul, and Herbert J. Biberman. "Breaking Ground." *California Quarterly* 2, no. 4 (Summer 1953, reprinted in Wilson, *Salt of the Earth: Screenplay*, 169–174. New York: Feminist Press, 1978.
Johnson, Gaye Theresa. "Constellations of Struggle: Luisa Moreno, Charlotta Bass, and the Legacy for Ethnic Studies." *Aztlan: A Journal of Chicano Studies* 33, no. 1 (Spring 2008): 155–172.
———. "'Sobre Las Olas': A Mexican Genesis in Borderlands Jazz and the Legacy for Ethnic Studies." *Comparative American Studies* 6, no. 3 (2008): 225–237.
———. *Spaces of Conflict, Sounds of Solidarity: Music, Race, and Spatial Entitlement in Los Angeles*. Berkeley: University of California Press, 2013.
Johnson, Gaye Theresa, and Alex Lubin, eds. *Futures of Black Radicalism*. London: Verso, 2017.
Kelley, Robin D. G. *Race Rebels: Culture, Politics, and the Black Working Class*. New York: Free Press, 1996.
Khasnabish, Alex. *Zapatismo Beyond Borders: New Imaginations of Political Possibility*. Toronto: University of Toronto Press, 2008.
Klein, Naomi. *No Is Not Enough: Resisting Trump's Shock Politics and Winning the World We Need*. Chicago: Haymarket, 2017.
Korstvedt, Benjamin M. *Listening for Utopia in Ernst Bloch's Musical Philosophy*. Cambridge: Cambridge University Press, 2010.
Kun, Josh. *Audiotopia: Music, Race, and America*. Berkeley: University of California Press, 2005.
———. "The Tijuana Sound: Brass, Blues, and the Border of the 1960s." In *Transnational Encounters: Music and Performance at the U.S.-Mexico Border*, edited by Alejandro L. Madrid, 231–250. New York: Oxford University Press, 2011.
Kurasawa, Fuyuki. *The Work of Global Justice: Human Rights as Practices*. Cambridge: Cambridge University Press, 2007.
Kurashige, Scott. *The Shifting Grounds of Race: Black and Japanese Americans in the Making of Multiethnic Los Angeles*. Princeton, NJ: Princeton University Press, 2008.
Lazos Vargas, Sylvia R. "The Immigrant Rights Marches (Las Marchas): Did the 'Gigante' (Giant) Wake Up or Does It Still Sleep Tonight?" *Nevada Law Journal* (Summer 2007): 780–825.
Leal, Mizraim, and Martin Perez (of Quinto Sol). Interview by Panquetzani. http://www.youtube.com/watch?v=AlEpl97d6EM.
Lear, Norman. *Even This I Get to Experience*. New York: Penguin Books, 2014.

Leonard, Kevin Allen. *The Battle for Los Angeles: Racial Ideology and World War II.* Albuquerque: University of New Mexico Press, 2006.

———. "'In the Interest of All Races': African Americans and Interracial Cooperation in Los Angeles during and after World War II." In *Seeking El Dorado: African Americans in California*, edited by Lawrence B. De Graaf, Kevin Mulroy, and Quintard Taylor, 309–340. Seattle: University of Washington Press, 2001.

Lesser, Gabriel, and Jeanne Batalova. "Central American Immigrants in the United States." *Migration Policy Institute*, April 2017. https://www.migrationpolicy.org/article/central-american-immigrants-united-states-2015.

Levitas, Ruth. "*In eine bess're Welt entrückt*: Reflections on Music and Utopia." *Utopian Studies* 21, no. 2 (2010): 215–231.

———. "Singing Summons the Existence of the Fountain: Bloch, Music, and Utopia." In *The Privatization of Hope: Ernst Bloch and the Future of Utopia*, edited by Peter Thompson and Slavoj Žižek, 219–245. Durham, NC: Duke University Press, 2013.

———. *Utopia as Method: The Imaginary Reconstitution of Society.* New York: Palgrave Macmillan, 2013.

Levitas, Ruth, and Tom Moylan. "Introduction: The Once and Future Orpheus." *Utopian Studies* 21, no. 2 (2010): 204–214.

Lipsitz, George. *American Studies in a Moment of Danger.* Minneapolis: University of Minnesota Press, 2001.

———. *Dangerous Crossroads: Music, Postmodernism, and the Poetics of Place.* London: Verso, 1997.

———. *Footsteps in the Dark: The Hidden Histories of Popular Music.* Minneapolis: University of Minnesota Press, 2007.

———. *How Racism Takes Place.* Philadelphia: Temple University Press, 2011.

———. *Rainbow at Midnight: Labor and Culture in the 1940s.* Urbana: University of Illinois Press, 1994.

———. *Time Passages: Collective Memory and American Popular Culture.* Minneapolis: University of Minnesota Press, 1990.

López-Lozano, Miguel. *Utopian Dreams, Apocalyptic Nightmares: Globalization in Recent Mexican and Chicano Narrative.* West Lafayette, IN: Purdue University Press, 2008.

Lorence, James J. *The Suppression of* Salt of the Earth: *How Hollywood, Big Labor, and Politicians Blacklisted a Movie in Cold War America.* Albuquerque: University of New Mexico Press, 1999.

Loza, Steven. *Barrio Rhythm: Mexican American Music in Los Angeles.* Urbana: University of Illinois Press, 1993.

Macías, Anthony F. "Bringing Music to the People: Race, Urban Culture, and Municipal Politics in Postwar Los Angeles." *American Quarterly* 56, no. 3 (September 2004): 693–717.

———. "California's Composer Laureate: Gerald Wilson, Jazz Music, and Black-

Mexican Connections." *Boom: A Journal of California* 3, no. 2 (Summer 2013): 34–51.
———. *Mexican American Mojo: Popular Music, Dance, and Urban Culture in Los Angeles, 1935–1968*. Durham, NC: Duke University Press, 2008.
———. "Rock con Raza, Raza con Jazz: Latinos/as and Post–World War II Popular American Music." In *Musical Migrations, Volume 1: Transnationalism and Cultural Hybridity in Latin/o America*, edited by Frances Aparicio and Cándida Jáquez, 183–197. New York: Palgrave, 2003.
Madrid, Alejandro L. *Nor-Tec Rifa! Electronic Dance Music from Tijuana to the World*. New York: Oxford University Press, 2008.
Mantler, Gordon. *Power to the Poor: Black-Brown Coalition and the Fight for Economic Justice, 1960–1974*. Chapel Hill: University of North Carolina Press, 2013.
Mariscal, George. *Brown-eyed Children of the Sun: Lessons from the Chicano Movement, 1965–1975*. Albuquerque: University of New Mexico Press, 2005.
Márquez, John. *Black-Brown Solidarity: Racial Politics in the New Gulf South*. Austin: University of Texas Press, 2014.
Martínez, Lisa M. "'Flowers from the Same Soil': Latino Solidarity in the Wake of the 2006 Immigrant Mobilizations." *American Behavioral Scientist* 52, no. 4 (Dec. 2008): 557–579.
Massey, Douglas S., and Karen A. Pren. "Unintended Consequences of US Immigration Policy: Explaining the Post-1965 Surge from Latin America." *Population and Development Review* 38, no. 1 (2012): 1–29. https://www.ncbi.nlm.nih.gov/pmc/articles/PMC3407978/?report=classic.
May, Elaine Tyler. *Homeward Bound: American Families in the Cold War Era*. New York: Basic Books, 1990.
McBroome, Delores Nason. "All Men Up and No Man Down: Black Angelenos Confront Refracted Racism, 1900–1940." In *City of Promise: Race and Historical Change in Los Angeles*, edited by Martin Schiesl and Mark Morrall Dodge, 59–84. Claremont, CA: Regina Books, 2006.
———. "Harvests of Gold: African American Boosterism, Agriculture, and Investment in Allensworth and Little Liberia." In *Seeking El Dorado: African Americans in California*, edited by Lawrence B. de Graff, Kevin Mulroy, and Quintard Taylor, 149–180. Seattle: University of Washington Press, 2001.
McCarthy, Jim. *Voices of Latin Rock: The People and Events That Created This Sound*. Milwaukee, WI: Hal Leonard, 2004.
McGirr, Lisa. *Suburban Warriors: The Origins of the New American Right*. Princeton, NJ: Princeton University Press, 2002.
Mehan, Hugh. "The Discourse of the Illegal Immigration Debate: A Case Study in the Politics of Representation." *Discourse and Society* 8, no. 2 (1997): 249–270.
Mendoza, Louis G., ed. *raúlsalinas and the Jail Machine: My Weapon Is My Pen*. Austin: University of Texas Press, 2006.
Millar, Bill. "Chicano Rock: Down Mexico Way." *Let It Rock* (September 1975): 16–17.

Mohl, Raymond A. "The Politics of Expulsion: A Short History of Alabama's Anti-Immigrant Law, HB 56." *Journal of American Ethnic History* 35, no. 3 (2016): 42–67.

Molina, Natalia. "Examining Chicana/o History through a Relational Lens." *Pacific Historical Review* 82, no. 4 (November 2013): 520–541.

———. *How Race Is Made in America: Immigration, Citizenship, and the Historical Power of Racial Scripts*. Berkeley: University of California Press, 2014.

———. "The Importance of Place-Makers in the Life of a Los Angeles Community: What Gentrification Erases from Echo Park." *Southern California Quarterly* 97, no. 1 (Spring 2015): 69–111.

Molina, Ruben. *Chicano Soul Music: Recordings and History of an American Culture*. Lubbock: Texas Tech University Press, 2017.

Muñoz, José Esteban. *Cruising Utopia: The Then and There of Queer Futurity*. New York: New York University Press, 2009.

Narváez, Peter. "The Influences of Hispanic Cultures on African-American Blues Musicians." *Black Music Research Journal* 22 (2002): 175–196.

Nevins, Joseph. *Operation Gatekeeper: The Rise of the "Illegal Alien" and the Making of the U.S.-Mexico Boundary*. New York: Routledge, 2002.

Noriega, Chon A. *Shot in America: Television, the State, and the Rise of Chicano Cinema*. Minneapolis: University of Minnesota Press, 2000.

Oguss, Greg. "Whose Barrio Is It?: *Chico and the Man* and the Integrated Ghetto Shows of the 1970s." *Television and New Media* 6, no. 1 (February 2005): 3–21.

Oropeza, Lorena. *¡Raza Si! ¡Guerra No! Chicano Protest and Patriotism during the Vietnam War Era*. Berkeley: University of California Press, 2005.

Ortega, Chato. "Chicano Reggae: The Story of Mark Moses Alvarado." http://www.texasreggae.org/docs/borderroots.pdf. URL no longer active.

Ortiz, Paul. *An African American and Latinx History of the United States*. New York: Beacon, 2018.

Pagán, Eduardo Obregón. *Murder at the Sleepy Lagoon: Zoot Suits, Race, and Riot in Wartime L.A.* Chapel Hill: University of North Carolina Press, 2004.

Peña, Manuel. *Música Tejana: The Cultural Economy of Artistic Transformation*. College Station: Texas A&M University Press, 1999.

Perales, Monica. "Fighting to Stay in Smeltertown: Lead Contamination and Environmental Justice in a Mexican American Community." *Western Historical Quarterly* 39, no. 1 (2008): 41–63.

Pfaelzer, Jean. "*Salt of the Earth*: Women, Class, and the Utopian Imagination." *Legacy* 16, no. 1 (1999): 120–131.

Poblete, Juan. "The Archeology of the Post-social in the Comics of Lalo Alcaraz: *La Cucaracha* and *Migra Mouse: Political Cartoons on Immigration*." In *Graphic Borders: Latino Comic Books Past, Present, and Future*, edited by Frederick Luis Aldama and Christopher González, 152–168. Austin: University of Texas Press, 2016.

Pratt, Mary Louise. *Imperial Eyes: Travel Writing and Transculturation*. London: Routledge, 1992.

Pulido, Laura. *Black, Brown, Yellow, and Left: Radical Activism in Los Angeles*. Berkeley: University of California Press, 2006.

Ramírez, Catherine. "Afrofuturism/Chicanafuturism: Fictive Kin." *Aztlan: A Journal of Chicano Studies* 33, no. 1 (Spring 2008): 185–194.

———. *The Woman in the Zoot Suit: Gender, Nationalism, and the Cultural Politics of Memory*. Durham, NC: Duke University Press, 2009.

Rando, David P. *Hope and Wish Image in Music Technology*. New York: Palgrave Macmillan, 2016.

Ransby, Barbara, and Tracye Matthews. "Black Popular Culture and the Transcendence of Patriarchal Illusions." In *Words of Fire: An Anthology of African-American Feminist Thought*, edited by Beverly Guy-Sheftall, 526–535. New York: New Press, 1995.

Redmond, Shana L. *Anthem: Social Movements and the Sound of Solidarity in the African Diaspora*. New York: New York University Press, 2014.

Reed, T. V. *The Art of Protest: Culture and Activism from the Civil Rights Movement to the Streets of Seattle*. Minneapolis: University of Minnesota Press, 2005.

Reyes, David, and Tom Waldman. *Land of a Thousand Dances: Chicano Rock 'n' Roll from Southern California*. Albuquerque: University of New Mexico Press, 1998.

Rivera-Servera, Ramón. "Musical Trans(actions): Intersections in Reggaetón." *Trans: Revista Transcultural de Música/Transcultural Music Review* 13 (2009): 1–13.

Robinson, Greg. *After Camps: Portraits in Midcentury Japanese American Life and Politics*. Berkeley: University of California Press, 2012.

Rogger, Basil, Jonas Voegeli, Ruedi Widmer, Zurich University of the Arts, and Museum für Gestaltung Zürich, eds. *Protest: The Aesthetics of Resistance*. Zurich: Lars Müller, 2018.

Rosas, Abigail. *South Central Is Home: Race and the Power of Community Investment in Los Angeles*. Stanford, CA: Stanford University Press, 2019.

Rosas, Anna. *Abrazando El Espíritu: Bracero Families Confront the US-Mexico Border*. Berkeley: University of California Press, 2014.

Rosenfelt, Deborah Silverton. "Commentary." In Wilson, *Salt of the Earth: Screenplay*, 93–168. New York: Feminist Press, 1978.

Rosove, John. "No Human Being Is Illegal! Elie Wiesel." *Jewish Journal* (March 8, 2017). http://jewishjournal.com/blogs/216216/no-human-illegal-elie-wiesel/.

Rueda, Claudia P. *Students of Revolution: Youth, Protest, and Coalition Building in Somoza-Era Nicaragua*. Austin: University of Texas Press, 2019.

Ruiz, Ramón Eduardo. *On the Rim of Mexico: Encounters of the Rich and Poor*. Boulder, CO: Westview, 1998.

Ruiz, Vicki. *From Out of the Shadows: Mexican Women in Twentieth-Century America*. Oxford: Oxford University Press, 2008.

Saldaña-Portillo, Josefina. "Who's the Indian in Aztlán? Re-Writing Mestizaje, Indianism, and Chicanismo from the Lacandón." In *The Latin American Subaltern Studies Reader*, edited by Ileana Rodriguez, 402–423. Durham, NC: Duke University Press, 2001.

Sánchez, George J. *Becoming Mexican American: Ethnicity, Culture, and Identity in Chicano Los Angeles, 1900–1945*. Oxford: Oxford University Press, 1995.

———. "What's Good for Boyle Heights Is Good for the Jews: Creating Multiracialism on the Eastside during the 1950s." *American Quarterly* 56, no. 3 (2004): 633–661.

Santa Ana, Otto. *Brown Tide Rising: Metaphors of Latinos in Contemporary American Public Discourse*. Austin: University of Texas Press, 2002.

Savishinsky, Neil J. "Transnational Popular Culture and the Global Spread of the Jamaican Rastafari Movement." *New West Indian Guide* 68, nos. 3–4 (1994): 259–281.

Scott, James C. *Domination and the Arts of Resistance: Hidden Transcripts*. New Haven, CT: Yale University Press, 1990.

Solnit, Rebecca. *A Paradise Built in Hell: The Extraordinary Communities That Arise in Disaster*. New York: Penguin, 2010.

Spencer, William D. "Chanting Change around the World through Rasta Riddim and Art." In *Chanting Down Babylon: The Rastafari Reader*, edited by Nathaniel Samuel Murrell, William David Spencer, and Adrian Anthony McFarlane, 253–265. Philadelphia: Temple University Press, 1998.

Spigel, Lynn. *Make Room for TV: Television and the Family Ideal in Postwar America*. Chicago: University of Chicago Press, 1992.

Stewart, Kathleen. *Ordinary Affects*. Durham, NC: Duke University Press, 2007.

Storey, John. *Radical Utopianism and Cultural Studies: On Refusing to Be Realistic*. New York: Routledge, 2019.

Tanny, Jarrod. "'A Bad, Bold, Big-Nosed Biblical Brother': Refashioning the Funny Jew in Post–World War Two America." *Journal of Modern Jewish Studies* 16, no. 1 (2017): 100–117.

Thompson, Peter. "Introduction." In *The Privatization of Hope*, edited by Peter Thompson and Slavoj Žižek, 1–20. Durham, NC: Duke University Press, 2013.

Truax, Eileen. *Dreamers: An Immigrant Generation's Fight for Their American Dream*. Boston: Beacon, 2015.

Van Pelt, Carter. "Big Mountain: Waking Up to Unity." 1994. http://incolor.ine braska.com/cvanpelt/bigmountain.html.

Vargas, Deborah R. *Dissonant Divas in Chicana Music: The Limits of La Onda*. Minneapolis: University of Minnesota Press, 2012.

Vargas, Zaragosa. *Labor Rights Are Civil Rights: Mexican American Workers in Twentieth-Century America*. Princeton, NJ: Princeton University Press, 2005.

Varzally, Allison. *Making a Non-White America: Californians Coloring outside Ethnic Lines, 1925–1955*. Berkeley: University of California Press, 2008.

Viesca, Victor Hugo. "The Battle of Los Angeles: The Cultural Politics of Chicana/o Music in the Greater Eastside." *American Quarterly* 56, no. 3 (2004): 719–739.

———. "Straight Out the Barrio: Ozomatli and the Importance of Place in the Formation of Chicano/a Popular Culture in Los Angeles." *Journal for Cultural Research* 4, no. 4 (2000): 445–473.

Vila, Pablo. "Identity and Empowerment on the Border." *NACLA Report on the Americas* 33, no. 3 (1999): 40–45.

Villa, Raúl. *Barrio-Logos: Space and Place in Urban Chicano Literature and Culture.* Austin: University of Texas Press, 2000.

Vincent, Ted. "Black Hopes in Baja California: Black American and Mexican Cooperation, 1917–1926." *Western Journal of Black Studies* 21, no. 3 (1997): 204–213.

Von Eschen, Penny M. *Race Against Empire: Black Americans and Anti-Colonialism, 1937–1957.* Ithaca, NY: Cornell University Press, 1999.

Wallerstein, Immanuel. "Remembering Andre Gunder Frank While Thinking about the Future." *Monthly Review: An Independent Socialist Magazine* 60, no. 2 (2008).

Weinberg, Carl. "*Salt of the Earth*: Labor, Film, and the Cold War." *OAH Magazine of History* 24, no. 4 (October 2010): 41–45.

Widener, Daniel. "Another City Is Possible: Interethnic Organizing in Los Angeles." *Race/Ethnicity: Multidisciplinary Global Contexts* 1, no. 2 (2008): 189–219.

———. *Black Arts West: Culture and Struggle in Postwar Los Angeles.* Durham, NC: Duke University Press, 2012.

———. "Perhaps the Japanese Are to Be Thanked? Asia, Asian Americans, and the Construction of Black California." *Positions: East Asia Cultures Critique* 11, no. 1 (2003): 135–181.

———. "Radical Rhythms: A Band Whose Time Has Come." *Against the Current* 78 (January/February 1999).

Williams, Raymond. "Utopia and Science Fiction." *Science Fiction Studies* 16, no. 5, pt. 3 (November 1978): 203–214.

Wilson, Michael. *Salt of the Earth: Screenplay.* New York: Feminist Press, 1978.

Young, Cynthia A. *Soul Power: Culture, Radicalism, and the Making of a U.S. Third World Left.* Durham, NC: Duke University Press, 2006.

Yúdice, George. "Afro Reggae: Parlaying Culture into Social Justice." *Social Text* 19, no. 4 (2001): 53–65.

Zamalin, Alex. *Black Utopia: The History of an Idea from Black Nationalism to Afrofuturism.* New York: Columbia University Press, 2019.

Zurawik, David. *Jews of Prime Time.* Hanover, NH: Brandeis University Press/University Press of New England, 2003.

Index

Abensour, Miguel, 7
Afro-Mexica reggae, 141–146; Cáñamo (band), 143, 144, 145; Cartel de Zion (band), 126, 143; De Raíz (band), 143; Elijah Emanuel and the Revelations (band), 144–145; Esencia (band), 143; influence of Bob Marley on, 141–142, 143, 144; influences on, 141–144; legacy of, 145–146; Los Astrorumberos (band), 143, 144; Maíz (band), 144, 148–149; Mexican identity of, 142; politics of, 144–146; utopian impulses of, 144; venues for, 143–144; Yumanos (band), 143
Alabama House Bill 56, 120
Albertson, Jack, 68; on character of Ed Brown, 82; on-screen chemistry with Freddie Prinze, 74
Allen, Thomas "Pappa Dee," 61–62
Alvarado, Mark Moses, 136, 137, 139, 148
Alvarez, Roberto, 132
American Civil Liberties Union (ACLU), 46
American Committee for the Protection of Foreign Born (ACPFB), 22
Amos, John, 85
Andrade, Ray, 76, 78–79, 81
Andreas, Peter, 130
anti-Korean War movement, 22, 37–38

anti-police brutality activism, 60, 150, 153, 154–155, 156
anti-racism, 10, 13, 19, 39–40, 69
Anti-Racist Group of Rethymno Students (Greece), 124
Anzaldúa, Gloria, 118, 137–138
Araiza, Lauren, 59
Arizona SB 1070 and HB 1070, 116, 120–121, 127, 131, 132
Arnold, Danny, 87
Arvizu, Ersi, 56
Arvizu, Mary, 56
Arvizu, Rosella, 56
Asociación Nacional Mexicana Americana (ANMA), 21–22
assimilation, 11, 52, 74
Atlanta Daily World, 23
Avila, Gil, 77
Aztlán, 10–11, 76, 134, 154, 162
Aztlan Underground, 138, 154–155

Baker, Ellen, 19, 33, 34, 35
Bald, Vivek, 158
ballot initiatives: in post-1992 Los Angeles, 64; upholding restrictive housing covenants, 47. *See also* California Proposition 21; California Proposition 187; California Proposition 209

Barkus, Mariona, 106–107
Barraza, Jesús, 102, 117–119, 121
Bayard strike. *See* International Union of Mine, Mill, and Smelter Workers, Local 890
Beatles, the, 53, 55, 59, 137
Benjamin, Walter, 1, 66
Bennett, Bob, 91, 92
Berger, Dan, 71, 72
Berlant, Lauren, 3, 5–6
Bernstein, Shana, 32, 47
Biberman, Herbert, 18, 22–23, 24–25, 27–28, 29, 31–32, 34, 36, 38, 40
Biberman, Sonja Dahl, 34, 36
Big Mountain, 134, 138, 147, 149–151; "Border Town," 138; "Deportation Nation," 149–151; *New Day*, 149–151
blacklisting: of actors, 18, 22; of *Salt of the Earth*, 18
Black newspapers, 23, 46, 50
Black Panther (film), 11
Black Panther Party (BPP), 59
Black Panthers, 58–59, 155
Blendells, the, 54, 57, 59
Bloch, Ernst, 5, 7, 127–128, 160
blueprint utopias, 6–7
Bob Marley Day celebration (Tijuana, Baja California), 126, 142
boogie-woogie, 49, 51, 52
borderlands and immigration: Arizona SB 1070 and HB 1070, 116, 120–121, 127, 131, 132; impact of globalization on, 127, 128–129, 130, 132, 133, 138, 141, 146–147; impact of NAFTA on, 109–110, 127–131, 139, 149; impact of neoliberalism on, 129, 141, 146; resilience of immigrants, 96, 98; surveillance and, 98, 110, 125, 129. *See also* border reggae; California Proposition 187; House Resolution 4437 (Border Protection, Antiterrorism, and Illegal Immigration Control Act); xenophobia and, 107, 112, 125

Border Protection, Antiterrorism, and Illegal Immigration Control Act (House Resolution 4437), 103–104, 114, 115, 131
border reggae: African Diaspora and, 148–149; commercialism and, 127, 130–131, 132, 146, 147, 160–161; dystopian contexts of, 129–130; gender politics of, 148; globalization and, 127, 129, 130, 132–133, 141, 146–147; influence of Rastafarianism on, 128, 133, 134, 137, 138, 140, 143–144; masculinity in, 147–148; pitfalls and possibilities of, 146–151; utopian impulses of, 126–130, 144, 146, 151. *See also* Afro-Mexica reggae; Chicanx reggae
Border Roots, 133, 136–138, 139, 148
Bourdieu, Pierre, 12
Bowditch, Rachel, 7–8
boycotts: banning of secondary boycotts, 170n14; of Coors beer company, 61; of *Salt of the Earth*, 18; threatened advertiser boycotts, 68, 79
Brown Bag Productions, 61
brown-eyed soul: in 1960s, 52–59; cultural foundations of, 45–52; definition of, 43; El Chicano and, 42, 52, 56, 60–61, 65, 83, 141; impact of Cold War on, 59–60; impact of Vietnam War on, 59; international and crosscultural connections, 57–58; legacy of, 62–67; origins of, 42–44; politics of, 58–59; popularity of, 57; in post-1968 era, 59–62; *rancheras* in, 51, 65; role of independent record labels in, 56–57; utopian impulses of, 43–44, 53, 57, 59, 62, 66–67; "Viva Tirado" (El Chicano), 42–43, 52
Burdon, Eric, 61
Burning Star, 64, 65
busing, Boston desegregation of, 68–69, 90–91

Byrd, Bobby, 142
Byrd, Samuel, 98

California Alien Land Law, 46
California Eagle (Los Angeles), 46, 50
California Proposition 21, 117, 131
California Proposition 187, 117, 131; impact on *NHBI* poster art, 96, 103, 109–114; intended purpose of, 109; protests against, 132; relation to NAFTA and neoliberalism, 109–110; unconstitutionality of, 109
California Proposition 209, 117, 131
California Proposition 227, 131
CalTrans immigrant crossing caution image, 115, 124
Camacho, Alicia Schmidt, 6, 19, 33, 36, 168n27, 170n12
Cannibal and the Headhunters, 14, 43, 53, 54, 55–56, 57, 59; "Land of a Thousand Dances," 55; tour with the Beatles, 59; "Whittier Boulevard," 54
Cantu, Caesar, 77–78
Caravan for the Rights of Refugees and Migrants, 124
Cardenas, Billy, 56, 57
Carillo, Yahaira, 123
Carter, Jimmy, 60
Castillo, Ana, 118
Center for Cultural Power, The, 117
Center for the Study of Political Graphics (CSPG), 96, 97–98, 99–104. *See also No Human Being Is Illegal: Posters on the Myths and Realities of the Immigrant Experience (NHBI)*
Central American Resource Center (CARECEN), 100, 105
Centro de Acción Social Autónomo (CASA), 58
Cervantes, Melanie, 117, 118–119, 120–121
Chacón, Juan, 24, 25, 26, 29
Chacón, Virginia, 21, 36
Chan, Edward, 11, 70

Chávez, Alex, 43, 57, 98
Chávez, Aurora, 21
Chavez, Cesar, 137, 157
Chávez, Ernesto, 58
Chávez-Ortiz, Ricardo, 106
Chavez Ravine, razing of, 47
Chicano Coalition, 79–80
Chicanx pop culture, 1–13; Black-brown connections in, 8–9; Chicanx cultural imaginary in, 6; Chicanx history and, 10–12; Chicanx utopias and, 7–13; commercialization of, 2–3, 6, 9; everyday utopias and, 7–8; postwar accessibility of, 3; racial and transnational crossings of, 3–4; revolution and, 1; social movements and, 4; utopia as cultural product in, 5; utopian visions and impulses in, 4–5. *See also* border reggae; brown-eyed soul; *Ngātahi: Know the Links*; *Salt of the Earth*; sitcoms, television
Chicanx reggae, 133–141; Big Mountain (band), 138, 147, 149–151; Border Roots (band), 133, 136–138, 139, 148; *corridos* integrated in, 51, 136, 137; influence of Bob Marley on, 126, 137, 140–141; Mexican identity of, 134; musical and cultural influences on, 134–135, 137; political activism in, 138–140; political influences on, 140–141; Quinto Sol (band), 65, 133, 134, 135, 136, 137, 138–139, 140, 142; Radio La Chusma (band), 133, 134, 137, 138; Rastafarmers (band), 133; Rising Roots (band), 133
Chico and the Man (sitcom): *All in the Family* compared with, 75; in authenticity of, 76, 83; barrio life in, 75–77, 79; charges of racism against, 76–77, 80–81; Chicano production staff members, 77–79, 81; contested Chicanx utopias in, 75, 76, 82–83; disruption of macho trope in, 177n13;

illusion of inclusion in, 88; Jewish identity and Jewishness in, 78, 79; legacy of, 93–95; masculinity in, 73, 77, 177n13; pilot episode, 68, 70, 88–89, 91–93; popularity of first season, 74; relationship between Chico and Ed, 74–75, 80; setting of, 68; themes of, 80; theme song, 77; threatened advertiser boycotts against, 68, 79; *Welcome Back, Kotter* compared with, 83, 84, 86, 88, 93. *See also* Albertson, Jack; Prinze, Freddie
Christian, Anna, 29
Citizen Engagement Laboratory (CEL), 117
Citizens Committee for the Defense of Mexican American Youth, 46
Clay, Sonny, 50, 141
Clifford, James, 159
Cold War: brown-eyed soul and, 59–60; Red-baiting, 13, 19, 20, 21; *Salt of the Earth* and, 19, 20, 21, 32, 33–34, 36, 37–40
Collette, Buddy, 49
commercialism, 127, 130–131, 132, 146, 147, 160–161
commodification, 2–3, 102, 127, 147
Community Relations Committee (CRC), 47
Community Service Organization (CSO), 47
Congress of Industrial Organizations (CIO), 21, 46
Cooper, Davina, 6, 19, 57, 69–70, 83, 98–99
corridos: border reggae and, 136, 137; brown-eyed soul and, 51
Council for Civic Unity, 46
critical race studies, 10
cruel optimism, 3
Cuban revolution, 58–59
Cuccinelli, Ken, 107
Cucher, Michael, 124

cultural imaginaries, 6
CultureStrike, 101, 116–117, 123–124

Dávila, Arlene, 2, 72, 98
Davis, Eddie, 56–57, 66
Davis, Mike, 63
Deal, Raoul, 122–123
deejays, 48, 53–54, 55, 57
Deferred Action for Childhood Arrivals (DACA), 122
Delgado, George, 59
Democratic Party Convention protests (2000), 63–64
Denning, Michael, 59
deregulation, 2, 98, 110, 130
desegregation, 48, 68
Development, Relief, and Education for Alien Minors (DREAM) Act, 104, 121–124
Dignidad Rebelde (DR), 118–119, 121
dissonance, 56
Dobbs, Lou, 131
Dolan, Jill, 5, 53
domesticity: Cold War cult of, 18, 20, 33–34, 35–36, 37; labor activism linked to, 35–36; in sitcoms, 72
domestic violence, 35
doo-wop, 49, 58
Doss, Yvette, 138
DREAM Act, 104, 121–124
Dreamers Adrift, 123–124
dystopias and dystopian visions: in border reggae, 129–130; in Cold War era, 39–40; *Ngātahi* and, 159; in Occupy movement, 100

East L.A. Sabor Factory, 64
East-Side Arts Alliance (ESAA), 119
Ejército Zapatista de Liberación Nacional (EZLN), 10, 132. *See also* Zapatistas and Zapatismo
El Chicano, 42, 52, 56, 60–61, 65, 83, 141

Empire Zinc Company, 21, 22, 35, 38. *See also* International Union of Mine, Mill, and Smelter Workers, Local 890
English-only movement, 103, 107
Esparza, Rubén, 115
Espinosa, Bobby, 42
essentialism, 8, 161
ethnocide, 2
everyday utopias, 6–8, 12, 44, 57, 98–99, 162
Executive Order 9066 (authorized relocation of Japanese Americans), 46

Farmer, Art, 49
Featherstone, Mark, 89, 100
Feliciano, José, 77
femininity, 33, 148
feminism: Hollywood filmmaking and, 34; mining industry and, 34; *Salt of the Earth* and, 32–37, 40
Ferguson, Roderick, 8
Fierro, Josefina, 37, 170n12
Figueroa, Ronnie, 53
Fischlin, Daniel, 4, 55
Flores, Quetzal, 65
Fogelson, Robert, 65
Ford, Gerald, 60
Fregoso, Chris, 143
Fuentes, José, 35
Fuentes, Julio, 86

Garcia, Carlos, 142, 144
Garcia, Frankie "Cannibal," 55–56
Garcia, Matt, 49
gender politics, 32–37; of border reggae, 34–35, 148; of Hollywood filmmaking, 34–35; in International Production Company (IPC), 34–35; of mining industry, 34–35; *Salt of the Earth* and, 32–37, 40
gender roles, 32, 36, 56
Gillespie, Dizzy, 45, 50

globalization: "from below," 4; influence on border reggae, 127, 129, 130, 132–133, 141, 146–147; influence on postwar Chicanx popular culture, 2; poster art on, 98
Global South, 39
Gomez, Octavio, 105–106
Gómez-Quinones, Juan, 38
Gonzalez, Hector, 66
Gonzalez, Martha, 65
González, Xico, 115
Gordin, Michael, 9, 12
Gray, Herman, 69, 159–160
Grossberg, Lawrence, 5
Guerrero, Lalo, 45, 174n52
Guerrero, Mark, 60, 83; "I'm Brown," 60; "Pre-Columbian Dream," 60; "Radio Aztlan," 60; "The Streets of East L.A.," 60
Gutierrez, Felix, 80

Hall, Stuart, 2, 6, 128
Haller, Melanie, 86
Hapeta, Dean, 152–161. *See also Ngātahi: Know the Links*
Harvey, David, 2
Hatch, Orrin, 121
Heble, Ajay, 4, 55
Hegyes, Robert: friendship with Freddie Prinze, 88; racial and ethnic identity of, 70–71, 74, 86–88
Hemsley, Sherman, 85
Hernandez, Ray, 123
Herrera, Little Julian, 48
heuristic utopias, 7, 168n35
Higgins, Chuck, 48, 54; "Pachuko Hop," 48; "Pancho Villa," 48; "Wetback Hop," 48
Hilton-Jacobs, Lawrence, 85
Hobsbawm, Eric, 39
Hollywood Latin, 45
Hollywood Ten, 18
Hong, Grace, 8

Hopkins, Samuel John "Lightnin'," 52
House Resolution 4437 (Border Protection, Antiterrorism, and Illegal Immigration Control Act), 103–104, 114, 115, 131
House Un-American Activities Committee (HUAC), 18, 20–21, 22, 26, 29
housing covenants, 47
Houston, Joe, 48
Howard, Robert, 77
Huntington, Samuel, 131
hypermasculinity, 89, 147, 161. *See also* masculinity

immigration. *See* borderlands and immigration
Immigration and Customs Enforcement (ICE), 131
Immigration and Nationality Act (McCarran-Walter Act), 20–21, 22, 33, 36, 37
Immigration and Naturalization Service (INS), 38, 106–107, 131
Immigration Reform and Control Act (IRCA), 96, 103, 104–105, 107–108, 109, 113
International Alliance of Theatrical and Stage Employees (IATSE), 18, 26
International Production Company (IPC): founding and purpose of, 18, 22; gender politics in, 34–35; Mine-Mill negotiations and collaborations, 25, 28–32, 34, 40. *See also Salt of the Earth*
International Union of Mine, Mill, and Smelter Workers, Local 890, 21–25, 30, 38; anti-war stance of, 38; border politics and, 38–39; Cold War context of, 36, 37–38, 39–40; IPC negotiations and collaborations, 25, 28–32, 34, 40; Ladies Auxiliary, 18, 21, 25, 31, 33. *See also Salt of the Earth*
intersectionality, 117–118, 123–124

Jackson, Donald, 17, 18, 26, 37–38, 39
Jacoby, Russell, 7
James, C. L. R., 1
Japanese American Citizens League (JACL), 46, 47–48
Japanese Americans, internment of, 46
Jarrico, Paul, 18, 22–23, 25, 27–28, 29, 31–32, 34, 38–39, 40
Jencks, Clinton, 23, 24, 26, 27
Jencks, Virginia, 21, 24, 29–30
Jewish identity and Jewishness: organizations, 47–48; in post-war music scene, 48–49, 50; in sitcoms, 68, 70–71, 78, 79, 85–88, 93
Johnson, Gaye, 8, 43, 46, 52, 128
Johnson, Jack, 50, 141
jump blues, 49, 51
Justice for Chicanos in the Motion Picture and Television Industry (Justicia), 75–76, 79
Justseeds Artists' Cooperative, 119–120

Kaltenborn, Sandy, 124
Kamathi, Dedon, 155–156
Kaplan, Gabe, 68; comedic career of, 84; Jewish contribution to *Welcome Back, Kotter*, 87; on New York as setting for television shows, 88; response to ban of *Welcome Back, Kotter*, 92–93; reviews of performance as Kotter, 89; role in success of *Welcome Back, Kotter*, 84–85
Kelley, Robin D. G., 5
Kenner, Chris, 55
King, Rodney, 63, 153
Kingston, Jamaica, 58
Klein, Naomi, 108–109
Komack, Jimmie: creator of *Chico and the Man*, 73, 75–76; creator of *Mr. T and Tina*, 94; criticisms of, 77–79, 94; "ethnic comedy" of, 73, 77; producer of *Welcome Back, Kotter*, 73, 83, 84–86, 88–90, 92–93; response to

Komack, Jimmie (*continued*)
    criticisms, 80, 81, 89, 90, 92–93; vision of race in America, 77–78, 80–81, 83, 86, 88, 90, 93
Komack Company, 73, 84
Kun, Josh, 50, 64, 138
Kurashige, Scott, 46
Kushida, Tats, 47–48

Laarman, Peter, 92
Laboe, Art, 55, 57
Labor Management Relations Act (Taft-Hartley Act), 22, 170n14
La Gran Marcha, 97, 103, 114–116, 118–120, 139
land loss, 39, 46, 159
Latinization, 73
Latinoization, 109, 131
Lazarus, Emma, 106–107
League of United Latin American Citizens (LULAC), 47, 76
Leal, Mizraim, 134, 136, 140
Leonard, Kevin Allen, 46
Levitas, Ruth, 4–5, 8, 43, 66–67, 157–158
Linden, Hal, 87
Lipsitz, George, 4, 55
Little Willie G, 53, 54, 57, 59–60
López-Lozano, Miguel, 109–110, 129
Los Angeles Riots (1992), 63
Los Lobos, 51, 52, 66, 137
Los Vaqueros, 59
lowrider culture, 66
Lowrider Japan, 66
Lowrider Magazine, 76–77
Lucero, Linda, 83

MacArthur Park, Los Angeles, 62–64
Macbeth, Hugh, Sr., 46
Macías, Anthony, 45, 49
Macías, Paul, 79, 176n1
MacPhee, Josh, 119
Madrid, Alejandro L., 145, 147
Magnificent Doll, 28

majority-minority demographics, 109, 131
Mardirosian, Vahaac, 77
Mariscal, George, 58
Marisol, 154, 155
Marley, Bob, 126, 137, 140–142, 143, 144
Márquez, John, 8–9, 150
masculinity: in border reggae, 147–148; of Chicano movement, 77, 177n13; in *Chico and the Man*, 73, 77, 177n13; class and, 85–86; disruption of macho trope in *Chico and the Man*, 177n13; hypermasculinity, 89, 147, 161; infantilization of Black masculinity, 94; public sphere associated with, 33–34; racialization and, 89, 94; in *Salt of the Earth*, 18, 33–34, 35; in sitcoms, 72–73, 77, 85–86, 89, 94; in *Welcome Back, Kotter*, 73, 85–86, 89
May, Elaine Tyler, 33
May Day immigrant rights marches, 63. *See also* La Gran Marcha
McCarran-Walter Act (Immigration and Nationality Act), 20–21, 22, 33, 36, 37
McCarthy, Joseph, 20
McMahon, John, 80
McNeely, Big Jay, 48, 49–50, 61
McWhinney, Joaquín "Quino": with Big Mountain, 134, 138, 147, 149–151; Chicanx activism of, 139–140; with Quinazo, 134, 136, 138, 139, 147; "Tierra Indígena," 138
Mendoza, Louis, 99
Mexican American Legal Defense and Education Fund (MALDEF), 76
Meyerson, Peter, 84
Miles, Malcolm, 89, 100
militarization, 127, 129, 133, 138, 140, 141, 146, 150
Mine-Mill strike. *See* International Union of Mine, Mill, and Smelter Workers, Local 890

Mingus, Charles, 49–50, 141
Minority Actors Committee (SAG committee), 28–29
Miracles, the, 53, 56
Miyata, Shin, 66–67, 162
Molina, Natalia, 8, 43–44
Molina, Ruben, 53–54
Montalvo, Joseph "Nuke," 152, 154, 157
Moraga, Cherríe, 118
Moreno, Luisa, 37, 170n12
Morton, Jelly Roll, 50, 51, 141
Moss, Carlton, 22, 24, 34
Mountjoy, Richard, 109
Movimiento, El (Chicano movement): Aztlán, 10–11, 76, 134, 154, 162; brown-eyed soul and, 42, 43, 44, 52, 60, 62, 83; Chicano Moratorium (anti-Vietnam War protest), 58, 71, 105–106; Chicanx reggae and, 133, 140–141; *Chico and the Man* and, 82, 83; El Chicano's "Viva Tirado" and, 52; masculinist ethos of, 77; murals, 157; poster art, 100, 102
Moylan, Tom, 43
multiculturalism, 48, 74, 90
Multi-ethnic Immigrant Worker Organizing Network (MIWON), 63, 176n87
Muñoz, José Esteban, 44, 53, 157

NAFTA. *See* North American Free Trade Agreement (NAFTA)
Narváez, Peter, 51, 52
National Council of La Raza (NCLR), 76
National Negro Labor Council (NNLC), 29
neoliberalism: activism against, 114–115, 153–154, 156; definition of, 2; for-profit prisons, 156; Fourth World War against, 153; impact on border reggae, 129, 141, 146; impact on immigration rights and policy, 98, 110, 112, 114–115, 125; impact on television, 71, 93; NAFTA and, 109–110, 129, 130–131; post-social moment as result of, 112; privatization, 2, 98, 112. *See also* globalization
newspapers: African American newspapers, 23, 46, 50; *Atlanta Daily World*, 23; *La Opinión* (Los Angeles), 105–106; Mine-Mill newspaper, 35–36; Spanish-language and Chicanx newspapers, 105–106, 140
Ngātahi: Know the Links (film): Aztlan Underground in, 138, 154–155; "By All Means Bring Unity" segment, 156; Chicanx Los Angeles in, 154–158; Culture of Rage in, 157; hip-hop in, 153, 156, 157, 161; inspiration for, 152; Kamathi, Dedon, in, 155–156; Marisol in, 154, 155; masculinity in, 161; Native Guns in, 156; "No More Prisons" segment, 155–156; Phoenix 51/50 in, 157; Santilla, Faith, in, 156; Shabaka, Macheo, in, 156; soundtrack of, 157; visions in, 157–162
NHBI. *See* No Human Being Is Illegal (NHBI), posters; *No Human Being Is Illegal: Posters on the Myths and Realities of the Immigrant Experience* (NHBI)
Ni de Aquí ni de Allá (Milwaukee exhibition), 123
Nielsen ratings, 71; Chicano audience's lack of voice in, 76, 79; of individual sitcoms, 71, 84; of shows about race, 71
Nixon, Richard, 60, 72
No Human Being Is Illegal (NHBI), posters: "Alto Arizona" (Yerena), 120–121; *Arizona Liberty* (Villalobos), 120; *Danger* (Anti-Racist Group of Rethymno Students), 124; *Don't Run* (Mexica Movement), 115; *Dream Act* (Deal), 122–

No Human Being Is Illegal (NHBI), posters (*continued*) 123; "DREAMERS, Education Is Our Liberation, Access Denied Since 2001" (Hernandez), 123; *English Only/Whites Only* (unknown artist), 107–108; *FRAID* (Alcaraz), 110–112; "Guess who pockets the difference?" (Common Threads Artist Group), 110; *If Capital Can Cross Borders, So Can We!* (Barraza), 118; *Illegal? No Human Being Is Illegal* (CARECEN and CARNET), 105; "Keep our families together" (Cervantes), 118; *Kein Mensch Ist Illegal* (Kaltenborn), 124; *La Dignidad No Tiene Fronteras* (unknown artist), 113; "L.A. Should Work . . . for Everyone" (Justice for Janitors), 108; "Ningún Ser Humano Es Ilegal" (AFSC), 100; *Ningún Ser Humano Es Ilegal: No Human Being Is Illegal* (Vallen), 100; "No US $$ for Death Squad Government in El Salvador" (unknown artist), 106; *Out of the Closets! Out of the Shadows! Into the Streets!* (Carillo and Salgado), 123–124; *Sitting Bull: No to HR 4437* (González), 115; "Undocumented Unafraid" (Rodriguez), 121; *Unidad Es la Vida/Unity Is Life* (Redback Graphix), 108; *U.S. Sanctuary Movement* (Barkus), 106–107; "Voices of Justice and Solidarity for Guatemala" (Vallen), 106; *We Are Not Criminals* (Esparza), 115; *Welcome to America* (Think Again), 113

No Human Being Is Illegal: Posters on the Myths and Realities of the Immigrant Experience (NHBI): collaborative utopia of, 99, 123–125; CSPG and, 99–104; everyday utopia of, 98–99; influence of IRCA on, 104–109; influence of La Gran Marcha on, 114–123; influence of Proposition 187 on, 109–114; "International Organizing for Justice" (exhibition section), 124; international reach of, 123–125; intersectionality of, 117–118, 123–124; origins and early history of, 102–104; radical utopia of, 98; title of exhibition, 99–100, 105, 124; utopian aesthetics of, 99, 112; utopian desire of, 99; utopian imagination of, 99, 100, 106, 108–109, 114–115, 124–125. *See also No Human Being Is Illegal (NHBI)*, posters

Noriega, Chon, 77
North American Free Trade Agreement (NAFTA), 64, 109–110, 127–131, 139, 149

Obama, Barack, 122
Occupy movement, 100
Olivares, Luis, 103
On the Waterfront (film), 39
Opinión, La (Los Angeles), 105–106
Oropeza, Lorena, 58
Ortega, Anthony, 49
Ortiz, Paul, 129–130
Otis, Johnny, 48–49
Ozomatli, 64–65, 137, 138

pachuco artists and songs, 45, 48, 134
Palillo, Ron, 83
Parker, William, 47
Peace and Justice Center (Los Angeles), 64–65, 139
Peet, Roger, 123
Perales, Monica, 139
Perez, Lawrence, 59
Perez, Martin, 136, 140
Pfaelzer, Jean, 19, 153
Phillips, William, 50–51
Phillips Music Company, 50–51
Pickett, Wilson, 55
Plyler v. Doe, 122

police brutality, 22; case of Rodney King, 63, 152; case of Ruben Salazar, 105–106; dystopian nature of, 159; protests and activism against, 60, 150, 153, 154–155, 156
pop culture. See Chicanx pop culture
poster art, 100–104; affordability of, 102, 104; circulated as GIFs, 102; impact of social media on, 102; as mobilizing force, 101–102. See also No Human Being Is Illegal (NHBI), posters; No Human Being Is Illegal: Posters on the Myths and Realities of the Immigrant Experience (NHBI)
Prakash, Gyan, 9, 12
Premiers, the, 53, 54, 57, 59
¡Printing the Revolution! (SAAM exhibition), 121
Prinze, Freddie: disruption of "macho" trope, 177n13; friendship with Robert Hegyes, 88; on-screen chemistry with Jack Albertson, 74; protests against casting of, 68, 76, 79; racial and ethnic identity of, 68, 70, 71, 76; response to critics, 81–82; suicide of, 75, 177n23
privatization, 2, 98, 112
privilege: of masculinities and gender, 34, 148; of nuclear and reproductive families, 36; power and, 163; wealth and, 163; white privilege, 69, 70, 132
Proposition 187. See California Proposition 187
Pulido, Laura, 58

Quetzal, 64, 65, 66, 138
Quinazo, 133, 134, 136, 138, 139, 147
Quinto Sol, 65, 133, 134, 135, 136, 137, 138–139, 140, 142

race: critical race studies, 10; neoliberalism and, 110, 153–154; normalizing of, 89–90; pop culture utopias and, 8–11; racial awakening in 1970s television, 71–74; racial utopias in sitcoms, 69–71, 72, 74; as social construct, 8
racialization: of film production team hierarchies, 34; of immigrants and immigration, 98–99, 125; interracial exchange and, 8, 167n13; masculinity and, 89, 94; musical traditions in racialized communities, 58, 65; representation of, 70, 72, 85, 89, 90, 92, 94; in sitcoms, 70, 72, 85, 89, 90, 92; social construction of race and, 8
racial profiling, 120
radical utopias, 7, 62, 98
Ramos, E. Carmen, 121
Rampart Records, 56, 66
rancheras, 51, 65
Rando, David, 54, 72, 114–115, 127, 133
Rap Declares War (War), 62–63
Rastafarianism, 128, 133, 134, 137, 138, 140, 143–144
Razteca identity, 134
Razteca reggae, 65
Reagan, Ronald, 47, 72, 107
Red-baiting, 13, 19, 20, 21
Redmond, Shana, 128, 151
Reed, T. V., 4, 12
Reese, Lloyd, 49
reggae. See Afro-Mexica reggae; border reggae; Chicanx reggae
resegregation, 43, 47, 53
Revolutions Per Minute project (RPM), 117
Revueltas, Rosaura, 18, 21, 27, 36–37, 170n12
Robeson, Paul, 28
Robinson, E. I., 47–48
Rodríguez, Favianna, 115–118, 120–121, 123, 162; on art as means of coping, 101; *Being Undocumented Is Not a Crime*, 115–116; *Legalización Ahora!*, 115; *Migration Is Beautiful*,

Rodríguez, Favianna (*continued*) 116, 121; *NHBI* posters by, 115–116, 121; *Nuestro Labor*, 116; president of The Center for Cultural Power, 102; role in CultureStrike, 116, 123; role in Taller Tupac Amaru, 117–118; on social media's impact on poster art, 102; "Undocumented Unafraid," 121
Rodríguez, Luis, 43, 140
Rolle, Esther, 73
Rosas, Abigail, 59
Rosenfelt, Deborah Silverton, 32, 36
Royal Chicano Air Force (RCAF), 115
Roybal, Ed, 47–48, 51
Ruiz, Isaac, 80, 81
Ruiz, Ramón, 50

Sacks, Alan, 84, 85–86, 88, 89, 93
Saldaña-Portillo, Josefina, 135
Salgado, Julio, 123–124
Salinas, Raúl, 99
Salt of the Earth (film): attacked by Donald Jackson, 17, 18, 26, 37–38, 39; blacklisting of, 18; Cold War context of, 19, 20, 21, 32, 33–34, 36, 37–40; creative process of, 25–26; depicted as "Race Film," 23; deportation of Rosaura Revueltas, 18, 21, 36–37, 170n12; discrepancies between real-life strike and, 27, 32–37; gender politics and, 32–37, 40; inspired by Mine-Mill strike, 21–24; IPC-union negotiations and collaborations, 25, 28–32, 34, 40; masculinity in, 18, 33–34, 35; mob violence and parade against, 17; plot of, 18; premiere of, 17; racial cooperation in, 23–24; racial politics in production of, 17–18, 24–32; renewed interest in, 18–19; reviews and press coverage of, 17–18, 23–24; as utopian project, 19–20, 23, 29, 32, 39–41
Sanchez, David, 77
Sanchez, Freddie, 61
Sanchez, Ramon "Chunky," 136–137
Sanchez, Rick, 136–137
Sandoval, Alicia, 76, 78, 176n1
Santana, 65, 137
Santana, Carlos, 50, 137, 148
Santos, Elioenai, 122
scat singing, 45
Scott, Debralee, 86
Scott, Howard, 61
Scott, James, 21, 158
Scottsboro Boys, 22
Screen Actors Guild (SAG), 26, 28–29
Sensenbrenner, Jim, 114
Serrano, Eddie, 43
Serrano, John, 80
"silo" archetypes, 11
Sisters, the (band), 56
sitcoms, television: *All in the Family*, 71, 72, 73, 74, 75, 85, 88, 94; *Barney Miller*, 71, 72, 73, 86, 87, 88; common production staff of, 73; common racial sensibilities in, 72–73; *The Cosby Show*, 94; *Different Strokes*, 85, 94; *Good Times*, 71, 72, 73, 85, 94; *The Jeffersons*, 71, 72, 85, 88, 94; lack of diversity in production staff of, 70; political and economic context of, 71–72; post–civil rights era and, 69, 73–75, 83, 84, 86, 93, 95; race relations in, 72–73; racial awakening in, 71; racialization in, 70, 72, 85, 89, 90, 92; racial utopias in, 69–71, 72, 74; ratings of shows about race, 71; *Sanford and Son*, 71, 72, 73, 74, 86; studio filming locations of, 70; urban settings of, 70; *What's Happening!!*, 71, 72. *See also Chico and the Man*; *Welcome Back, Kotter*
Sleepy Lagoon Defense Committee (SLDC), 46
Smithsonian American Art Museum (SAAM), 121

Sondergaard, Gail, 36
stereotypes and stereotyping: in *Chico and the Man*, 77, 80, 82; in entertainment industry, 28; in *Mr. T and Tina*, 94; in *Salt of the Earth*, 25; in *Welcome Back, Kotter*, 87, 89, 92
Stewart, Kathleen, 7
Storey, John, 7, 62, 98–99, 140
Strassman, Marcia, 86
surveillance: of border dwellers, 129; of immigrant communities, 98, 110, 125; in postwar United States, 3; of urban areas, 98
systematic utopias, 7, 168n35

Tafoya, Alfonso, 82
Taft-Hartley Act, 22, 170n14
Taller Tupac Amaru (TTA), 102, 117–118
Taniguchi, Kenji, 51
Tanny, Jarrod, 87
Teatro Nacional de Aztlán (TENAZ), 76, 78, 79, 176n1
Temptations, the, 53, 56
Tenayuca, Emma, 37, 170n12
terminology, 15–16
Tesso, Andy, 59
Thee Midniters, 14, 51, 53, 54, 55, 57, 59–60; "The Ballad of Cesar Chavez," 60; "Chicano Power," 60; influences on, 53; "Land of a Thousand Dances," 53, 55; "Whittier Boulevard," 53–54
Thompson, Peter, 144
Tilley, Hellen, 9, 12
Tirado, José Ramón, 42
Torrez, Lorenzo, 31–32
Tosti, Don, 45
Travolta, John, 85, 92
Treaty of Guadalupe Hidalgo, 39
Tribute to the Legends concert and festival (Tijuana, Baja California), 126, 142
Trump, Donald, 107, 122, 149, 150

Undiscovered America (Los Angeles mural), 152
United Farm Workers movement, 105
United Farm Workers of America (UFW), 59
United Latin American Citizens (LULAC), 47
utopias and utopian visions: of Afro-Mexica reggae, 144; blueprint utopias, 6–7; of border reggae, 126–130, 144, 146, 151; of brown-eyed soul, 43–44, 53, 57, 59, 62, 66–67; in Chicanx popular culture, 1; collaborative utopias, 99, 123–125; contested Chicanx utopias in *Chico and the Man*, 75, 76, 82–83; definition of, 4–5; deliberate "concrete" utopias, 7; as end game, 10, 19; everyday utopias, 6–8, 12, 44, 57, 98–99, 162; failed utopian vision of *Welcome Back, Kotter*, 83, 86, 88, 89–90, 93, 95; heuristic utopias, 7, 168n35; as ongoing struggle, 10, 19; racial utopias in sitcoms, 69–71, 72, 74; radical utopias, 7, 62, 98; of *Salt of the Earth*, 19–20, 23, 29, 32, 39–41; systematic utopias, 7, 168n35; utopian aesthetics, 99, 112; utopian imagination in *NHBI*, 99, 100, 106, 108–109, 114–115, 124–125; wishful "abstract" utopias, 7; of Zapatistas, 10

Valens, Ritchie, 49
Vallen, Mark, 100, 106
Varela, Migdia, 78–79
Vargas, Deborah, 56
Vargas, Zaragosa, 38
Ventura, Patricia, 11, 70
Viesca, Victor, 64, 132, 138
Vila, Pablo, 142
Village Callers, 53, 56, 66
Villalobos, Roy, 120
Vissicaro, Pegge, 7–8
Viva Zapata! (film), 39

War (band), 60, 61–63, 65, 83; popularity of, 61–62; *Rap Declares War*, 62–63
Watts, Los Angeles, 47, 48, 49, 50, 156
Watts Riots/Rebellion (1965), 47, 52–53
Welcome Back, Kotter (sitcom): analysis by AFT of, 92; banned by WCVB (Boston), 68–69, 90–92; *Chico and the Man* compared with, 83, 84, 86, 88, 93; failed utopian vision of, 83, 86, 88, 89–90, 93, 95; gender in, 86, 87, 89; illusion of inclusion in, 88; Jewish identity in, 68, 70–71, 85–88, 93; legacy of, 93–95; LGBT depictions in, 85; masculinity in, 73, 85–86, 89; multiracial aspects of, 86–89; Nielsen ratings, 71, 84; pilot episode, 70, 88–89, 91–93; racialization and, 72, 85, 89, 90, 92; setting of, 68–69; Sweathogs (students), 68, 70–71, 83–91, 93, 94; themes of, 84, 89; writers of, 84. *See also* Hegyes, Robert; Kaplan, Gabe; Sacks, Alan
Wells, Carol, 102–103, 104–105
White, Barry, 57
whiteness, 14, 52
white privilege, 69, 70, 132
White Shadow, The (television series), 71, 72–73, 85, 86, 94
white supremacy, 11, 70, 108
Widener, Daniel, 8
Wiesel, Elie, 100, 105, 124
Williams, Frances, 162; influence of Paul Robeson on, 28; influence on *Salt of the Earth*, 24, 27–35; joins IPC, 22, 28–29; political activism of, 29; political career of, 29
Wilson, Gerald, 42, 45, 49
Wilson, Michael, 22, 25, 30, 31, 34, 38–39, 40
Wilson, Pete, 109, 111, 132
Wolper, Dave: criticisms of, 77–79; executive producer of *Roots*, 73; response to criticisms, 80; vision of race in America, 83, 89, 90, 93
Wolper Productions, 73, 83, 84
Wonder, Stevie, 54
Wood, Brenton, 54–55, 61; "Gimme Little Sign," 54; influences on, 55; *Oogum Boogum*, 54; "The Oogum Boogum Song," 54
Woodman, Britt, 49
Woodman, Coney, 49
Woodman, William, 49
World War II, 43–48, 51, 64

xenophobia, 107, 112, 125

Yerena, Ernesto, 120–121
Young, Cynthia, 58, 59
Yúdice, George, 129

Zamalin, Alex, 44, 76, 99
Zapatista Army of National Liberation (EZLN), 10, 132. *See also* Zapatistas and Zapatismo
Zapatistas and Zapatismo: influence on border reggae, 129, 132, 135–136, 138–139, 140–141, 145; influence on brown-eyed soul, 65; influence on Joseph "Nuke" Montalvo, 157; influence on *NHBI*, 118; practices and principles of, 10; utopianism of, 10
Zoot Suit Riots, 46
zoot suits, 45, 48, 49, 134
Zurawik, David, 87